Architecture and Beauty

Architecture

and Beauty

CONVERSATIONS WITH ARCHITECTS

ABOUT A TROUBLED RELATIONSHIP

YAEL REISNER WITH FLEUR WATSON

WILEY

A John Wiley and Sons, Ltd, Publication

This edition first published 2010
© 2010 John Wiley & Sons Ltd

Registered office
John Wiley & Sons Ltd, The Atrium, Southern Gate, Chichester, West Sussex, PO19 8SQ,
United Kingdom

For details of our global editorial offices, for customer services and for information about how to
apply for permission to reuse the copyright material in this book please see our website at
www.wiley.com.

Executive Commissioning Editor: Helen Castle
Project Editor: Miriam Swift
Assistant Editor: Calver Lezama

ISBN 978-0-470-99784-0

Cover design, page design and layouts by Jeremy Tilston, The Oak Studio Ltd
Printed in Italy by Printer Trento Srl

Contents

Dedication

To Yehudit and Joseph Yoshko Reisner
and
To Peter and Alexander
YAEL REISNER

For Finn and Hope
FLEUR WATSON

Acknowledgements

Thank you to the interviewees who provided such good conversations and were genuinely keen to express their views. Also to the architects' image archivists who were so patient with my selections.

Thank you to Helen Castle for her wise advice and support, and to Calver Lezama and Miriam Swift for a great collaboration.

To Fleur for her kindness and brilliance; a rare combination from which I was very lucky to benefit.

This book is dedicated to my father Joseph Yoshko Reisner – a most loveable person who died before his time and who introduced me to Modern culture. To my mother, Yehudit Reisner, who introduced me to insistence and care.

To Peter – the groovy man in my life – and to Alexander, the dearest of all. I am indebted to them both for their genuine encouragement and tolerance of my long-term obsession with the book's subject matter.

YAEL REISNER

Thank you to Martyn Hook whose valuable insights and talents are of continual inspiration.

Also to Desmond and June for their unconditional support and belief in integrity, persistence and education.

To Helen Castle and the team at Wiley for their unwavering support and encouragement.

Thank you to the interviewees for their generosity and engagement with this book's compelling thematic.

And, of course, to Yael Reisner for her friendship, faith in a collaborative process and tireless commitment to this publication.

FLEUR WATSON

Architecture

and Beauty

GENESIS OF A TROUBLED RELATIONSHIP

Yael Reisner

THE ARTIST'S ROLE IN SOCIETY has fluctuated significantly over time and across different cultures – from Rembrandt and Vermeer's indulgent portraits for the Dutch aristocracy in the 17th century, through to Dada and Marcel Duchamp challenging the very question of what art might be in the early 20th century. Regardless of their position, an artist's embracement or rejection of 'artistic beauty' is often at the core of their work. In recent times artists have been pressured to justify the creation of their work and forced to offer evaluations of its contribution to society; the resulting commentary usually returns to questions of aesthetics. For example, the recent controversy over British artist Damien Hirst's *For the Love of God* (2007) – a diamond-encrusted skull valued at £50 million – revolved around the beauty of the diamond and its value in direct comparison to the 'value' or content of the object as an artwork; arguably a deliberate ploy by the artist, despite the ongoing vigorous debate.

The visual artist may feel an obligation to communicate the intent of his or her work beyond the sublime and add qualitative value through exegesis, providing critical explanation, personally or through others, in exhibition catalogues, art magazines and the general media in an attempt to locate the work in its cultural and historical context. The composer, on the other hand, may look to an appreciation of his or her work as quantified by the recording, the performance and market exposure, all of which reinforce an acceptance of the quality of the music. The practice of architecture shares many of these concerns, yet the pressure for architects to quantify their work through non-emotive evaluation and justification has tended to fluctuate through history. Yet, since the wide dissemination of the values of Modernism, many of the vanguard architects of the past 70 years have deliberately generated their architecture without a primary consideration

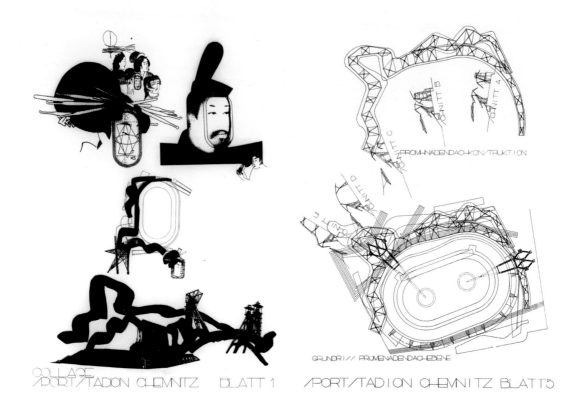

COLLAGE
/PORT/TADION CHEMNITZ   BLATT 1   /PORT/TADION CHEMNITZ BLATT5

for its appearance.[1] Indeed, architectural discourse is dominated by the commentary of almost every aspect of the architectural process except aesthetics[2] – a fact that has driven the architect's intention to a point of mystique and, increasingly, alienation from public understanding.

The genesis of this book's subject matter came as a consequence of a long preoccupation with what I refer to as the 'troubled relationship' between architects and the content of their architecture, as well as its relationship with form and aesthetics.[3] Good architecture and brilliant buildings are mostly judged by their capacity to produce an aesthetic experience, yet many outside the architectural profession are surprised to discover that architectural design is neither led by, nor generated through, a process that is engaged with aesthetical issues or visual thinking. Indeed, the diversity of response among the interviewees in this book reveals, in itself, the complexity of this inherently troubled relationship. For many, beauty is a concept that does not hold any value within architecture, while for others it has regained its importance and relevance through the framework of a new definition. For example, Frank Gehry sees 'beauty' as something

ABOVE ENRIC MIRALLES AND BENEDETTA TAGLIABUE (EMBT), CHEMNITZ SPORTS STADIUM COMPETITION ENTRY, CHEMNITZ, GERMANY, 1995

The early montages of the Chemnitz Sports Stadium are imbued with the confidence of Enric Miralles and Benedetta Tagliabue's unique freethinking process and use of associative metaphors. Miralles died tragically in 2000 at the age of 45. Many of the projects designed between 1995 and 2000 were realised by 2008 with Tagliabue leading the EMBT office.

'pretty and soft' and unconnected with buildings, while Thom Mayne finds the term difficult within itself though he defines it as being 'compelled' to a particular type of architecture. For Gaetano Pesce, beauty is simply perfection, a notion he views as outdated and out of step with the fallible nature of human existence. Paradoxically, beauty can also be the very raison d'être of architecture: for Finnish architect Juhani Pallasmaa it provides the promise of a better human world, while for Odile Decq, to be in denial of the importance of beauty is the rejection of a basic human right. The concluding interviewee, the young Argentinean architect Hernan Diaz Alonso, provides a starkly contemporary viewpoint: for him beauty is integrally embedded within a playful exploration of the grotesque and horrific.

This poignant struggle is also encapsulated in the classic dyad of 'content and form' and how, as a principle, it is understood or perceived by architects of our time. As Juhani Pallasmaa eloquently describes in his interview: 'The discipline of architecture is "impure" in the sense that it fuses utility and poetics, function and image, rationality and metaphysics, technology and art, economy and symbolisation. Architecture is a muddle of irreconcilable things and categories.'[4] Thus, it seems that the cultural and artistic facet of architecture is often undermined in favour of the more rational,[5] pragmatic[6] requirements of the discipline[7] and, as such, drives this rarely confronted 'troubled relationship'.

RIGHT TEL AVIV, ISRAEL, EARLY 1980s

The beauty of the Modernist white city of Tel Aviv was an unexpected cultural statement that shocked many visitors from the 1930s through to the 1960s. Yet many of the city's socialists chose to turn a blind eye to its visual qualities, resulting in a lack of care for, and dilution of, the city's aesthetic nature in favour of practical, utilitarian, socioeconomic and political issues.

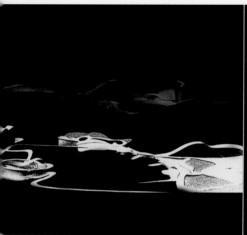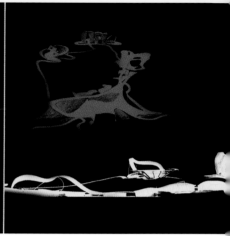

The historic struggle between architectural content and form – particularly within the second half of the 20th century – resonates with me at a distinctly personal level and has, over time, provided the provocation for my engagement with the difficult position that beauty holds within architecture. Since my youth I have always admired beautiful objects and adored the look of new things. I believe I was born with a sensitive eye which was developed during my childhood and adolescence[8] despite growing up in the context of the socialist,[9] Modernist and cosmopolitan culture of the provincial city of Tel Aviv in the 1960s. The Israeli collective identity of the time and sense of place lay in an idealisation of modernity and simplicity, where ideological debates were prevalent, and aesthetic 'indulgence' was absent, frowned upon and treated as reminiscent of the old habits of the European bourgeoisie. I suspect that the Modernist socialist attitude of the people of Tel Aviv was the major reason why their city's new beauty[10] became diluted and has been badly treated. 'Content' was satisfying and more significant; as Tel Avivians often remark: 'We don't argue about taste and smell.'[11]

Yet my persistent attitude towards the look of things was mostly triggered by my father,[12] who rarely missed an opportunity to tease his daughter[13] for her appreciation of things simply because of their appearance. I was accused of adoring empty vessels rather than admiring 'content' produced by intellectual activity (which was, in my father's opinion, worth critically appraising). Our conflict was reinforced daily by a famous Hebrew saying – 'Don't look at the jar but at its content' – which finds its parallel in the English saying 'Don't judge a book by its cover', though it does not translate as directly.

Projecting from my paternal influence was my observation that most intellectuals do not have a developed 'eye' with which to truly appreciate the range of values that can be captured within the 'look of things' – an observation that seemed underwritten by the context of socialism. Indeed, there appeared to be no genuine interest in looking; instead a deliberate setting of a blind eye to a visual set of references, creating a lack of visual sensibilities over time. I, therefore, assumed that being an intellectual meant the application of the written word through literature and poetry, and even theatre, to develop a quite different set of sensibilities; it did not matter if any object was defined by its ugliness, its originality of form, its beauty or its reflection on culture as it would always be reduced to the status of a merely decorative phenomenon. As I began to question this attitude my growing frustration fed my conviction and, in turn, the need for this book. This dialectic informs my research and drives my distrust of the collective message of cultural theory – and, more specifically, in architectural discourse – that the 'content' of cultural and creative output is more important than its 'appearance', and that the notion of 'beauty' is often misinterpreted as being devoid of intellectual depth.

Living in London since the early 1990s[14] I have been struck by the disappointing fact that architecture is predominantly discussed in terms of ethics, content or activity, and much less in terms of its imagery, look, visual values, composition or architectural language. While teaching at the Bartlett School of Architecture, I had the opportunity to listen to a large number of lectures given by internationally renowned architects[15] and I could not help thinking that the architectural discourse of the time shared attitudes with the arguments I had heard in my youth; tragically it seemed to me that many architects had lost their conviction of the cultural importance of aesthetics and its ties with individuality. I hoped to find satisfaction in the shift that 'digital architecture' brought to the international stage, with its focus on form and appearance rather than on content. Yet, disappointingly, the digital movement's famous protagonists elevated the status of conceptual objectivity and pursued a 'rational' design process via computational processes. The rise of computer-generated design valued 'automated', 'pseudo-scientific' and intellectualised characteristics where originality evolved from intrinsic procedures derived from mathematics and not from an individualistic, aesthetic approach.

From a historical perspective, the origins of this troubled relationship throughout the 20th century can be traced to the beginnings of Functionalism where the Modernist ethos was embedded in socialist ideologies.[16] Since the 1930s architectural discourse has been dogged by the Modernist ambition to avoid being driven by aesthetics and, in turn, the desire not to involve the 'self' or 'subjectivity' during the design process.[17] Resistance to an architecture generated through emotion and visual thinking was a result of pressure from the Modernist 'apologists' who succeeded in creating an architectural discourse that

OPPOSITE YAEL REISNER (WITH MARO KALLIMANI, ANDY SHAW, KENNY TSUI AND LORENE FAURE), FAMILY HOUSE PROPOSAL, SPACE FOR LISTENING TO MUSIC, KFAR SHMARYAHU, ISRAEL, 2004–07

Since 1999, through teaching and practice, Reisner's work has been preoccupied with investigating a 3-D condition of spatial complexity. It is an exploration reflected in her students' work, such as that by Marjan Colletti and Aniko Meszaros. In 2004, Reisner coined the term 'depth-scape' to describe an aesthetic exploring spatial depth. In this interactive domestic installation she examines the mediation of light and acoustic effect with soft and hard materials and 3-D forms. 'Manifold Silhouettes', as seen here, is one of the atmospheric phases.

distorted the early Modernists' content, eliminating their aesthetic bias. Reyner Banham, the British architectural historian, explains in *Theory and Design in the First Machine Age* (1960)[18] that the aesthetics of the early Modernists (such as Gerrit Rietveld, Mies van der Rohe and Le Corbusier) carried a symbolism as the authentic reflection on time,[19] which was part and parcel of the aesthetics of their buildings[20] in the 1920s. Nevertheless, that authenticity was discarded or ignored in the 1930s by their apologists (Sigfried Giedion, Alberto Sartoris and Lewis Mumford),[21] who skewed interpretation of the Modernists' ethics dramatically away from the intended, highly symbolised aesthetic approach, and explained it as architecture driven by functionality.[22] As Banham suggests: 'Nowhere among the major figures of the '20s will a pure Functionalist be found.'[23] From a contemporary viewpoint, we can conclude that the apologists succeeded in influencing the architectural discourse of the time and pursued an agenda that sidelined aesthetics as a generator for the architecture of the 20th century; the generating forces had to be related to the world of utility. Additionally, through critique of the Expressionist artists of the 1920s, personal expression was increasingly seen as an unworthy pursuit, underwriting an exclusion of the self and any individualistic tone from new work. As the historian Wolfgang Pehnt suggests in quoting the zealous words of the artist and poet Uriel Birnbaum: 'The Messianic attitude of the Expressionists seemed like mischievous caprice, if not indeed inspired by the devil.'[24]

Architects have often resisted imposing personal values on their work beyond the required objectives or through mere subjectivism. One understands from the historian and urban theorist Colin Rowe[25] that an emphasis on the notion of being objective, beyond the cerebral characteristics of generating work, led many architects to generate their architectural design based on facts, data, analysis, programme, function, and so on. Rowe identifies the conflicting characteristics of the Modernist architects' intention to manifest objective qualities in their work and simultaneously reflect authentically on the time in which they live. In his book *The Architecture of Good Intentions* (1994), he writes: 'From Mies van der Rohe there follows possibly the most succinct statement of what – until not very long ago – was to be considered modern architecture's avowed aim: Essentially our task is to free the practice of building from the control of aesthetic speculators and restore it to what it should exclusively be: building.'[26] This statement captures the belief that architects have an obligation to advance the objective needs of society; as Mies wrote in 1940: 'We find the only solutions of that time to be ... where objective limits were imposed and there was no opportunity for subjective license.'[27] So emerge the two opposite notions of 'objective limits' and 'subjective license', informing the psychology of the era. As Rowe confirms: 'That opposition: "objective limits" and "subjective license", was a crucial component of the architecture thought of the time, and indicated that one is good and the other is highly dubious.'[28]

Hence the resistance of Modern architects to embrace a subjective will, or at least admit to its role in the creation of their architecture, begins. The popular mantra extracted from the European Functionalist ethos of 'form follows function' clearly reinforces the repression of individualistic expression and the utilitarian facet of Modernism that became the dominant attitude. Surprisingly, as Rowe points out, at the time no one actually admitted the incompatibility of the two concepts, shifting between an idea of the architect as the servant of technology, the impersonal and the super-important 'facts', and an idea of the architect as the executive of the *Zeitgeist*, responding to the unconscious demands of the day, interpreting his aesthetic preferences as prophetic intuitions.[29]

The Modernist intellectual attitude is also captured by the well-known British social historian Eric Hobsbawm,[30] who wrote in the 1990s: 'Films depended on books from the start.'[31] That is, the underlying message is the most significant value that comes with a film, though Hobsbawm clearly recognises the visual powers and importance of the cinema. In his book *Age of Extremes* (1994), Hobsbawm expands on his thoughts: 'One of the most obscure questions in history; and for the historian of culture, one of the most central, is the very phenomenon that brilliant fashion designers,[32] a notoriously non-analytical breed, sometimes succeed in anticipating the shape of things to come better than professional predictors.'[33] This comment succinctly expresses a refusal to recognise that intellectual depth can be captured in visual imagery generated intuitively by an individual's insight and a lack of respect for the image unless it carries strong social and political content, or a 'utilitarian task'. The intellectualisation of the thought process[34] is generally prevalent in our culture and it has led to further support of the rational faculties[35] as evidenced in architecture's design process.[36] As Walter J Ong explains, democracy's 'public opinion' took over individual taste and power.[37]

It took until the late 1970s for emotional content to re-emerge in architecture and for aesthetically driven design to achieve positive status while facilitating the role of the 'eye' once more.[38] This new architectural spirit was led by the dynamic work of Frank Gehry, Zaha Hadid, COOP HIMMELB(L)AU and Daniel Libeskind[39] and propelled into international prominence by the exhibition 'Deconstructivist Architecture', curated by Mark Wigley with Philip Johnson at New York's Museum of Modern Art (MoMA) in 1988.[40] The exhibition's enticing title distracted from the content of the architecture displayed, hijacked the architectural scene and ignited a fire among many architects who seemingly had an incredible thirst for philosophy or for a cerebral authority rather than for embracing an emotional, authorial voice to lead their architecture.[41] While resoundingly important and highly successful, the 'Decon' show really indicated the end of a discussion[42] and, immediately afterwards, the philosophy of Jacques Derrida[43] strengthened as one of

OPPOSITE MARJAN COLLETTI (MArch, BARTLETT SCHOOL OF ARCHITECTURE, UCL), THE BASKING, HAMPSTEAD, LONDON, 1999

Colletti's design is an entirely organic digital proposal beyond the common aesthetics of NURBS surfaces, abstract scapes or parametric skins. The 2-D spline – the only design element – follows the logical and structural thoughts of the designer: considering inhabitation, function and presence of the building. In the garden, a floating swimming pool – like a humongous flower – grows out of the pond and blossoms regularly, changing its shape depending on the season.

The 'Basking'
A house in Hampstead, London.

Section

Plan of

the primary authorities in the design process.[44] Thus content became more significant than aesthetics, underpinning a return to the historical architectural tradition of rejecting the 'self', with all its emotional involvement, as an authority.

During the 1990s the use of computers became a prevalent phenomenon in architectural schools and offices and influenced the design process tremendously by enabling more complexity in architectural organisation, three-dimensional forms and structure along with virtual representation and simulations. With this radical shift, the first wave of influential 'digital architects'[45] arrived on the architectural scene – such as Greg Lynn, Lars Spuybroek, Marcos Novak, Mark Goulthorpe (dECOi) and Mark Burry (SIAL). Collectively and individually they took the architectural discourse of the time by storm, drawing on mathematics and the influence of the work of philosopher Gilles Deleuze to provide joint authorities for generating the work and, in turn, swinging the focus back to form and, apparently, cerebral aesthetics. However, rationality prevailed and the architect's 'eye' and individuality were removed from the design process, but this time in the name of new objectified computational technologies and production. Content – as it was often claimed – became fused with form, and form was arrived at through cerebral computational process and technique.

In many cases not only was 'subjectivity' rejected, but also, among those architects influenced by the French philosopher Henri Bergson's notion of intuition,[46] psychological intuition was substituted and the architect's personal creative authority became cerebral. Bernard Cache, an industrial designer and influential figure within digital architecture, confirms its intent as he saw it in the late 1990s: 'The architect is an intellectual worker whose mode of production is increasingly governed by digital technologies ... which are

OPPOSITE ANIKO MESZAROS (MArch, BARTLETT
SCHOOL OF ARCHITECTURE, UCL), PLANT ANIMA,
VENETIAN LAGOON, ITALY, 1999

This vision for a new landscape connects Venice with
the inland, cleans the Venetian Lagoon and creates a
new aesthetic related to water, culturally and
ecologically, above and under, physically and
metaphysically. The scheme employs biotechnological
knowledge to create an interactive hybrid, live
organism interwoven with a man-made matrix and
controlled by a collaborative team of scientists and
architects over time by an in-situ laboratory.

hostile to random, fluid, moving or virtual architecture, and to all approaches that perpetuate the age-old myth of the capricious architect-artist.'[47] There were others who could see a different future: in 2004 Lars Spuybroek, who was the first to assert that the digital scene had evolved into a cultural pursuit, wrote: 'The computer has reached a cultural stage, finally. The years that it was used for dreaming of perfect shape grammars and design automation ... those years are over.'[48] Certainly, with the benefit of hindsight, Spuybroek's encouraging words seem prophetic of the work of many emergent digital practitioners today.

When embarking on the research material to explore my preoccupation, I felt it was critical to establish direct contact with the architectural elite and chose to interview architects who are, or were, highly influential among fellow architects and students of architecture – usually architects whose work I respect and find attractive, though I do not necessarily agree with their schools of thought. There are 16 interviewees in the book, who provide a rich cross-section of opinion but who do not necessarily represent the widest range of views. Collectively they represent only a small sample of a potentially large number of architects with equally valuable opinions who might have been included. I met most of them two or three times over a span of nearly three years (2004 to 2007). All are, or have been, leading architectural educators and are generally considered mavericks who have moved architecture forward through talent, originality, integrity and individuality. I drew on my own experience struggling with the troubled relationship in an attempt to understand each architect's value system and to draw out their views on the subject.

The 16 conversations resulted in a resonant, explorative and starkly diverse set of positions – Frank Gehry exposes the poignancy of self-expression in architecture in democratic societies. Peter Cook hankers for the time in history when architects engaged in passionate battles over their different styles. Eric Owen Moss believes architecture encompasses a colossal breadth of experience in art, history and prosaic pragmatics, and that the expression of these things has built up the integrity of architects as individuals reflecting on their times. Will Alsop argues that individuality is the very thing that architects can offer, believing in the 'diverse' and the 'speculative' and fighting long, arduous battles with British critics and conservatives. Like Odile Decq, Wolf D Prix vehemently believes that architectural practice should not be separated from architectural theory and research;[49] that architecture functions as both a reflection of an architect's cultural background and as a general register of culture. While Zaha Hadid's ideology is masterfully captured within her architectural paintings and drawings, presenting a new vision and an original way of communicating architecture.

OPPOSITE CJ LIM/STUDIO 8 ARCHITECTS, THE BAKER'S GARDEN, SOHO, LONDON, 2008

'The garden-bakery is deciphered through its temperature within the cloak of darkness. The fire from the clay ovens brings a glow to the making of fresh bread, which fills the garden with topiaries of smells and steam', (CJ Lim, London, 2008). It is interesting to observe Lim's impulse against the planar Modernist aesthetic (flat or curved) as shared by other architects such as Hernan Diaz Alonso, Lebbeus Woods and Reisner's own work. While a particularity of aesthetic arguably unites them, each architect works from a diverse range of thoughts and activities, and using different design tools and mediums.

BELOW PHILIP BEESLEY, ORGONE REEF, INSTALLED IN LONDON AND BIRMINGHAM, 2004

'The project probes the possibilities of combining artificial and natural processes to form an uncanny, hybrid ecology ... Osmotic action that pulls moisture ... the intrusion of larger organisms ... would encourage a living turf to accumulate, intermeshed within the lightweight matrix. The structure would eventually decay and be replaced by this growth ... a poignant alternative to the Modern version of progress' (Exhibited at the Design Centre in Store Street, London, 2004).

For Zvi Hecker, architecture is an expression of the human soul in its ever-changing condition, whereas Juhani Pallasmaa points to the missing presence of the 'self' and believes that architects should rely on personal experience and imagination to fuel their work. Lebbeus Woods believes that a progressive world must engage with social and ethical aspects rather than technological progress. For Gaetano Pesce, new imagery imbued with cultural messages is paramount; he employs new materials with innovative technologies in juxtaposition to figurative elements. For Thom Mayne it is the very uniqueness of architecture that allows it to operate on so many levels – conceptual, social, cultural, historical, urbanistic – loading multiple perspectives into single frames. Greg Lynn and Mark Goulthorpe claim that content is always fused with form; their interest is focused on form generated by computational processes. KOL/MAC LLC – unlike many of their digital colleagues – bravely introduced lateral thinking to the computational process in the mid-1990s, though they still reject any suggestion of deterministic formalism. Hernan Diaz Alonso, as the youngest (and final) interviewee, has liberated himself from the cerebral design process and many of the rules of his digital colleagues, and in doing so, has permeated his work with individualism and personality.

As an architect who has spent years battling with the suppression of the 'eye' and the 'I' and their role in the design process, I especially identify with the American psychologist James Hillman[50] who wrote: 'This curious refusal to admit beauty in psychological discourse occurs even though each of us knows that nothing so affects the soul, so transports it, as moments of beauty – in nature, a face, a song, an action or dream.'[51] And, as he suggests, 'We are left with fractals and wittily named particles by definition non-sensate of theoretical physics,[52] the puns and parodies of architecture, and the language games of philosophical analysis resulting in a severe dissociation between what is thought, said, and written and what the senses see, the heart feels, and the world suffers.'[53]

More architects should confidently accept the need to generate architecture with an authorial voice, embrace an intuitive eye and lateral thinking, seize impulses and become individualistically speculative. Within this publication, Thom Mayne and Hernan Diaz Alonso serve as two examples of architects who embrace their own cultures and integrate these into their work. For example, Thom Mayne's Caltrans District 7 Headquarters in downtown Los Angeles (2001–04) is an elegant, monumental and significant landmark that successfully portrays elements of Angelino culture while demonstrating the key characteristics of Morphosis's architecture. It is highly intense and energetic with angular folded elements that peel away from the structure's large-scale block to reveal a human scale that effortlessly defines the public entry. Hernan Diaz Alonso has turned digital discourse on its head by introducing his authorial voice into the design process. He has pursued a new architectural aesthetic that breaks away from the planar Modernist language into an architecture of organic growth, leaving the digital preoccupation for volumetric continuous wrapping far behind. He focuses his intensity, instead, on what might fill in the imaginary 'missing volume' and, although he engages cutting-edge computational processes, he is refreshingly unapologetic about using his taste, culture and aesthetic to corrupt the logical process.[54]

By integrating their own cultures into their work, these architects demonstrate a conviction to engage with the generation of their designs through a unique aesthetic discourse that explores an original architectural language, as well as atmosphere that

Digital render. Diaz Alonso is interested in the resultant form and image of that form rather than in a discourse regarding process. Consequently, he is critical of the self-righteous nature of many architects and the manner in which they claim the importance of process to their work. According to him: 'The purity of the work lies in the final effect.'

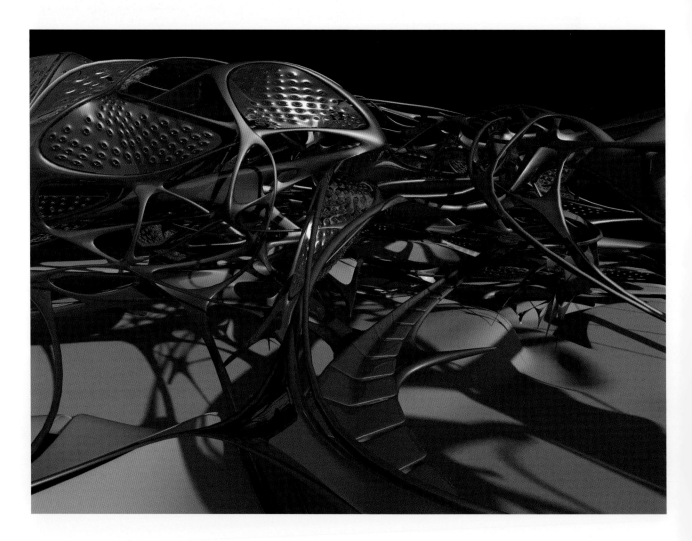

This pivotal installation is a departure from Woods's earlier work although it still relates to his original notion of 'heterarchical space' – a design for a world that consists of spontaneous lateral network of individuals. It is a spatial field that explores interior qualities by celebrating internal objects, giving the viewer a keen sense of spatial awareness.

affects people's comfort levels and emotions. If architects can be empowered to pursue this paradigmatic shift in practice and discourse, we may well arrive at an architecture of enough diversity to bring with it 'the beautiful'. Beauty,[55] as a concept for our age, a work of the individual for other individuals, an authentic product for a pluralistic global time, is not a singular idea. The beautiful is seen by many and is therefore an 'uncontrollable beauty'.[56] It is time to argue that architecture's 'aesthetics' have the power to synthesise values, poetics, pragmatic constraints and overbearing cultural issues, and at the same time cohere to the construct of the architectural design.

Notes

1. For example, at the end of the 1940s, Peter and Alison Smithson engaged with the notion of 'New Brutalism', where they denied aesthetic considerations while designing the Hunstanton High School in Norfolk. In the 1950s, Aldo van Eyck called for a return to humanism as a generating force of architectural design. In the 1970s, Christopher Alexander from Berkeley University School of Architecture wrote his influential book *Pattern Language*, which prescribed templates for good design. At London's Architectural Association (AA), John Frazer, the forefather of the computational process in architectural design, continued to advocate his theory of 'Evolutionary Architecture' – an approach that evolved from the 1970s to the 1990s where the logic of the 'genetic code' was borrowed and became the generator of form. In Australia, Glenn Murcutt – a Pritzker Prize laureate – claimed that his architectural process had no connection with aesthetics, while Italian architect Gaetano Pesce also suggested he was not led by aesthetic values throughout his career. The digital architect Mark Goulthorpe continues to suggest that his computational process is not led by an aesthetic discourse.

2. Yet paradoxically, some colleagues, critics and members of the general public blame architects for being driven by stylistic decisions. For example, in the April 2007 issue of *BD Weekly* – a weekly magazine read by most architects in the UK – a front-page headline claimed: 'Public wants space not style'. It reported: 'Over-design is creating public spaces that people don't want to use ... A new report, "The Social Value of Public Spaces", for the Joseph Rowntree Foundation, attacks key aspects of current government policy concerning public space.' Or, as the headline read in March 2008, 'Starchitects are merely stylists, says RMJM's boss. Peter Morrison calls on architects to regain status of "master builder" in unprecedented attack.'

3. It was Mark Cousins (from the AA, London) who asked me one simple yet challenging question many years ago that opened up this obsession of mine: 'What do you really hate within your world of architecture?'

4. Zvi Hecker describes the ongoing challenge of being both a professional and an experimental practitioner: 'The architect is always within a schizophrenic situation because on one hand he is a professional, and on the other he is within the creative process of searching, experimenting, and developing the design.' Zvi Hecker, interview with Yael Reisner, 8 September 2004.

5. Leon van Schaik explains that the source of the architects' troubles with their mastery is that the notion of architectural professionalism, as we understand it, originated at the beginning of the 19th century when architecture was perceived and defined as technology. Van Schaik emphasises that architects continue to confuse their 'knowledge base': 'When architecture was professionalised in the early 19th century, it was done on the basis that the unique area of knowledge that this profession had custody of – in the interests of serving the public disinterestedly – was that of a master builder ... The error was that this placed technologies at the forefront, instead of quality that all humans strive for. In medicine and the law, technology serves in pursuit of health and justice ... but defined as technology, architecture is impoverished as a practice and fails as a profession. The impoverishment stems from a limited definition of what is appropriate architectural knowledge. I propose a wider, more inclusive definition.' Leon van Schaik, *Mastering Architecture: Becoming a Creative Innovator in Practice,* John Wiley & Sons Ltd, Chichester, 2005, p 176.

6. Diagrams often take the lead here. One of the most recent examples is the Hamburg Science Centre by OMA. Planned for completion in 2011, it is beginning to represent the 'appearance of the impeccable logic', to use Colin Rowe's great phrase. Colin Rowe, *The Architecture of Good Intentions: Towards a Possible Retrospect*, Academy Editions, London, 1994, p 25.

7. The expression 'hegemony of the eye' appeared during the 20th century as a critical phrase, evidence of which is given in many important books. See, for example: David Michael Levine, *Modernity and the Hegemony of Vision*, University of California Press (Berkeley and Los Angeles, CA), 1993; Walter J Ong, SJ, *The Presence of the Word*, Yale University Press (New Haven), 1967; Martin Jay, *Downcast Eyes: The Denigration of Vision in Twentieth-Century French Thought*, University of California Press (Berkeley and Los Angeles, CA), 1994; Juhani Pallasmaa, *The Eyes of the Skin: Architecture and the Senses*, John Wiley & Sons Inc., New York, 2005.

8. In 1786, Goethe wrote in his diary, *Italienische Reise*: 'It is evident that the eye is educated by the things it sees from childhood.'

9. To be precise, one must add that the socialist attitude of Israelis was reinforced by the Jewish iconoclastic tradition.

10. As I grew up in the Modernist, white city of Tel Aviv, I gradually became aware how its beauty, as much as its cultural statement, shocked most visitors. Yet the socialist mentality shared by most of its inhabitants makes them turn a blind eye to visual references. Tel Aviv's beauty was diluted and badly affected by years of a prevailing socialist attitude that focused on practical, utilitarian, socioeconomic and political issues, and categorically left aesthetics behind.

11. Another very prevalent Hebrew expression that cuts off any conversation politely, since it comes to the conversation as a reminder of an agreed consensus. A variation of the expression also exists in German: '*Über Geschmack lässt sich nich streiten*' – 'on style we do not argue'.

12. Towards the end of the 1960s I entered my teens. At home, 'indoor' life was saturated with many vivid discussions about people, books, theatre and film. Most of these emanated from that very jolly Austro-Hungarian-Jewish intellectual, my father, a chemical engineer whose heart belonged to European Modernist culture.

13. Though he loved me dearly and put forward his views to 'rescue' me from what he saw as a shallow attitude to life, or my indulgence in silly, girlish occupations.

14. I was a student at the Architectural Association (AA) School of Architecture from 1982 to 1987 – years when aesthetics was very much part of the debate in London.

15. During that decade it struck me that many of the vanguard architects appearing at the Bartlett would often go to significant lengths to state that the choices they made within their architectural process had no connection to aesthetics. This view was put forth by Kathryn Findlay, Thom Mayne, Mark Goulthorpe and Gaetano Pesce among others, and each time with a different perspective.

16. It is important to note that I write this from the perspective of personal impression and based on an understanding of recent architectural events. That is, from the perspective of a designer-architect and not of an architectural historian. Rather than attempting to present archival material, I am speculating through my intimate understanding of the architects' work and through my reading of mainstream books that discuss historical events. My intention is to discuss what I feel is a path that simply went too far.

17. 'Alexander Baumgarten coined the term "aesthetics" in 1735 ... to indicate a new kind of investigation of the "sensual", showing that sensuality is not just – as Rationalist philosophy had claimed – the source of "obscure and unclear" ideas, inferior to and thus to be superseded by reason, but the "analogon" to reason.' See Christoph Menke, 'Modernity, subjectivity and aesthetic reflection', in Peter Osborne (ed), *From an Aesthetic Point of View: Philosophy, Art and the Senses*, Serpent's Tail, London, 2000, p 40. Interestingly, 'aesthetics' and 'subjectivity' are two terms that were interrelated within the same document written by Baumgarten. He coined the term 'aesthetics' to mean taste, or 'sense', of beauty, thereby inventing its modern usage and tying it to a personal attitude.

18. Reyner Banham, *Theory and Design in the First Machine Age*, Architectural Press, Butterworth-Heinemann, Oxford, 1997, first published in 1960.

19. 'De Stijl adopted Mondriaan's abstract art since it reflected the "de-personalisation of art" and symbolized a universal beauty. Reinforced concrete was considered as a mechanical and impersonal tool too. Thus creating the illusion of weightlessness, or of structural homogeneity ... That symbolism appealed to the Modernist heroes.' Ibid, p 240.

20. 'As we can see in the work of: De Stijl; Gerrit Rietveld, "Schroeder House", Utrecht, 1925; Mies van der Rohe, "Project for a Brick Villa", 1923; Le Corbusier, the "Pavilion de l'Esprit Nouveau", Paris, 1925; or Le Corbusier's "Les Terrasses", Garches – the most complete demonstration of Le Corbusier's aesthetics of 1926.' Ibid, p 240.

21. 'Most of those apologists came to it late, five years after it roughed out, and they were not from Holland, Germany, and France, that had done most to create the new style. Sigfried Giedion, Swiss, caught only the tail end of this process, in 1923; Sartoris, Italian, missed it almost completely; Lewis Mumford, American, was too remotely placed to have any real sense of the aesthetic issues involved.' Ibid, p 320.

22. 'Giedion, Sartoris, and Mumford, who all believed that the cultural-political environment wouldn't accept new aesthetics unless based on logical and economical grounds.' As this quote suggests, rational logic, such as in Functionalism, was in the apologists' view more convincing. Ibid, p 321.

23. Ibid, p 162.

24. Written by the Austrian artist and poet Uriel Birnbaum in his book *Der Kaiser und der Architekt*, Thyrsos-Verlag, Leipzig and Vienna, 1924. As Pehnt explains: 'Adolf Behne in Berlin in 1927 was one of the first of the architects and architectural critics in Germany to sense the changing climate. Thinking of the De Stijl group in Holland and the avant-garde in France he announced the rejection of crafts, the renunciation of sentimental enthusiasms, and the end of the rule of caprice.' Wolfgang Pehnt, *Expressionist Architecture*, Thames & Hudson, London, 1973, p 194. Thus, already in the mid-1920s, 'subjectivity' as exercised by architects in the first two decades of the 20th century was considered 'old-fashioned', especially by German Expressionists such as Bruno Taut and Hans Poelzig who both believed in the intuitive call of the individual.

25. Colin Rowe was an architect, academic and the Andrew Dickson White Professor of Architecture at Cornell University in Ithaca, New York, until his death in 1999.

26. Colin Rowe, *The Architecture of Good Intentions: Towards a Possible Retrospect*, Academy Editions, London, 1994, p 24.

27. Ibid, p 21. Quote from Mies' writings of 1940.

28. Ibid, p 21.

29. In 2002, digital architect Mark Goulthorpe interestingly made a related argument – albeit focused on the emphasis on computational design processes throughout the 1990s – where he revealed his doubts about the potential of many digital processes to be 'poetic' in a Bachelardian sense. The two arguments are similar in their doubts regarding what evolves with the 'removal' of the 'self' and its effect on the outcome of the design process.

30. Eric Hobsbawm, *Behind the Times: The Decline and Fall of the Twentieth-Century Avant-Gardes*, Thames & Hudson (London), 1998.

31. Ibid, p 12.

32. Hobsbawm related his argument to fashion only because it engages with the masses on a fundamental level.

33. Eric Hobsbawm, *Age of Extremes: The Short Twentieth Century, 1914–1991*, Abacus, London, 1994, p 178.

34. Walter Ong explains in his book, *The Presence of the Word*, that the development of abstraction in visualisation and its cerebral interpretation of what we see started with script and the alphabetic typography of the 15th century, leading to the invention of 'perspective' and later to the increased use of maps. See WJ Ong, SJ, op cit. As architects we witness how, in the 20th century, this attitude has stimulated an intellectual affinity with diagrams, informational data visualised in graphs, or digitalised mathematical design methods; all affect architectural design.

35. Since ancient times, architecture has more often than not been a result of a cerebral approach and abstracted expression, whereas sculptural content – most often located in space – has incorporated feelings.

36. Besides, the historian Marvin Perry reinforces the observation that, having witnessed scientific revolutions since the 15th century, Enlightenment philosophers had been encouraged to trust in the rational faculties. See Marvin Perry, *An Intellectual History of Modern Europe*, Houghton Mifflin Company, Boston, MA, 1993. As we can see, that inclination became even more entrenched in the 20th century, where mechanisms and processes in nature (as explained by scientists) were borrowed by many other disciplines, including architecture.

37. Taste and smell are personal and reflect on subjective feelings. As Ong explains, 'During the 18th century when individuals got free from the Feudal society they were forced to make decisions and develop their own attitude. That's why and how "taste" became a new concept and "subjectivity" was a new invented term at that time. But that "relationship of the human life-world to the complex world of the senses" changed once more with 20th-century democracy.' WJ Ong, SJ, op cit, p 5.

38. The vanguard architects of the mid-1980s believed vehemently in self-expression and rejected the imposition of their will. This resulted in the desire for the architect-designed space to be free and open to the inhabitant, allowing him or her to decide how to organise it. Frank Gehry pursued a similar direction with the view that a building should act as a container with interiors that are flexible and changeable. Wolf D Prix's 'open system' used the roof structure as a 'differentiator' so that the programme could change underneath its expanse. Lebbeus Woods's projects are about self-organisation, while, throughout the 1990s, Will Alsop ensured his designs were non-deterministic by employing strategies such as meeting public groups, organising open and active workshops for individuals related to the projects, and collaborating with those who would inhabit or interact with a project. Despite this, Alsop believes that the architect still holds the right to 'have the last word'.

39. This 'new spirit' was expressed in the work of other architects who were not exhibited in the seminal show at MoMA despite being influential from the early 1980s. Examples include Günther Domenig, Richter-Gerngross, Gaetano Pesce, Gordon Matta-Clark and James Wines. It is arguable that they were not included because their work did not fit within the Derridean theme of 'Deconstructivism'.

40. The exhibition's catalogue dealt with fragmented language that is now recognised as Deconstructivist but not at all with the emotional impact of the architecture. It was written in a very analytical and dry manner, reinforced by a choice of images that illustrated the cerebral text. This reduced the emotional expression in each work, though the architecture exhibited by Frank Gehry, Zaha Hadid, Daniel Libeskind and COOP HIMMELB(L)AU clearly demonstrated a personal creative authority and an imagination driven by emotions.

41. A reminder of an 18th-century argument: 'The Romanticism with the plea for the liberation of the human emotions, and the free expression of personality and imagination, challenged the Enlightenment's stress on Rationalism. The Enlightenment philosophers and the Romantics both believed in the individual's personal significance. But, the Romantics blamed the Philosophers for separating people from their feelings, and crushing their spontaneity and individuality in order to fit all life into mechanical framework, soulless thinking machines.' Marvin Perry, op cit, p 174.

42. That exhibition brought an end to a short decade, the late 1970s to late 1980s, that was typified by freer architecture. James Wines's book *De-Architecture* (published a year before the MoMA exhibition in New York) reminds us that architecture is 'the most public of arts' and that 'de-architecture's basic premise is that art, not design, is the supreme mission of a building, and that the creative process must be revised to reflect this objective.' James Wines, *De-Architecture*, Rizzoli, New York, 1987, p 118.

43. 'Deconstruction' is a term used in philosophy, literary criticism and the social sciences, popularised through its usage by Jacques Derrida in the 1960s. Peter Eisenman, Bernard Tschumi and Mark Wigley were influenced by him, while Frank Gehry, COOP HIMMELB(L)AU, Zaha Hadid and Daniel Libeskind never referred to Derrida's writing.

44. Following in the footsteps of Eisenman and Tschumi, the 'Decon' exhibitors and Wigley's curatorial approach, Dutch architect Rem Koolhaas also became an important influence on the architectural scene, although his more recent work has a more inclusive and ambiguous agenda.

45. 'Digital architects' embrace a complete computational design process using the computer as a design tool from early sketches, developed drawings, drawn models and working drawings through to final products manufactured and produced by rapid-prototyping machines. It is about the CAD/CAM (computer-aided design and computer-aided manufacturing) path of design and production. Other architects use computers alongside non-digital tools and have different agendas, modes of conceptual thinking and psychology.

46. 'Bergson basically says, "intuition is when you have a technique and you can envision the evolution of that technique at another level, and intuition is seeing that kind of extrapolation of something into the future before you've mastered it".' Extract from conversation between Yael Reisner and Greg Lynn in September 2004.

47. *L'Architecture d'Aujourd'hui*, 349, Nov/Dec 2003, pp 96–7. Cache's zealous words are a reminder of the mid-1920s and mid-1930s' critique on the Expressionist artists and architects who were regarded as capricious and too emotional.

48. Lars Spuybroek, *NOX: Machining Architecture*, Thames & Hudson, London, 2004, p 4.

49. Very strong evidence for this crucial relationship lies in the fact that all the interviewees are involved in academic discourse, which is where experimental architecture is taking place.

50. James Hillman, an American psychologist, is considered to be one of the most original of the 20th century. Hillman was, for 10 years, Director of the CG Jung Institute in Zurich. He is a founding fellow of the Dallas Institute of Humanities and Culture, publisher of Spring Publications, and Editor of *Spring: A Journal of Archetype and Culture*. See Bill Beckley with David Shapiro, *Uncontrollable Beauty: Toward a New Aesthetics*, Allworth Press, New York, 1998, p 405.

51. James Hillman, 'The practice of beauty: an essay', in Bill Beckley with David Shapiro, op cit, p 263.

52. As someone who enjoyed studying science before turning to architecture, and who sees the value of acquired knowledge, I still find the number of references to science by architects overdrawn and unbalanced.

53. James Hillman, op cit, p 266.

54. Thus Diaz Alonso's projects are an expression of the new architectural aesthetic he embarked on in 2002 and 2003. This has a clear affinity with other architects' modes of expression. For example, Lebbeus Woods's The Fall installation in Paris (2002), the Canadian architect Philip Beesley's Orgone Reef 'inverted landscape' travelling architectural installation (2004), and CJ Lim's Virtually Venice project (2004), exhibited in the British Pavilion at the Venice Biennale. This aesthetic approach is also presented in Lim's and Studio 8's more recent project, The Baker's Garden (2008). And here, in my students' projects from 1999 (Marjan Colletti and Aniko Meszaros), representing the early buds; or in my own project, Manifold Silhouettes (2004–07), which demonstrates an aesthetic approach I have been striving for along with other architects since the turn of the century. Others exploring this field, to name just a few, include marcosandmarjan (Marcos Cruz and Marjan Colletti) in London, Evan Douglis in New York, and Servo and Dennis Dollens in Los Angeles. These projects, though very different architecturally, show an aesthetic affinity. They stem from a completely different direction of thought and activity, using different design tools and mediums.

55. As the American critic Dave Hickey writes: 'In images … beauty was the agency that caused visual pleasure in the beholder … I direct your attention to the language of visual affect – to the rhetoric of how things look – to the iconography of desire – in a word, to beauty!' From the essay 'Invisible dragon', published also in Bill Beckley with David Shapiro, op cit. pp 15-16, first published in Dave Hickey, *The Invisible Dragon: Four Essays on Beauty*, Art Issues Press, USA, 1993.

56. After the inspiring book *Uncontrollable Beauty*. Bill Beckley with David Shapiro, op cit.

Frank O Gehry
A WHITE CANVAS MOMENT

THE GUGGENHEIM MUSEUM IN BILBAO (1997) propelled architect Frank O Gehry's work onto the world stage and cemented his status as one of the few architectural 'names' that instantly registers recognition within the collective public consciousness. The building's seductive, expressive form, heroic interiors, glistening titanium-clad exterior and contextual, photogenic presence ensured that the project was widely celebrated and published through the mass media, becoming one of the most resonant buildings of the 20th century.

Predating Bilbao by 20 years, Gehry's own house in Santa Monica (1978), Los Angeles, had already established his reputation within the international architectural community. This richly layered, spatial composition employed construction techniques to create a visual toughness and rawness through its lack of craftsmanship. The strategy succeeded in capturing a sense of the extraordinary derived from ordinary means, and resulted in a poetic and innovative composition. Gehry's aspiration to create a new and expressive American architectural language that aligned itself with the LA art world rather than with the LA architectural preoccupations of the day, was prophetic of his later work, and was significantly developed in, for example, the startling forms of the Vitra Design Museum in Weil am Rhein, Germany (1989), the DZ Bank Building in Berlin (2000), the Walt Disney Concert Hall in downtown Los Angeles (2003) and the hotel at the Marqués de Riscal Winery in Elciego, in the Rioja region of Spain (2006), among others.

OPPOSITE GEHRY RESIDENCE, SANTA MONICA, LOS ANGELES, CALIFORNIA, USA, 1978

Gehry's own house in Santa Monica was the first project to establish his reputation within the international architectural community. This richly layered, spatial composition employed construction techniques to create a visual toughness and rawness through its lack of craftsmanship. The strategy succeeded in capturing a sense of the extraordinary derived from ordinary means, and resulted in a poetic and innovative composition.

Now 80 years old, Gehry remains a vital and integral presence in his large office, travelling often for his projects which are scattered throughout the US, Europe and the Middle East, yet driving and directing the design process at both the micro and macro level. The latter indicates his strong work ethic and total commitment to his practice – released only by his Sunday ritual of ocean sailing. Unassuming and quietly spoken, Gehry admits that his congenial personality masks an inquisitive and fiercely ambitious mind. Driven by his passion and expert knowledge of fine art, classical and contemporary

music and literature,[1] he believes that the human condition should be the leading driver of the design process. His work transcends professional and public boundaries through its humanistic, expressive yet highly experimental form – all factors that resulted in him being awarded architecture's highest honour, the Pritzker Prize, in 1989.

Frank Gehry's career as an architect evolved from a childhood dominated by poverty but enriched by the embracement of culture: 'My mother always took me to art museums and classical music concerts,' he recalls. 'My parents were very poor, but my mother had studied violin as a child and so her belief was that I should be exposed to cultural things. My father – who was not educated at all – won awards for window dressing. He was this tough kind of guy who spoke street English,[2] but he had a yearning to design and he used to talk about his window installations and show me pictures of the work.' Continuing, he explains: 'There was no sense of "design" within our house, yet when my mother could afford it, she bought beautiful objects that were different than any of our friends' interiors. I remember seeing and noting the difference in their character.'

Encouraged by his family to pursue his ambitions, Gehry began his studies in fine arts and ceramics before studying architecture at the University of Southern California and Harvard's Graduate School of Design. Although he didn't draw naturally, Gehry quickly learnt to sketch and communicate his work with dexterity, partly influenced by his ongoing connection with the work of the university's art students: 'I didn't draw very much as a child but I was very interested in art. When I was accepted into architecture after studying fine art I kept a relationship with the department and continued to be interested in the art students' work.'

While studying at Harvard, Gehry was introduced by his tutor, Joseph Hudnut, to the notion of creating a new American architectural language appropriate for the time: 'Joseph Hudnut would take us on long walks through Boston and talked about "American" architecture. That was when it really hit me ... that an ambition to create an American architecture was something to strive for and that meant you had to find a new language because one didn't really exist yet. How do you do something when nobody is doing it yet? I felt optimistic about America and so it was all about finding new ways.'[3]

Post graduation, and after taking his first position with Victor Gruen Associates, Gehry began to realise that his architectural ambition differed starkly from those of his colleagues who were engaged with a Functionalist aesthetic and were uninterested in pursuing an engagement with art. As a result, he gravitated to the graphic designers and artists within the office who supported his direction: 'In Gruen's office, I became friends with the graphics staff rather than the other architects who were critical of my position.

OPPOSITE GEHRY RESIDENCE, SANTA MONICA, LOS ANGELES, CALIFORNIA, USA, 1978

Gehry's aspiration was to create a new and expressive American architectural language that aligned itself with the LA art world rather than with the local architectural preoccupations of the day. He wanted to explore the possibilities of bringing the qualities he admired within painting to architecture: 'I wanted to see ... in particular, how could a building be made to look like it's in process? And how could the expressive and compositional attitudes of painting be explored in a building?'

BELOW LEWIS RESIDENCE, LYNDHURST, OHIO, USA, 1989

The still life compositions of the Italian painter Georgio Morandi informed Gehry's aspiration to create a better scale for an architectural experience. He explains: 'I was looking at how to break down the monolithic Modernist building into pieces that could break down the scale and create a different urban model.' This strategy was rigorously pursued within the Lewis Residence – a house that was never built yet provided an important reference point for many of Gehry's later projects.

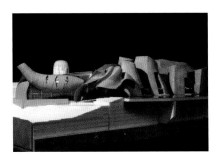

We used to go to all the galleries together so I knew a lot of LA artists[4] and became very familiar with their work. I felt that they approved of me and encouraged me. In a sense they were my team.'

The decision to strike out on his own and establish his own practice in 1962[5] provided the opportunity for Gehry to pursue his interest in self-expression and explore the possibilities of bringing the qualities he admired within painting to architecture.[6] He found the work of Georgio Morandi – a well-known Italian painter in the 1970s[7] – particularly resonant and was influenced by the artist's still-life paintings derived from everyday sources as well as his compositional arrangements. Unable to find support or establish a discourse with the local architectural community, Gehry continued to consolidate his relationships with artists, relating more easily to the emotions expressed in the LA art world[8] than in the local architectural establishment of the time.[9]

Gehry firmly rejects the notion that self-expression is a capricious act within the design process. Conversely, he believes that signature and democracy are integrally interlinked and, in fact, when an architect suppresses his or her emotions within the design process, it is an act that 'talks down to people' and does not allow a full engagement with architecture. Certainly, the role of self-expression and its legitimacy in architecture is a

ABOVE LEWIS RESIDENCE, LYNDHURST, OHIO, USA, 1989

Gehry firmly rejects the notion that self-expression is a capricious act. Conversely, he believes that signature and democracy are integrally interlinked and, in fact, when an architect suppresses his emotions within the design process, it is an act that 'talks down to people' and does not allow a full engagement with architecture.

BELOW FRANK GEHRY'S PORTRAIT SITTING ON A CARDBOARD CHAIR MODEL FROM HIS 'EXPERIMENTAL EDGES' SERIES, EARLY 1980s

Gehry states: 'Not imposing yourself means you have to modify your feelings to a lower level of expression and I believe that is "talking down" to people. If you take an idealistic approach then it follows that if every human being delivers to the table their best efforts, then society is elevated because the individuals' efforts add up to a whole.'

familiar issue within architectural discourse,[10] and one that resurfaces with a sense of self-righteousness within the digital realm. As a result, Gehry's position is consolidated by years of battling criticism that his architecture is too derivative of the art world – too sculptural and self-expressive. His response to this critique is clear and direct: 'To deny the validity of self-expression is akin to not believing in democracy – it's a basic value … If you believe in democracy then you must allow for personal expression.'[11]

Gehry references other creative disciplines as having a healthier relationship with the notion of an embodied signature within the work: 'Any suggestion of an architect having a signature is a colossal put-down. Yet, it's not the same for any other discipline within the performing arts – cinema, music or art.' He explains that his process is disconnected from critical discourse: 'I just get on with the work and do it – it doesn't seem worth the discussion, or trying to convince people. I think there is a consistent denial as to what constitutes excellence and I'm very uncomfortable with the notion that you do one building and then suddenly there's an idea of being a "star" architect – that's so deprecating.'

Despite the public accolades, Gehry found that success had a less positive effect on his practice: 'I completed the Guggenheim Bilbao in 1997 and it was a big success, number one on the hit parade, yet I didn't receive any more museum commissions though Renzo Piano had many. And the Walt Disney Concert Hall was also number one on the hit parade – it works like a dream. Yet still no calls – Herzog & de Meuron and Jean Nouvel have all had commissions.' He continues: 'When I finished Bilbao there was a museum conference in London with curators and directors such as Nicholas Serota of the Tate Modern and they all spoke against my design.'

Despite this disparity between Gehry's perceived success and the reality of working commissions, he maintained his commitment to a personalised approach and has seen the critique come full circle: 'Now there's a backlash because the extension to MoMA[12] has totally failed. The neutral white cube ideology is turning and now I am beginning to get hired for museum projects again, such as the new Guggenheim Museum in Dubai.'

Gehry describes his design process as working from the 'inside out', and yet the exteriors of his buildings often look very different than the interiors. His friend, artist Robert Wilson, has described this approach to an interior/exterior relationship by drawing an analogy with the way that an orange skin is very different from its interior.[13] Gehry also returns to the compositions of Morandi to inform his aspiration to create a better scale for an architectural experience, explaining: 'I was looking at how to break down the monolithic Modernist building into pieces that could break down the scale[14] and create a different

ABOVE VITRA INTERNATIONAL MANUFACTURING FACILITY AND DESIGN MUSEUM, WEIL AM RHEIN, GERMANY, 1989

Gehry advocates signature within artistic endeavour: 'Any suggestion of an architect having a signature is a colossal put-down. Yet, it's not the same for any other disciplines within the performing arts – cinema, music or art ... I think there is a consistent denial as to what constitutes excellence and I'm very uncomfortable with the notion that you do one building and then suddenly there's an idea of being a "star" architect – that's so deprecating.'

urban model[15] based on European references. I think it's intriguing that Rem Koolhaas seems to be doing large-scale work in the spirit of Le Corbusier – it's strange to me that the Modernist approach is coming back as a model.'

For Gehry, Mies van der Rohe's renowned Barcelona Pavilion (1929) was the ultimate expression of 'form follows function', yet he points out the contradictions inherent in the ideology: 'I think that the Barcelona Pavilion is the most successful Modernist example of the interior and exterior as one thing. Yet the connection between the walls and the ceiling and the engineering to achieve that effect is hidden from view. So the irony is that the small scale defies what they were aspiring to do.'

In contrast to the Modernist ideology, though Gehry may begin his design process with functional requirements the form will not necessarily be related directly to programme. 'I have always maintained that the building is a container or "shell" and that the interior has to be flexible and changeable as most buildings will change use over time. The separation between interior and exterior is also realistic for budgets and changing functions. I don't, however, just build a container and then jam programme in; I always work from the inside out, but with flexibility and an "open-ended" system.'

This 'inside out' strategy is supported by Gehry's technique of working with many physical models[16] as preliminary 'sketches' in order to gain a strong sense of organisation and scale for each project. 'I work with models to plan in a very conventional way and organise the building from the interior,' he explains. 'So before I draw I know the scale and the spatial proportions and I've got the design pretty well established in my brain. When I eventually sketch I'm pretty close to the reality and even though the drawings look "squiggly", when you see them next to the finished building they look pretty close to the built form.'

For Gehry, thinking through making models and sketching is simply a method for unearthing ideas rather than any kind of objectification of the model itself. He eschews any preciousness about the process: 'It's simply a method for intuitive expression – you find something and then you're opportunistic with that idea. It's like a pussycat with a ball of thread; you start pushing and you don't know what's going to happen and then something falls and you chase after it – "it" being the intellectual opportunity.'[17]

RIGHT VITRA INTERNATIONAL MANUFACTURING FACILITY AND DESIGN MUSEUM, WEIL AM RHEIN, GERMANY, 1989

Gehry usually begins his design process with functional requirements but the form will not necessarily be related directly to programme. He explains: 'I have always maintained that the building is a container or "shell" and the interior has to be flexible and changeable ... The separation between interior and exterior is also realistic for budgets and changing functions ... I always work from the inside out, but with flexibility and an "open-ended" system.'

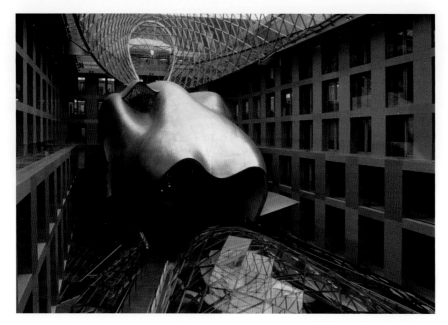

However, Gehry tempers his passion for pursuing opportunity with each new project with an innate respect for site and cultural context[18] – a preoccupation he shares with other LA-based architects such as Thom Mayne and Eric Owen Moss.[19] While all three architects acknowledge that this preoccupation is occasionally borne out of the pragmatics of budget where partly using conventional construction techniques can create freedom for experimentation, they also have individual concerns. Mayne's aspiration lies in the desire to imbue his work with memory, while Moss believes it is a connection with a historic continuum that drives his process. However, for Gehry it is a more personal agenda – the desire to be a self-described 'do-gooder' that comes from his Jewish upbringing. 'The essence of the Jewish faith is: "Do unto others as you would have others do unto you",' he explains. 'So if you take that ideology to architecture then you have to consider that a building is a neighbour to somebody or something. I think that the Guggenheim Bilbao was successful in creating a relationship with its neighbours and I feel that's the golden rule – be a good neighbour.'[20]

Gehry's aspiration to be neighbourly, open and accessible is also reflected in his wariness of a forced connection between cultural theory and architectural practice, particularly where it has the potential to contribute to misleading or misappropriated meanings: 'French philosophy and its relationship to architecture has lost me. I actually met Jacques

Derrida once and talked to him about "Deconstruction" as it related to architecture, and he said that the way it was presented within the Museum of Modern Art's "Deconstructivist Architecture" show[21] wasn't his intent. Personally, Derrida's philosophy didn't actually interest me so I felt it was opportunistic to use the word "deconstruction" for the purpose of the exhibition. As a consequence, when people looked at my house at that time, and heard the word "deconstruction", they would say "oh that's it!'" As a result, I felt I'd been hijacked and misappropriated.[22]

Gehry resists the word 'beauty' as being representative of values with which he struggles to find a connection: 'The connotation of "beauty" for me is that it represents pretty and, therefore, the association is "soft" – I'm not interested in that in a building.' Undoubtedly, the term sits uncomfortably with his architectural language, which early on in his career pursued a rough, tough aesthetic. And while it has evolved into the refined and elegant collage within projects such as the Guggenheim Bilbao, his aesthetic continues to feel at odds with any traditional notion of beauty. Elaborating, Gehry explains: 'Beauty is in the eye of the beholder so I find that my understanding of what is beautiful and what is ugly is pretty wide and open compared to others. It's a visual thing and difficult to define. Artists talk about it being tough and there's a certain toughness to my aesthetic.'

Despite Gehry's discomfort with the term 'beauty', he is much more at ease with the expressive nature of his work than the majority of his contemporaries; his architectural language is derived almost completely from the self and is completely fluid with no fixed preoccupation.[23] His preoccupation with quality of light within his architecture is a direct result of living in Canada during his early adolescence, coupled with his deep affinity with

ABOVE HOTEL AT MARQUÉS DE RISCAL, ELCIEGO, (ALAVA) SPAIN, 2006

Gehry works with a multitude of models as preliminary three-dimensional 'sketches': 'Before I draw I know the scale and the spatial proportions ... When I eventually sketch I'm pretty close to the reality and even though the drawings look "squiggly", when you see them next to the finished building they look pretty close to the built form.'

BELOW GUGGENHEIM MUSEUM ABU DHABI, ABU DHABI, UNITED ARAB EMIRATES, 2007

Despite the popularity and success of the Guggenheim Museum in Bilbao, it was over a decade before Gehry was commissioned to design another museum. Although he weathered criticism for his expressive approach, he has maintained his position and has watched the critique come full circle.

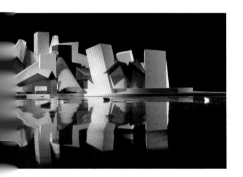

Nordic architecture and particularly the work of Alvar Aalto whose studio he visited in 1972: 'I feel that I relate to Aalto more than any other architect because of that experience. But nobody sees that in me for some reason.'[24]

Gehry's engagement with his work is derived more from the process of his architecture rather than the end form or building – what he calls a 'white canvas' moment. 'I feel a brotherhood with artists because they have a moment of truth when they face a white canvas. And I imagine that's a very threatening moment in one's life,' he explains. 'Here you are, you've got the canvas and the paint so what marks will you choose and why? What inspires you to start and what makes you decide on your approach?'

Holding this deeply felt kinship with the artist's intuitive process, Gehry reflects on his own architectural methodology: 'Every artist I know just starts working, they don't have any preconceived ideas. They might be informed by their personal history or by their knowledge of art history, but then they bring to the work their own particular time. It's just intuitive, it happens, it informs itself as it goes along. I always look back at buildings when they're finished and say: "How the hell did that happen?" I never record my process and so I don't know and I don't want to know ... that would tighten up the process so I couldn't do anything.'

Characteristically, Gehry returns to another art reference point to succinctly sum up his position: 'Within the architectural process the critical point comes when you've solved the project and the site, you've established the building's budget, timescale, technical issues and organisation[25] and now you're ready to make it into something. Then you have the same "moment of truth" as an artist where you have to decide on form, composition, colour, texture, and you make a deeply personal commitment to a building or project. Ultimately, my moment of truth is just as threatening for me as it must be for the guy with the white canvas.'

Interviews
Gehry's office, Los Angeles, 13 December 2006
Gehry's office, Los Angeles, 16 December 2006
Del Rey Yacht Club, Marina Del Rey, Los Angeles, 28 July 2007

Notes

1. 'I'm pretty well educated. I've been involved with a lot of art and studied architectural history pretty damned thoroughly. I appreciate the interaction between architecture and great classical music and I understand the relationship between architecture, literature, art, painting and sculpture. I'm not a scholar, but I do have some sense of it.' Frank Gehry, interview with Yael Reisner, 28 July 2007.

2. Frank Gehry's father was born in New York before moving to Canada, and his mother was born in Poland. Gehry was born in Toronto, and at the age of 18 moved to Los Angeles with his parents.

3. *Frank O Gehry, Kurt W Forster*, Art and Architecture in Conversation, Series, Cantz, Germany, 1999, conversation between Frank O Gehry and Kurt W Forster with Cristina Bechtler. Santa Monica, California, 24 August, 1997, p 60.

4. 'I connected with the work of the LA artists because there was feeling in the work that I could respond to and have an emotional experience.' Frank Gehry, interview with Yael Reisner, 13 December 2006.

5. As Gehry recalls: 'The first person who recognised me was Esther McCoy, the architectural historian renowned for her specialised knowledge on RM Schindler. She wrote about the Danziger House for an international magazine and that was first time that I ever received any attention past the borders of California.' Interview with Yael Reisner, 13 December 2006.

6. 'I'm looking at painting all the time, so one part of architecture that I felt an interest in exploring was how to bring these ideas to buildings. The tradition of Mondrian's paintings affecting architecture is an old story. I wanted to see what else we could learn from paintings. In particular, how could a building be made to look it's in process? And how can the expressive and compositional attitudes of painting be explored in a building?' In Frank Gehry, *Frank Gehry: Buildings and Projects*, Rizzoli, New York, 1985, p xiii.

7. Many architects from the 1960s and early 1970s also referenced the visual arts – albeit with different approaches – instigating a genuine spirit of change after two decades of design led by a utilitarian ethos. At the Architectural Association in London, the Archigram group looked at a wide range of visual sources. The Russian Constructivists were revisited by Elia Zenghelis, Rem Koolhaas and Zaha Hadid (who at the time was a student of Zenghelis and Koolhaas). In New York, James Wines was also engaged with the issues arising from the art world. In Vienna, COOP HIMMELB(L)AU was influenced by the Viennese painter Arnulf Rainer, who was engaged with emotional paintings, while Tel Aviv-based architect Zvi Hecker was influenced by the artist Mario Merz.

8. Other artists Gehry met included: Robert Irwin, John Altoon and his wife, Jasper Johns, Robert Rauschenberg, John Chamberlain, Viva, Paul Morrissey, Claes Oldenburg, James Rosenquist, Don Judd and Carl Andre. *Frank O Gehry, Kurt W. Forster*, Art and Architecture in Conversation Series, Cantz, Germany, 1999, conversation between Frank O Gehry and Kurt W Forster with Cristina Bechtler. Santa Monica, California, 24 August, 1997, pp 60-1.

9. 'Who was doing Architecture in LA in the 1960s? John Lautner started to wane for me, Ray Kappe was friendly but rather distant, Bernard Zimmerman was cranky about my work. So the architectural milieu was not accessible to me. Schindler was gone, I met Neutra a few times, but didn't find him very exciting to be around.' Ibid, p 63.

10. Since the fall of German Expressionism, personal expression has been widely viewed by architectural critics as a capricious act. As Wolfgang Pehnt writes: 'Adolf Behne was the first of the architects and architectural critics in Germany ... to announce [in Berlin in 1927] ... [this is] the end of the rule of Caprice ... What had hitherto been celebrated as an expression of a general will now appeared as pure subjectivity. 'The personal, individualistic work will be more out of place ... than ever before ... Objectivity [is] the highest thing of which we are capable.' Wolfgang Pehnt, *Expressionist Architecture*, Thames & Hudson, London, 1973, p195.

11. 'Not imposing yourself means you have to modify your feelings to a lower level of expression, and I believe that is "talking down" to people. If you take an idealistic approach then it follows that if every human being delivers to the table their best efforts, then society is elevated because the individuals' efforts add up to a whole. Conversely, if each individual within a society downplays their best efforts and modifies it to a lower level of expression, then it's ultimately like self-flagellation. They are beating themselves because they have to pay for their sins and the sins of their forefathers.' Frank Gehry, interview with Yael Reisner, 13 December 2006.

12. The competition for the expansion of New York's Museum of Modern Art (MoMA) was won by the Japanese architect Yoshio Taniguchi in 1997, and the work completed in 2005.

13. According to Wilson: "Bauhaus was formful as functional. The outside revealed the inside. With a fish and an orange the skin is very different than the interior.' *Frank O Gehry, Kurt W Forster*, Art and Architecture in Conversation Series, Cantz, Germany, 1999, conversation between Frank O Gehry and Kurt W Forster with Cristina Bechtler. Santa Monica, California, 24 August, 1997, p 72.

14. 'I wasn't the only one with that approach ... Jim Stirling ... Aldo Rossi ... we went different ways ... I think I related more to Stirling at the time, and probably also to Lou Kahn, who was interested in breaking down the building except that when Kahn broke them down they kept their unity.' Ibid, pp 29–31.

15. Gehry describes the design process for the Wynton Guest house in Wayzata, Minnesota (1987): 'These are people who are very neat and clean ... what they really wanted ... was that it had to look like a sculpture ... That's when I started thinking, well, if I made a still life ... a Morandi "three big bottles and three little bottles", in order for each piece to retain its "objecthood", then the thing had to have the crack. It had to have the separation, it couldn't be a continuous structure.' Ibid, p 25.

16. 'I make lots of models and sketches – it just helps me to think and my team use them to make hundreds of models per project.' Frank Gehry, interview with Yael Reisner, July 2007.

17. Gehry believes in a lateral, creative design process: 'I just gave a talk in Atlanta to 7,000 neuroscientists on the topic of "creativity". I explained that if I knew what I was going to do before I started the design process then I wouldn't do it, so it's a bit like the cat with the ball; you become opportunistic, you discover things and then you work with them, which leads to another discovery and growth. They loved it; that's the way they work, so I do believe that this is a good model.' Interview with Yael Reisner, 16 December 2006.

18. Many of Gehry's buildings have a wing that is box-like and generic, as seen in the Walt Disney Concert Hall, Los Angeles (2003) or the hotel at the Marqués de Riscal Winery in Elciego, in the Rioja region of Spain (2006). In addition, the projects of Morphosis through the 1990s often utilised a rectangular plan with the new, innovative architectural parts expressed through the section. Eric Owen Moss also retains traces of existing structures and juxtaposes his dialectical expressions.

19. An approach that is distinctly different than their European counterparts such as Zaha Hadid, COOP HIMMELB(L)AU, Hans Hollein, Jean Nouvel, Peter Cook and others. As Gehry explains: 'I understand that if you are in Europe it's a different context and it can become oppressive.' Interview with Yael Reisner, 16 December 2006.

20. Gehry states: 'I worry about mega-projects such as Rem Koolhaas's CCTV in China, which I like because they are Corbusian in scale and attitude. It's like a brave new world or metropolis but very impersonal. I think you can go to that scale and invent a new world, but you need to remember the individual.' He cites Archigram as having successfully expressed a vision for the future with an understanding of humanity: 'It's clear to me that Archigram invented the language for the new world, and that's what we are doing now. Their models of the city are still relevant today. I don't think that anybody has come up with a better one for the future. They tapped electronics, robotics, everything. My only problem with their position at the time was that there wasn't the level of art content that I could relate to.' Interview with Yael Reisner, 16 December 2006.

21. 'Deconstructivist Architecture', Museum of Modern Art (MoMA), New York, 1988, curated by Mark Wigley and Philip Johnson. This seminal exhibition featured the work of seven architects: Peter Eisenman, Bernard Tschumi, Frank Gehry, Zaha Hadid, COOP HIMMELB(L)AU, Daniel Libeskind and Rem Koolhaas.

22. As Gehry recalls: 'I took part in the exhibition and I shut my mouth about how I felt – I didn't do anything. I don't think I even went to the conferences they had. I don't remember participating because I didn't know how to talk about Derrida. And in any case, Derrida said they really misunderstood him.' Interview with Yael Reisner, July 2007.

23. As Gehry has often stated: 'I think my ideas are derived more from paintings than sculptures, but I'm all over the place with my influences. Whenever I go to a museum I fall in love with something, yet each time I see it differently from the last time. I am interested in all of the arts such as music and literature. I would never be just monochromatic, I always take a broad outlook.' Interview with Yael Reisner, 13 December 2006.

24. While architectural critics may not be attuned to Gehry's Nordic sensibilities, Peter Cook has for many years drawn his students' attention to Gehry's affinity with the manner in which Nordic architects handle natural light, as is evident in Sigurd Lewerentz's St Peter's Church in Klippan, Sweden (1966).

25. According to Gehry: 'As architects we have plumbing and building departments and clients, and so it's presumed that these elements eclipse and neutralise the moment of truth, but I don't believe that's true.' Interview with Yael Reisner, 28 July 2007.

Zvi Hecker

A RARE ACHIEVEMENT

BORN IN POLAND IN 1931, architect Zvi Hecker grew up in Europe during the turbulent times of the Second World War and eventually fled Cracow in fear of the advancing German army. He spent much of his formative years in the city of Samarkand in Uzbekistan[1] before returning briefly to Cracow to face the increasing communist influence over his home city. In rejection of another oppressive regime, Hecker and his family relocated to Israel in 1950, taking refuge in a temporary camp near Haifa in an ex-British military camp. Despite these difficult circumstances, Hecker settled and quickly enrolled to continue his architectural studies[2] at the Technion in Haifa.[3]

Now, at the age of 77 and in excellent health, Hecker is a humorous gentleman with a fondness for telling anecdotes about the various artists and writers he admires rather than engaging in dry, academic discourse. Yet his calm and warm personality conceals a provocative mind that is quick to challenge the status quo and make an astute point with only a few well-chosen words – a characteristic that is also present in his dynamic architecture.[4] Hecker gives great importance to the aesthetic decisions that underpin his architecture and is open and willing to discuss the influence of form, expression and style within his work – a fact that sets him apart from many architects who reject any role of aesthetics in the design process. It is a sentiment that Hecker finds bemusing, quoting the late Modern master Alvar Aalto as saying: 'To take the idea of form out of architecture is like taking the idea of heaven from religion!' Indeed, in stark contrast to his peers, Hecker's practice manifesto embraces esoteric values: 'Architecture is an act of magic; it hides more than it reveals.' To this end, he believes that architecture is a true art form and an expression of the human soul.

OPPOSITE BAT YAM CITY HALL, BAT YAM, ISRAEL, 1963

Breaking away from the aesthetic of the white city of Tel Aviv, in an attempt to create a new identity for a local new town, Bat Yam is influenced by ancient regional tradition, biblical and historic European references along with progressive architectural ideas. The ancient typology of the cool, shadowed, inner courtyard for hot climates was part of the inspiration for the project's working and meeting spaces.

ABOVE **ABOVE** BAT YAM CITY HALL, BAT YAM, ISRAEL, 1963

Searching for a new architectural expression grounded the new building with historical references. As Hecker explains: 'Neumann always looked for historical precedents and one can see that the project's main staircase was referenced from the city hall of Florence, the bench around the building from Palazzo Strozzi and the main interior hall from Tony Garnier's Hôtel de Ville in Bois de Boulogne.'

Zvi Hecker decided that architecture was his vocation at the tender age of 13 while attending school in Samarkand.[5] The young Hecker studied and drew the ruins of Muslim architecture, forming a deep connection with design practice. Recommencing his studies post-war and relocating from Cracow to Israel in 1950, he found a new and influential mentor within the Technion's Faculty of Architecture: Alfred Neumann, a Czech architect from Brno[6] who had studied under Peter Behrens in Vienna before working for Adolf Loos and Auguste Perret. As Hecker reflects: 'We were still in a refugee camp after arriving in Israel, but the first thing I did was go to the Technion. I was horrified! I had completed one semester in Cracow before leaving and the presentation of the projects and graphics were incredibly beautiful. On an introductory tour of the School of Architecture,[7] I saw transparent pieces of paper with drawings, cut roughly in different sizes, drawn in hard pencil and very difficult to read. You could imagine my disappointment!' Explaining further, Hecker suggests: 'I think the programme was focused on strict utilitarianism. It was a transitional period and the great German-speaking architects from Austria and Germany like Richard Kauffman,[8] Leopold Krakauer and Heinrich Rau had already left the Technion. However, and thank God, when I was in my second year of studies Alfred Neumann joined the Faculty of Architecture.'

BAT YAM CITY HALL, BAT YAM, ISRAEL, 1963

The climate in this part of Israel dictates an outdoor lifestyle for most of the year. As Hecker explains: 'We enriched the programme of what was a strict office building with the addition of public functions that could be used by both the bureaucrats and the citizens of Bat Yam, including a reflecting pool, a performing stage and a small amphitheatre, as well as ventilation towers located on the roof, to encourage public gatherings and events.'

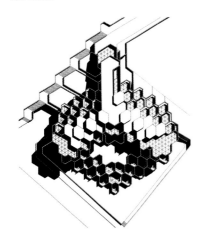

DUBINER HOUSE RESIDENTIAL COMPLEX, RAMAT GAN, ISRAEL, 1963

From the early 1960s Hecker was one of the Israeli avant-garde architects who broke away from the Modernist Cartesian grid and moved towards a polyhedral lattice. The Dubiner House apartments were situated along a hexagonal lattice to generate the dynamic overall form.

After completing his architectural studies, Hecker moved to Tel Aviv where he set up practice with young local architect Eldar Sharon.[9] Together they enjoyed early success with their competition-winning scheme for a city hall for the new city of Bat Yam, south of Tel Aviv. Challenged and encouraged by this achievement, Hecker approached his long-time mentor Alfred Neumann to join the partnership – a move that would also enable Neumann to realise his first building within Israel. As Hecker explains: 'I thought Neumann was simply a genius who should have the opportunity to build. For his part, he insisted that the work was to be wholly collaborative.' He continues: 'For Neumann, architecture was not about geometry but expression.[10] He talked about Bat Yam being the equivalent to Tel Aviv as Pompeii was to Rome. He always looked for historical precedents and one can see that the project's main staircase was referenced from the city hall of Florence, the bench around the building from Palazzo Strozzi, and the main interior hall from Tony Garnier's Hôtel de Ville in the Bois de Boulogne.'

The Bat Yam project effortlessly combined European references with biblical ones: for example, the building's brightly coloured concrete panels in hues of blue, red and gold according to the colours of King David.[11] Continuing, Hecker adds that the design was underpinned by a desire to create a sense of presence for the new building: 'We really

LEFT DUBINER HOUSE RESIDENTIAL COMPLEX, RAMAT GAN, ISRAEL, 1963

The complex is built on the slope of a steep hill along which each apartment has its own private entry. The units can be approached from the bottom of the hill, where cars can be parked in a courtyard, before ascending through stairs and ramps within the open but shaded spatial labyrinth. Alternatively, visitors can climb up the hill via the open stairs before turning towards their chosen floor. Here Hecker articulates the journey of walking through the entry space to give the sense of being inside and protected by the architecture, even when outside it.

tried to elucidate the essence of the design. Neumann believed that even a small city like Bat Yam should have its own character, so we put the city hall in the most exposed position on the piazza, which was rectangular in form like the piazza of Pompeii. We enriched the programme of what was a strict office building with the addition of public functions that could be used by both the bureaucrats and the citizens of Bat Yam, including a reflecting pool, a performing stage and a small amphitheatre, as well as ventilation towers located on the roof, to encourage public gatherings and events.'

Every part of the project refers to a historical and cultural context, yet the building is as much a masterpiece of engineering[12] and geometry as it is a portrait of a new city inspired by cultural influences. Sadly it has lapsed into a total state of disrepair – a fact that Hecker finds overwhelming: 'It's still there but it is completely destroyed. I never go there because I suffer when I see what has become of the building.'[13]

The geometry within the completed project is difficult to detect while the camouflaging elements remain, but Hecker continues to use hidden geometries to guide the building's narrative and aesthetics. In turn, this creates a spatial dynamic that is charged, complex and exotic. The materiality adds another 'episode' of complexity to the project: the 'poor' materials that wrap the building's spiralling walls are put together in a manner that pays homage to the Arte Povera movement.

While his architectural language has varied over the years, Hecker's core values can be traced back to the strategies that his mentor, Neumann, instilled within his student and partner – an inspiration that manifests itself in Hecker's trademark courtyard strategy.[14] The courtyard became Hecker's overarching design preoccupation and a testing ground for new concepts, contextual cultural critique, forms and 'hidden' geometries throughout his collective work. With each project the strategy became more dynamic with an emphasis on the journeys created around, through, inside and outside the varying courtyard configurations. 'For me there are two kinds of architecture: one where you walk around the building in admiration, and the other where you walk into the building,' Hecker explains. 'I prefer the latter. Such architecture demands forms that simultaneously reveal their internal and external lives. I would like people to feel like they are inside the building even if they are outside.' As a result, nearly all of Hecker's projects explore the concept of what he describes as a 'city walk',[15] employing the deliberate device of directing the visitor along a series of progressions and delays through the building – much like a journey through a city.

Hecker's extraordinary forms are generated by an intense relationship with geometry within his design process in which he lays down what he describes as 'line networks' that become a system of 'geometric scaffolding'. He references the strategy back to the influence of Frank Lloyd Wright, recalling: 'It was Frank Lloyd Wright who first considered geometry as scaffolding, which is later taken off. And for me, geometry – or as I would prefer to call it, mathematics – is a necessary logic, the foundation underlying my work.' As a result, the mathematical grid and geometry that underpins Hecker's work is concealed while the cinematic unfolding of 'happenings' or 'episodes'[16] work against the scaffolding to give focus to his evocative architectural language and the unique aesthetic of his buildings.[17]

LEFT SPIRAL HOUSE APARTMENT COMPLEX, RAMAT GAN, ISRAEL, 1990

Hecker adds a provocative tone in using the cheap, slate stone commonly used for low-cost fences, pavements and buildings in the 1970s and 1980s, particularly in the Arab-Israeli villages and towns. This cultural commentary captures an ordinary, anti-bourgeois expression for a residential block. As Hecker explains: 'I accept that projects such as the Spiral House can also be viewed as a comment on society and its many contrasts and contradictions.'

BELOW SPIRAL HOUSE APARTMENT COMPLEX, RAMAT GAN, ISRAEL, 1990

Architecture generated through customised geometries became an intrinsic battle for Hecker within his design process so that every new project gave birth to a new language. The Spiral House's spectacular beauty is ruled throughout by mathematics.

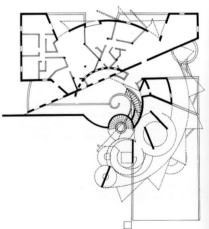

SPIRAL HOUSE APARTMENT COMPLEX, RAMAT GAN, ISRAEL, 1990

Writing in his diary in 1994, Hecker says: 'The Spiral incompleteness is also its poetry, because poetry is the most precise expression of our need for precision. Expressive as it is, The Spiral can't be fully understood. It speaks too many languages at one and the same time. It speaks in Arabic about the human condition when sheltered by the high walls. It argues in Hebrew in the sheer necessity to bring the muscles and materials together, but it is quite fluent in Russian when construction becomes architecture. Its Italian is very Baroque, as spoken in Piedmont by Guarino Guarini. The Spiral is a Tower of Babel in miniature.'

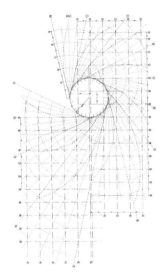

ABOVE HEINZ-GALINSKI SCHOOL, BERLIN, GERMANY, 1995

Nearly all of Hecker's projects explore the concept of what he describes as 'city walks', where the architect directs the visitor along a series of progressions and delays through the building – much like a walk through a city. In the Spiral House, and more so in this Jewish school in Berlin, Hecker's language becomes more complex and exotic due to his preoccupation with the dynamic sunflower geometry that generates the form. He privileges this geometry over all other design issues and pulls in free elements as 'happenings' and 'episodes' to camouflage its strength.

Hecker's approach to geometry is a distinctly personal one that drives the narrative for each project. One can trace his geometric preoccupations through the early 1960s, beginning with the square, and developing through the 1970s to static polyhedral geometries. In the early 1980s he embarked on a series of projects that explored the dynamic 'sunflower geometry',[18] with the intention of creating a sense of gravitated momentum within his work. Thus, the underlying geometry became increasingly difficult to detect within his projects and, coupled with the contradictory qualities of added 'happenings' or 'episodes', resulted in increasingly charged, complex and exotic spatial experiences.

For example, the spiral of the celebrated Spiral House apartment complex in Ramat Gan (1990) started with a geometry based on the sunflower, customised to lead upwards and further camouflaged by snake-like forms. Hecker describes these narrative elements as appearing 'only when the geometry and the structure are very clear. Then one can camouflage this so-called precision. That is also how the snakes were introduced first to guard the paradise and then to frighten the neighbour who constantly complained about the Spiral House being built next to his lot.' Hecker also introduces 'poor' materials to wrap the building's spiralling walls,[19] recalling the Arte Povera style.[20] He describes the strategy as 'an attempt to express human thoughts and emotions using the most ordinary materials – it's a noble aim that I think sums up what architecture is about.'

For the competition-winning Heinz-Galinski School in Berlin (1995), Hecker created a journey that led the occupant to the building's courtyards and opened expansively to the sky. He suggests that despite the complexity of the design, he was surprised to hear the project being described as 'wild'.[21] 'I thought that the design was so mathematical and clear, so how could it be wild?' he says. 'But then I understood that the geometry produced during design development became a kind of wild geometry; unique for the particular place and programme and not translatable for any other projects in the future.' While all of Hecker's projects employ a similar design process, they result in buildings that are imbued with a disparity of architectural language, materials, ideologies, contextual commentary and individual form.

'Architecture is an expression of the human soul in its ever-changing condition. It is a human art, never humane enough,' Hecker states empathically. He considers himself as a 'professional architect' first and an artist second, suggesting: 'If someone considers me an artist, then it probably means that they view my architecture as art; however it doesn't change the reality of my profession.' He believes that regardless of one's status, any artistic value lies in the quality of the workmanship and, as a result, he is quick to embrace visual language: 'I have no problem using the words "style" and "expression" because, in my opinion, art is not a profession. It is a marker of quality work. Everybody can be viewed as an artist if they produce work of the highest standard: for example, a

ABOVE HEINZ-GALINSKI SCHOOL, BERLIN, GERMANY, 1995

Appearing for the first time as a metaphor in the Spiral House, the 'snakes' (corridors) of the Heinz-Galinski School form part of its cross-circulation system. Part of the sunflower's 'line network', they intensify the dynamic qualities of the architectural language, enriching the experiential qualities for the children who walk, run, play, study and talk within the building.

OPPOSITE HEINZ-GALINSKI SCHOOL, BERLIN, GERMANY, 1995

The sunflower geometry used for the school resulted in a very different and unique architecture. As Hecker explains: 'I understood that the geometry produced during design development became a kind of wild geometry; unique for the particular place and programme and not translatable for any other projects in the future.'

brilliant chef or a talented fashion designer could be viewed as an artist. Conversely, the text that we read in our daily newspaper is not literature – we throw it away the next day. So artists are not recognised for their profession, but for their achievements. Architecture is an incredibly rare human achievement and I would say that an architect is very seldom an artist.'

He also views the architect's role as a very difficult path to navigate between the expectations of professional practice and that of the avant-garde world of the artist: 'In the end, I would like to consider myself a Functionalist in my own way.[22] Function helps to limit choices and to distinguish architects from those who build sculptures on an architectural scale. Function is also linked to human needs, movement and, eventually, to human scale.' He continues: 'Yet an architect is always within a schizophrenic situation because, on one hand, he is a professional and, on the other, he is within the creative process of searching and developing the design. The beginning of the process is an experiment – much like creating a dish that is not yet cooked and ready to be served. So the architect must admit that the design is still not perfect and is only in development.'[23]

For Hecker, the roles of ethics and aesthetics are intimately intertwined and his position is made clear through the disparate aesthetic that runs through his body of work. He suggests that architects have the ability to capture culture in form and material,[24] although he believes that architectural expression cannot be approached directly. Nevertheless, while Hecker refutes that he thinks directly about encapsulating a project's ideals, many of his projects are resonant with cultural qualities. The Palmach Museum, for example, successfully captures the building's cultural significance and creates a distinctive group 'portrait' through form, materiality and ultimately its aesthetic.[25]

Hecker believes that beauty must originate and grow from a point of critique or a generating source. In his architecture, this manifests itself in his endless preoccupation with the complex relationship between his chosen geometries and their camouflaged elements to create a meaningful journey through experience. In addition, he suggests that a focus on function within the architectural process is characterless within itself. 'Just as yeast gives bread more volume, a refined taste and a beautiful form during baking, so too does the inclusion of clients' needs, movement, scale and personality enrich the functionality of architecture and direct its aesthetic value.'

Undoubtedly, Hecker's originality, sensitivity and refined aesthetic expressed through his architectural practice is integrally linked to his early experiences of political oppression and his belief in the power of art to transcend human experience and find beauty in the most difficult of circumstances. 'For me beauty means hope. The real hope for humanity

BELOW HEINZ-GALINSKI SCHOOL, BERLIN, GERMANY, 1995

'Everybody can be viewed as an artist if they produce work of the highest standard,' Hecker states emphatically. 'For example, a brilliant chef or a talented fashion designer could be viewed as an artist. Conversely, the text that we read in our daily newspaper is not literature – we throw it away the next day. So artists are not recognised for their profession, but for their achievements. Architecture is an incredibly rare human achievement and I would say that an architect is very seldom an artist.'

HEINZ-GALINSKI SCHOOL, BERLIN, GERMANY, 1995

Hecker views the architect's role as a very difficult path to navigate between the expectations of professional practice and that of the avant-garde world of the artist. He declares: 'In the end, I would like to consider myself a Functionalist. Function helps to limit choices and to distinguish architects from those who build sculptures on an architectural scale. Function is also linked to human needs, movement and, eventually, to human scale.'

RIGHT PALMACH MUSEUM, TEL AVIV, ISRAEL, 1996

Many within the Israeli community have embraced Hecker's Palmach Museum and view the building as a distinctive group portrait of the 'Palmachnics' that has been created through form, materiality and, ultimately, aesthetics. However, Hecker refutes the analogy, believing that architectural expression cannot be approached directly and is achieved by having 'faith in how to make the materials speak' in the spirit of the artist.

ABOVE PALMACH MUSEUM, TEL AVIV, ISRAEL, 1996

As Zvi Hecker wrote in his diary on 15 July 1998, when Israel celebrated its 50 years of independence: 'The Palmach Museum of History is essentially a landscape. It is a landscape of the dreams that have made Israel a reality. The form of this landscape is homage to the ideals that Palmach stood and fought for. They are also the invisible foundations that carry the load built in 50 years of Israel's independence.'

lies in art. The mistake that communist regimes make lies in forbidding artists to make art, and that's why communism inevitably collapses – it's not because of economic mismanagement, it's because people will always want to find ways to create art,' he declares. 'Unfortunately, in much of today's architectural discourse, aesthetics is seen as a kind of substance that can be added to a building, but I believe beauty must originate and grow from creative thinking. It's not an assortment of dry spices – nature does not distinguish between beauty and ugliness. It's pure human invention and that is why it changes constantly.'

Interviews
Venice Architecture Biennale, Venice, 8 September 2004
Hecker's office, Berlin, 2 March 2007

Notes

1. Samarkand is now the second largest city of Uzbekistan. As Hecker recalls: 'At the beginning of the Second World War, my family were picked up by the Russian army and, under the order of Stalin, transported first to Siberia at the very far east border with Japan. Then, following the agreement between Stalin and the Polish government in exile in London, all of the Jewish Pole prisoners in Siberia were released and permitted to go to the south of Russia via Iran and to Palestine to join the British army. However, following this path didn't work out for us, and so we stayed in Samarkand until the end of the war.

2. Relocating meant that Hecker was required to master a third language, Hebrew, along with his native Polish and Russian in order to recommence his studies.

3. The Technion, or the Israel Institute of Technology, in Haifa was for many years the only institute in Israel with a faculty of architecture.

4. Hecker recounts an anecdote to illustrate the provocative nature of his work: 'Bruce Goff once told me that when Frank Lloyd Wright came to Norman, Oklahoma, for a lecture, Goff showed him his latest work. In response Frank Lloyd Wright asked: "Bruce, who are you trying to scare?" In much the same way I have become used to similar reactions to my work.' Zvi Hecker, interview with Yael Reisner, 2 March 2007.

5. Hecker studied under the mentorship of his drawing teacher, Izhak Palterer, who was unable to complete his own architectural studies due to the outbreak of the Second World War and shared a similar history to Hecker's family.

6. Neumann was born in Brno, Czechoslovakia, and worked in South Africa before returning to Prague at the outbreak of the Second World War due to concerns for the safety of his parents. He ended up in the Theresienstadt concentration camp for the duration of the war.

7. The Dean was Yohanan Ratner, Israel's ex-Chief of Staff and the first Israeli Ambassador to Russia, who gave Hecker a private tour of the Technion during the summer when all of its facilities were closed.

8. 'Richard Kauffman came to Palestine from Germany in 1920. During the British mandate, Kauffman planned more than 150 settlements, kibbutz, neighborhoods and towns. The modernist approach of Kauffman and other contemporary architects in the 1930s created the typical Israeli aesthetic and especially Tel Avivian architecture.' Ran Shechori, 'The State of the Arts: Architecture in Israel' (text updated, 1998); see www.mfa.gov.il/MFA/MFAArchive/2000_2009/2002/7/Architecture (accessed in 2005).

9. Eldar Sharon was the son of the influential Israeli architect Arie Sharon, a Bauhaus graduate from before the Second World War, who was a partner in an established office (Idelson Sharon) in Tel Aviv. Eldar Sharon was working from a small space within his father's office.

10. A preoccupation held by few young Israeli architects at the time.

11. This biblical reference was an unusual approach in a period when Israel was psychologically and culturally very modern, and evolved from the ambition to create a new local identity based on a historical framework.

12. The complex structure of the Bat Yam City Hall literally hangs from its roof.

13. Hecker is clearly upset about the condition of the Bat Yam City Hall. When asked about its possible renovation, after a long silence he says, sighing: 'It's not possible to renovate it. No, it's destroyed. I never go there. I did all the working drawings personally and all the negotiations with the contractors so for me it's very sad.' Interview with Yael Reisner, 2 March 2007.

14. Hecker recalls: 'Neumann's suggestion on how to make architecture was to "make a courtyard, and then to build around it", and it seems that I still follow this advice.' Interview with Yael Reisner, 2 March 2007.

15. Hecker's projects all engage with and develop the 'city walk' typology, as can be seen in the Bat Yam City Hall (1963), Dubiner's House residential complex, Ramat Gan (1963), Spiral House apartment complex, Ramat Gan (1990), Heinz-Galinski School, Berlin (1995), Palmach Museum, Tel Aviv (1996) and his most recent project, the Royal Dutch Military Police complex near Schiphol International Airport, Amsterdam, which is currently under construction.

16. The notion of 'happenings' and 'episodes' is particularly relevant to Hecker's camouflaging counterparts. The English academic Colin Rowe described 'happenings' and 'episodes' thus: 'The normative has a kind of use as a surface or background for the display of the deviant? I think it means that amongst other things ... the Ground stimulates the intimate apprehension of the Figure ... which is also the balance between Scaffolding and Happening and Grid and Episode.' Lecture, 1975. Colin Rowe, *As I Was Saying: Recollections and Miscellaneous Essays – Volume Two, Cornelliana*, The MIT Press, London, 1996, p 67.

17. 'The Palmach Museum is a good example where the design is based on a mathematical grid and yet the geometry is difficult to detect.' Zvi Hecker, interview with Yael Reisner, 8 September 2004.

18. 'The sunflower is one of the most spectacular examples of the Fibonacci series, and is also known as the "Golden Proportion". The growth of the sunflower seeds is determined by two intersecting sets of sinuous spirals.' Zvi Hecker, email to Yael Reisner, 14 October 2008.

19. The walls of the Spiral House are wrapped provocatively with flat, cheap stones. The use of this material references the cheap fences of the Arabic-Israeli villages where the stones are commonly used. The project is a resonant example of Hecker's battle with a disciplined geometrical system while also adding 'episodes' throughout his architecture.

20. Both the Spiral House and the Palmach Museum are strong examples of the Arte Povera movement within architecture. In Hebrew, the term translates to 'Dalut Hachomer', or 'Poor Materiality'. The movement had a local authenticity and was common among many Israeli artists during the 1970s and 1980s, though it failed to resonate in Israeli architecture.

21. Hecker recalls: 'I remember that when you visited me in February 1990, you were the first to see the models of the Jewish School and you commented: "What a wild project." At the time, I was surprised by your comment and later I wrote a short article in the Aedes exhibition catalogue that mentioned your reaction.' Interview with Yael Reisner, 2 March 2007.

22. 'James Stirling wrote in an introduction to his projects that the theory of Functionalism is still the driving force for him. And I would agree with this sentiment.' Zvi Hecker, interview with Yael Reisner, 2 March 2007.

23. Hecker has suggested that: 'Forgetting and not knowing is not the same. A real artist produces new material; and he is expected to do that very precisely; dealing with things he didn't know from before.' Zvi Hecker in conversation with Kristin Feireiss, in Kristin Feireiss, *Zvi Hecker: The Heinz-Galinski School in Berlin*, Ernst Wasmuth Verlag GmbH & Co, Tubingen/Berlin, 1996, p 29.

24. Here he speaks of 'faith in how to make the materials speak' in the spirit of the artist, and recalls a story he once heard that prior to beginning a painting, Renoir kissed his canvas in anticipation.

25. The Palmach was the regular fighting force of the unofficial army of the Jewish community for seven years during the British Mandate in Palestine. Its members contributed significantly to Israeli culture and ethos. Being a Palmach member was considered a way of life and held associations with notions of modesty, poverty and culture.

Peter Cook

ARCHITECTURE AS LAYERED THEATRE

PETER COOK IS A WARM, ENERGETIC AND PASSIONATE ENGLISHMAN – always impatient to do something new and catch, enjoy, gossip or revel in another creative day. His architectural frame of reference is wide, democratic and imbued with an inherent curiosity to learn and discover new ideas, expressions or emerging practice – what he calls his 'sniff' for talent. He has a naturally inquisitive personality, honed by years of practice and experience into a highly tuned, discerning 'eye'. His sensibility is essentially English[1] and evolves from the regional characteristics that he is most comfortable with: the seaside 'tack' that hugs the coastline and the minor towns dotted across the countryside with their expansive gardens layered with sequential, polite procedures and rituals that reveal hidden secrets.

As a member of the maverick and culturally incisive architectural collective Archigram,[2] Cook found international fame early in his career. However, it is, arguably, his longstanding commitment to teaching architecture that has cemented his reputation as an innovative thinker and inspirational educator.[3] As a result, he was awarded a Knighthood in 2007 – the first to be bestowed upon an architect for services to architecture *and* education. Post-Archigram, Cook's architectural practice took many forms of metamorphosis[4] and produced mainly speculative projects, drawings and books over an intensely productive 30 years. Now in his early 70s, Cook is relishing the long-awaited opportunity to consistently build through his most recent collaborative, Studio CRAB.[5] The practice currently has several projects under construction including a theatre in Verbania, Italy, and a social housing project in Madrid. The upcoming projects cement Cook's transition from paper architecture to built form along with the widely published 'Friendly Alien' art museum in Graz, Austria.[6]

A self-described 'journalist' by nature, Cook has been an architectural commentator and critic over the past 50 years, with a regular column in the Architectural Review and, most recently, as the curator of his architectural Store Street chat show series held at the Building Centre in London's West End each month. Well known as an articulate and theatrical orator, Cook is the consummate conversationalist – a master of the English language both verbally and in text. His self-described 'elliptical method of conversation' allows a freeform discussion where one begins with a topic and talks around the subject, never engaging directly yet exploring and extrapolating in order to return to the original point.[7] Indeed, Cook's personality is imbued with juxtapositions and contradictions, a position that he openly embraces, suggesting that his preference is for 'considering a number of positions and possibilities and retaining the right to harden up the definitions at the least likely moment; to scramble the sets of values; to introduce totally non-architectural anecdotes and to hold an ambiguous position that is not necessarily disclosed, but perhaps unearthed by one's friends, bit by bit.' It is a revealing anecdote that also serves to aptly sum up Cook's architecture – a magical, layered and theatrical world where ambiguity is an asset and all is not what it seems.

Peter Cook admits he has little time or patience for most other subjects besides architecture – yet the sphere of what he feels is relevant to architecture is broad and inclusive.[8] Once within it, diversions are welcomed, discussed at length and, most often, embraced. While Cook's usual mode of operation is in collaboration with others, he also enjoys time alone to think, draw, write, manipulate and transform his thoughts and observations into ideas. An independent thinker and prolific designer, Cook is also a 'maker and shaper' of schools of architecture, books, magazines, events, exhibitions and art institutions – in short, the 'stuff' that keeps him interested and motivated to pursue a wider appreciation of architecture.[9]

BELOW ROOM OF 1000 DELIGHTS, 1970

As Cook describes: 'The drawing captures a sense of release and I was trying to say that architecture should parallel a sense of release from gravity or from the rational. So I was trying to communicate that feeling through a picture. The image is mostly drawn and painted, but it's also partly collage, which gives you a level of image you can't get by hand, so it's a sort of pictorial use of collage.'

RIGHT SPONGE PROJECT: 'GUNGE', 1975

Cook claims repeatedly that he does not have a natural drawing ability, but that he was eager to learn pictorial skills as a youth. His early drawings were highly influenced by the French Beaux-Arts tradition and, over time, became more pictorial, colourful and layered. He believes in the importance of communicating one's ideas quickly and seeks to create memorable and dramatic imagery.

ABOVE TRONDHEIM LIBRARY (WITH CHRISTINE HAWLEY, TRONDHEIM, NORWAY, 1977

As Cook explains: 'The Trondheim library is really a city. It was a piece of landscape or a piece of building pretending to be a landscape that really had a city inside it. It was a trick – it was saying it looks like countryside but actually it's inhabited. I don't really honour the countryside; I want to take the city to it and I want to melt the city a bit so it can absorb bits and contain countryside.'

Cook is an acute observer of architecture and its relationship to contemporary culture, and a prolific collector of ideas and propositions. As such he is in constant engagement with the world that surrounds him – a skill he attributes to his itinerant childhood: 'My dad was Quartering Commandant in the British Army,' he explains. 'We moved about 13 times from when I was 3 to 15,[10] and so I became adept at a kind of pictorial recognition of my environment. In a sense, I was trained to absorb towns, because I lived in and visited so many. So I built up a vocabulary to recognise and describe different town layouts and I became fascinated in them in much the same way that people might collect stamps or fossils. I collected castles and I bought books so I could tick them off as I saw them, and I remember "collecting" about 20 castles in all before I moved on to become more interested in the positioning of Roman cities.'

His transient upbringing exposed Cook to a diversity of experience that, in turn, fed his emerging passion for the culture of architecture: 'I became fascinated with architecture very early on in life,' he confirms. 'Personally, I think architecture's an enormously broad church. It's such a rich culture and there are so many strands that lie within it.' His colourful, dramatic and layered drawings are highly regarded internationally[11] and continue to hold great influence within architectural education and discourse. He insists,

Cook has explored the idea of metamorphosis and the notion of time cycles since the mid-1970s. Layering, ambiguity, surprise and theatricality were all enhanced through his work and speculation and inventiveness were, and still are, an important part of the design process.

The idea of constant change was applied here to a piece of land in West Berlin. As Cook recalls: 'Let's take ... a piece of America to it. Let's give it a grid; a skyscraper and a square ... hybrids develop ... The fungoid growth is also a child of my architectural methodology ... I like the idea of cactus as architecture. Marvelous! The cactus – nasty, spiky, funny, blobby.' Peter Cook, *Six Conversations*, Architectural Monographs No 28, Academy Editions, London, 1993, p 24.

'A layered theatrical world where ambiguity is an asset and all is not what it seems.' This quote is an apt and revealing description of Cook's architecture and reinforces his English or 'Northern European' position and the cultural characteristics that he is most comfortable with – the English countryside and famous gardens and parks, layered with sequential procedures and hidden secrets.

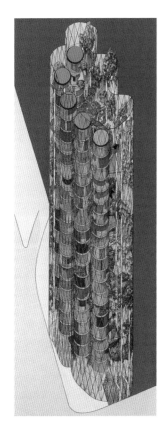

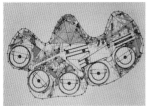

however, that he did not hold a natural talent for drawing,[12] recalling: 'I never felt that I was a good artist, although culturally I had strong ideas. I was also not sufficiently good as a gadgets sort of a person, so I forced myself to be able to communicate by drawing.'[13] He suggests that his distinctive technique was a result of his early architectural education at Bournemouth College of Art rather than through his subsequent graduate studies at the Architectural Association (AA)[14] in London: 'We were brought up on a Beaux-Arts curriculum at Bournemouth – in fact, it was the last architecture school in England still doing it. We had to send what were called "testimonies of study" to the RIBA in London for assessment and there were very specific demands; for example, submitting coloured elevations was mandatory.[15] So I was taught to draw with much more intensity than many architects.'

Cook passionately believes in the power of drawing to create memorable, dramatic imagery[16] – what he terms the 'theatre' of architecture – and is an expert in communicating ideas quickly through pictures.[17] His early Archigram drawings were highly experimental, producing powerful commentary on how buildings, towns and cities might evolve. As an example, he cites his famous drawing Room of 1000 Delights (1970): 'The drawing captures a sense of release and I was trying to say that architecture should parallel a sense of release from gravity or from the rational – that's why a key element is the person on the surfboard because I imagined that you might feel released from gravity when surfing. So I was trying to communicate that feeling through a picture.' He continues: 'As I remember it, the image is mostly drawn and painted, but it's also partly collage, which gives you a level of image you can't get by hand – so it's a sort of pictorial use of collage.'[18]

Insisting that an architect's natural process is to use images to work through ideas, Cook declares: 'How would you do it any other way? As an architect you use observation and pictures as a way of organising your thoughts. If you take one of my most famous schemes such as 'Plug-In City' (1964), I still did the plan first before doing the axonometric and elevation but I don't believe the plan has ever been published. I think it hardly exists anyway – only on graph paper. The axonometric was immediately made by overlaying the plan in the traditional way, and the interesting bits were worked up in the extrusion. The sequence of drawings such as plans and sections might be in existence, but the key thing to communicate the idea was the image of what it actually looked like!'

He explains that he often starts a drawing by using a conventional grid in order to set up a tangible framework to react against: 'It's a compositional thing. It gives one scale, rhythm and something to bounce off; it's like having a site. I think it must be similar to the way that composers move onto a key or a playwright has planned that the play is

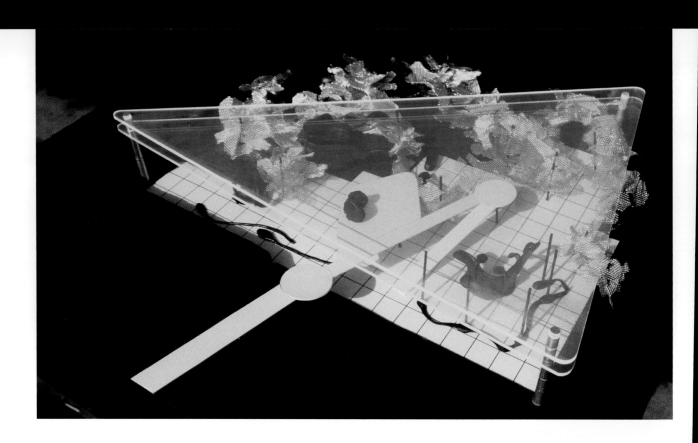

ABOVE VEG HOUSE, MONTREAL, CANADA, 1996

Cook recalls: 'The Veg House is the first project in which I was developing the idea of bugging the trees with sound and things, on a bigger scale, but it is really an encapsulated version of that, developed. Aesthetically, it was a better result than the earlier Kawasaki Information Museum and, again, I used the triangle with the grid to bounce up against it.'

going to be for four persons, six persons, in three acts, etc. You can't just "float" so you decide that you're going to jettison the grid – but I'd be at sea without the grid because it gives you something to bounce against.'[19] Elaborating, Cook suggests that the metaphorical image is equally as important for his process: 'I need it in the same way that I like the figurative metaphor.[20] It's difficult not to come up with metaphors because it's generative and helps to kick you off. The metaphor comes pretty early in the design process; as soon as you're getting a "sniff" for the building and once you've got the metaphor you know you're up and away.'[21]

Cook's architectural language is imbued with a sense of delight and exuberance that is reflected in his choice of metaphorical references and reinforces his position that 'being "po-faced" is the worst thing for me.' He explains that the actual imagery is always consciously – and occasionally subconsciously – associative or even quotational: 'It helps to evoke imagery through association such as "plug-in", "animal", "hulk", "bird", "vessel", "Arcadia", "field", "spooky", like a "bat", "beaver" and "fried egg". It's a quality that you can trace through the work of various English architects who enjoy the strategy, such as Alison Smithson's "mat" and "clusters", Cedric Price titles such as the "Architect as Fat Man", James Stirling's projects and so on.'

Certainly, Cook's ability to generate architecture from lateral observations, second-hand anecdotes and the oddness of daily life share a commonality with the traditions of English observational newspaper columnists, cartoonists and comedians.[22] He has a natural curiosity in human behaviour, acknowledging: 'I'm interested in funny phenomena that I can connect with my architectural process and that's because I'm a creative magpie, picking from here and there. I have a typically English, quizzical, slightly jokey "Isn't that funny? Put that in my back pocket for another day" viewpoint rather than a dogmatic attitude about architectural culture.' His particular 'brand' of Englishness advocates the expression of delight in architecture and questions the pursuit of 'puritan, rational, meek and aesthetic' values. As he explains: 'There's always been a flamboyant wing of English culture that likes fun and games,[23] amusement and a "look, here's a funny thing in the corner" attitude, and I'm definitely from that perspective. There's a famous quotation that suggests that good architecture should have "firmness, commodity and delight":[24] Firmness – it must stand up; Commodity – it must be able to deal with activity; and Delight – three elements together. While many other cultures only aspire to firmness and commodity, the English also want Delight!' Cook is, however, resistant to the idea that his inherent 'Englishness'[25] is in some way anti-Modernist: 'I was full on into Modernism,' he exclaims. 'My natural inclination is towards the pictorial, but I think Modernism was a very useful cult. Essentially I'd describe myself as an English theatrical pictorialist and so my architecture uses a Modernist ethic to sustain part of it while also enjoying a pictorial ethos to sustain the balance.'

The laboured relationship between content and form within architectural discourse is a source of frustration for Cook, who exclaims: 'Content-scmontent! I think that the "tight" attitude towards typologies or "types of activity" is no longer of any interest. It depends upon your attitude towards activity; so, for example, when you give a lecture in a school then you are being, to some extent, an actor, or if you're shopping then you're strategising in terms of time or resources in a similar way to a military general.' He concedes that his position takes a contradictory line to that of many of his colleagues: 'I'm quite willing to believe that the hierarchy of importance that I place upon things will be different from another architect's. If you choose to articulate the movement system, or the skyline, then that's your choice. Form is part of that[26] and it comes out of articulation, so if you're a visual person you articulate visually.'

For Cook the connection is much more aligned with the pursuit of theatre than that of programme: 'In my view, there's no "divine right" that a building should be one thing or another. For example, if you go into a town hall then it's very much like going into a college or a block of flats. So if you want to articulate the business of "going in" or if you want to articulate the significance of the courtyard, then that becomes form. I simply don't honour content as much as many architects. It all depends what you want it to be, and the content in architecture is theatre. I think architecture is theatre and I think buildings – if they're interesting – have theatre in them.'

BELOW TOWER FOR MEDINA CIRCLE (KI'KAR-HA'MEDINA), TEL AVIV, ISRAEL, 1997

Cook is a natural orator and a master of his self-described 'elliptical method' of conversation: 'I may be considering a number of positions ... retaining the right to harden up the definitions at the least likely moment; the right to scramble the sets of values; the right to introduce totally non-architectural anecdotes; the right to hold an ambiguous position that is not necessarily disclosed.' Peter Cook, *Six Conversations*, Architectural Monographs No 28, Academy Editions, London, 1993, p 6.

Cook states: 'It's difficult not to come up with
metaphors ... It's generative, it helps and it tells you
where you want to be ... The metaphor comes pretty
early in the design process; as soon as you're getting a
'sniff' for the building and once you've got the
metaphor you know you're up and away ... Being "
po-faced" is the worst thing for me. The actual imagery
is always consciously – and occasionally subconsciously
– associative or even quotational.'

The notion of 'architecture as theatre' is an essential element of Cook's collective work,
providing the conceptual framework that drives many of his projects. Recalling the widely
published Kunsthaus in Graz, completed in collaboration with Colin Fournier in 2003, he
explains: 'The Kunsthaus has a definite sense of theatre. The two key rooms are
intentionally hidden and the ground floor is an enclosed continuation of the street. When
you enter there is a "mouth" and "tongue" that invites you to go up into the unknown;
you can't actually see what's up there so the tongue licks you up and you glide up into
what is being exhibited. Then you repeat the process as you move through the levels.'

Enjoying the description, he continues: 'There's one place where you can be released –
the "naughty nozzle" – and finally you are rewarded with the view. Yet even then, it's
not actually related to everyday life because the view is from the top of this special
object in the town and of a special object – the 'castle'. It's an episodic journey where
the city is revealed to you in the same way as a stage in the theatre and it's this theatrical
process that then provides the form.'[27] The theatrical aspect of the interiors was further
enhanced in the museum's exterior street elevation through collaboration with Berlin-
based architects John deKron and Carsten Nikolai of realities:united who designed an

RIGHT KUNSTHAUS GRAZ (WITH COLIN FOURNIER),
GRAZ, AUSTRIA, 2003

Cook and Fournier collaborated with structural engineer
Klaus Bollinger, from Bollinger + Grohmann, who
designed the innovative structural concept of using
curvaceous walls as a substitute for structural columns
to achieve the art museum's large, open galleries.

Berlin-based architects realities:united were commissioned to design a complete media technology integration system for the Kunsthaus Graz. The permanent light and media installation, entitled BIX, uses standard industrial fluorescent light tubes to transform the building's outer biomorphic skin from its translucent blue acrylic glass panels into a low-resolution greyscale computer display and encourages users to interact with the architecture.

innovative communicative display skin for the building. The concept and application consisted of a BIX permanent light and media installation where artists can interact with and receive a live response from people on site.[28]

The Kunsthaus' interactive skin feeds into many of Cook's other longstanding preoccupations and devices for providing a generative and sequential sense of theatrics whithin his work: 'It relates to my interest in a vocabulary or "palette" to describe form, and I borrow ideas from vegetation,[29] machines[30] and many other things to extend architecture beyond the classical or Modernist vocabulary,' he explains. 'I'm interested in palette in response to theatre. First I give an idea theatre, then decide on the palette, and then I break the rules of the palette but bounce off a grid.' Cook's explorations of the qualities of metamorphosis and cyclical change also continue to form a cornerstone of his practice through a long list of individual and collaborative projects:[31] 'As I was brought up by the seaside my natural response to the idea of metamorphosis is simply that an English coastal town has to absorb many more people in the summer and, as a result, its elements must metamorphose.' Musing on the topic, he asks: 'One of my favourite metamorphic conditions is found in coastal marshland where the water will insidiously creep among the mud and the growths and then go again. Is it land or is it sea?'[32]

Undoubtedly, Cook has produced projects and buildings that are striking and provocative yet it is difficult to claim that his work – while pictorial – has ever engaged with a concern for conventional aesthetics. 'The concept of aesthetics is a construct and a way of manipulating forces. For example, you can have an aesthetic of a conversation by introducing different subtopics such as balance, surprise and intrigue,' he declares. 'The Modernist aesthetic was a specific language and much of Modernism is linked to socialism and indirectly to a form of ascetic puritanism. You only have to read the text of

ABOVE KUNSTHAUS GRAZ (WITH COLIN FOURNIER), GRAZ, AUSTRIA, 2003

Cook describes the experiential sequence of the Kunsthaus: 'When you enter there is a "mouth" and "tongue" that invites you to go up into the unknown; you can't actually see what's up there so the tongue licks you up and you glide up into what is being exhibited ... There's one place where you can be released – the "naughty nozzle" – and finally you are rewarded with *the* view ... it's this theatrical process that then provides the form.'

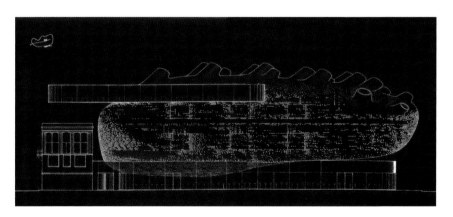

LEFT KUNSTHAUS GRAZ (WITH COLIN FOURNIER), GRAZ, AUSTRIA, 2003

Cook and Fournier aspired to make the building's acrylic exterior skin livelier by using light in keeping with Cook's early elevation drawing. To achieve their vision, the architects approached John deKron and Carsten Nikolai of realities:united to collaborate and produce an innovative lighting and media solution.

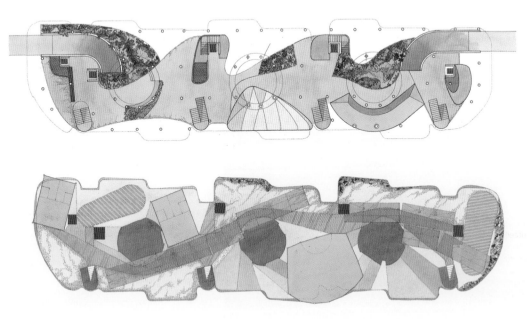

RIGHT PINTO MILLENNIUM MASTERPLAN (WITH
SALVADOR PÉREZ ARROYO AND EVA HURTADO),
PINTO, SPAIN, 2001-04

As Cook describes: 'The task was to put 30,000 people
alongside a small "dormitory" town about 25
kilometres (15.5 miles) south of Madrid. By
establishing a deck, I made a place where the
"flâneurs", or the boys and girls of the town, might
gather. By lifting the main buildings off the ground on
piloti I suggested that kiosks and market stalls could
flourish, gaining a "lively" atmosphere that is lacking in
most new developments.'

OPPOSITE VALLECAS HOUSING (WITH SALVADOR
PÉREZ ARROYO AND GAVIN ROBOTHAM), MADRID,
SPAIN, 2005

When the Pinto project did not proceed, some of the
ideas were utilised in the Vallecas Housing scheme
where the architecture explored a similar theme.
According to Cook: 'Up on legs, kiosks under, sport on
top – there's no street life proposed in that area but
the kiosks will bring life. The kids will hang around and
people will buy bread, dry cleaning, etc, and it will
create a little bit of life.'

someone like Hannes Meyer[33] to feel the moral insistence.' Cook advocates an
engagement with delight and holds an inherent mistrust of overly righteous values: 'I
was always irritated by piety: I'm too much of a natural hedonist. Yet I still proceed in a
design with a mental checklist that involves "right" or "wrong" decisions, "rules",
"sequences of action" that have been trained into me from the Modernist ethic.'[34] As a
direct reaction to this heritage, Cook's architecture eschews the dogmatic and pursues an
inclusive and often irreverent agenda: 'Pictorialism inevitably involves delight – the same
delight that enjoys of ice cream, bright colours and "fruitiness". It can be quite useful for
a designer to bounce aspects of a scheme back and forth between the "procedural" and
the "delightful".'

He also rejects the notion that architecture is most rigorous when produced within strict
constraints or a dogmatic approach, viewing such rules as representative of an oppressive
and stale attitude to architectural design. Conversely, he admires the individualistic
approach of 19th-century architects who actively worked in competition with each other
to promote their differing architectural styles and values. 'The Battle of the Styles in
England in the 19th century is a fascinating era for me. Essentially the period was about
a conflict of ideas and a battle between groups of people who were vehemently opposed
to each other. I think I respond to the extremism and the passion of these people.[35]
Undoubtedly, my motivation in Archigram largely came through reading about the
"Frulicht"[36] people in Berlin in 1917 and the Battle of the Styles in England in the 19th
century – that architecture could raise passion and I find that absolutely fascinating.'[37]

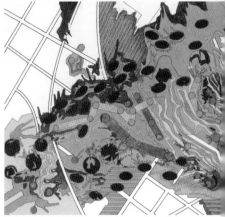

On the topic of drawing, Cook muses: 'What is drawing? It's a way of organising your thoughts. You're doing architecture, which is 'stuff'... and you use paper because it's quick and there it is, so you draw it. Now whether you call that image, I can't define. It's rather the same with language: to me language is a means of communication; image is a means of putting on paper what you're trying to do.'

On the topic of beauty, Cook is equally eclectic and inclusive in his tastes: 'I like the very "sleek" and I like the very "crumbly". What I find irritating and rather boring are the buildings that use normal classical procedures to enforce architectural conventions such as "the windows *have* to be mathematically placed" and "the door *must* have a certain amount of articulation" – I'm completely bored by that.' Instead, Cook believes surprise and intrigue are most resonant to the concept of beauty: 'I like a lot of ugly buildings, but they're original. I'm more interested in ideas and originality than I'm interested in something that is beautiful: not that I'm anti-beauty, but I can't single it out.[38] I'm interested in originality and special-ness, so something might look ugly but interesting, and something might look very beautiful, but if it doesn't do something that you didn't expect then it doesn't interest me.' He continues: 'When you've been involved in architecture for over 60 years as I have, then you can feel as if you've seen it all before. So when you land in a place and suddenly you see something intriguing and say "Ah, that's an odd thing" – that's interesting, because it articulates in a different way.'

Characteristically, Cook concludes his position with clarity yet great optimism, declaring: 'I want to *enjoy* architecture and *enjoy* doing it. I take the view that if it gives *me* a buzz, then that buzz might just transmit across to the observer or dweller. Being "po-faced" about architecture is the worst possibility for me. I'm more intrigued by something being interesting than beautiful. I suppose that I'm a child of one's time in that I'm a bit suspicious of something that tries to be beautiful. What I'm really saying is that while I don't mind beauty, I want it to emanate from ideas!'

Interview
Venice Architecture Biennale, Venice, 11 September 2008

Notes

1. Cook refers to his sensibility as 'Northern European'. Interview with Yael Reisner, September 2008.

2. Archigram was founded in 1961, and the group completed in 1963. Its members were Peter Cook with Warren Chalk, Ron Heron, David Green, Dennis Crompton and Mike Webb. The highly experimental architectural collective transformed the way architecture was viewed both in the UK and internationally, and was awarded the RIBA Gold Medal for Architecture in 2003.

3. He is currently Professor of Architecture at the Royal Academy of Arts in London, Emeritus Professor of the Bartlett School of Architecture, University College London and of the Städelschule art academy in Frankfurt. He also holds teaching positions at the École Spéciale d'Architecture in Paris and the Technical University of Lund in Sweden.

4. Archigram (1961–75); in collaboration with Christine Hawley (1975–97); Spacelab with Colin Fournier (1997–2004); in collaboration with Salvador Pérez Arroyo and Eva Hurtado for Pinto's masterplan and urban design study, Spain (2001–04); and, most recently, as a partner of CRAB Studio with Gavin Robotham, Salvador Pérez Arroyo and Juan Barrado (2005–).

5. CRAB Studio was established in 2005. Its four partners are Peter Cook, Gavin Robotham, Salvador Pérez Arroyo and Juan Barrado.

6. The Kunsthaus Graz was designed by Peter Cook with Colin Fournier (Spacelab) and completed in 2003.

7. It is a strategy that Cook puts into practice within his legendary critiques where the ideas within a student presentation will be thoroughly discussed, explored and expanded upon without the need for a direct assessment of success or failure – a value judgement seemingly too crude for Cook's teaching approach.

8. Cook quotes a military analogy to describe the notion that architecture is a difficult combination of utility, technology and artistic response: 'It's like saying that military history is a tricky combination between generals' intentions, economic pressures and whether the soldiers had enough sleep. It's a tricky combination because it's complex, not because it's inherently tricky. Architecture involves almost anything and you steer your way between whatever fascinates you.' Peter Cook, interview with Yael Reisner, 11 September 2008.

9. Cook's father was responsible for providing accommodation for allied troops and foreign prisoners of war during the Second World War – a role that had an impact on his young son. As Cook recalls: 'Why architecture for me? Maps I think ... I wanted to make towns and I still like making towns. My dad was Quartering Commandant and I used to go to his office in Leicester and there were all these maps with pins on them. I was fascinated by them and I started drawing maps almost immediately from the age of four to my teens. I would be in the car with him and he had to go and visit all sorts of big mansions all over the Midlands. On one occasion I went with him to a field near Leicester and he said: "We'll put it there." A few months later we went to the same field and there were 2,000 Italian prisoners of war in a compound with huts and watchtowers. What a great game this was.' Peter Cook, interview with Yael Reisner, 11 September 2008.

10. As Cook recalls, he moved many times as a young child: 'From the age of 3 I was in Northumberland, then County Durham, before that I was in Cardiff. The first place I consciously recall was Leicester, but I vaguely remember Whitley Bay, near Newcastle. Then Darlington where I went to kindergarten, Leicester until I was 10, half a year in Norwich, Ipswich for two and a half years continuously, then Letchworth (which is in Hertfordshire, a famous garden city) when I think I was about 13 years old, then Colchester, back to Ipswich and Southend-on-Sea, where I was actually born, and then Bournemouth.' Peter Cook, interview with Yael Reisner, 11 September 2008.

11. Cook's drawings are held in the collections of the Museum of Modern Art (MoMA), New York; the Centre Pompidou, Paris; the Deutsches Architekturmuseum (DAM), Frankfurt; FRAC Centre, Orleans; the Victoria & Albert (V&A), London; and the Japan Architect' collection, Tokyo; and also in many private collections.

12. 'All the people I have and currently collaborate with draw naturally: David Greene and Ron Herron, Christine Hawley, CJ Lim, Colin Fournier, and Gavin Robotham and Salvador Pérez Arroyo of CRAB. We communicate more quickly because we draw. Also, drawing enables you to jump from device to mannerism to reference. Model making is too consistent and slow. If you can draw you can invent anything and twiddle the pencil as you talk; the drawing soon looks like something – even something that the model maker wouldn't easily be able to fashion and the developer wouldn't even grasp.' Peter Cook, interview with Yael Reisner, 11 September 2008.

13. Cook has recently published a book about drawing as communicating, entitled *Drawing: The Motive Force of Architecture*, John Wiley & Sons Ltd, Chichester, 2008.

14. Cook recalls: 'At the AA, the drawing style was about imitating Le Corbusier with little spots of colour; like a Corb drawing. As a student, I hit the Corb lot as my teachers; like the famous quote from Peter Smithson: "Mies is great but Corb can communicate." Well, I hit the Corb lot and they were more expressive and more interesting to me. Mies and this rational thing – I've never got it. I think it was with me once you were released from the school, and being very opinionated, I could do individual work – I used what I knew or what I liked to use. And Bournemouth was much more influential in some ways than the AA.' Peter Cook, interview with Yael Reisner, 11 September 2008.

15. 'Around the third year the Bournemouth College as a whole, the art school, had a competition. You could compete for prizes. I did the unthinkable – I put in a drawing in the stage design section. I won the prize for stage design and I did it with a very spooky, funny design which was a bit architectural but was done in gouache. I was well taught in terms of drawing, more than most architects.' Peter Cook, interview with Yael Reisner, 11 September 2008

16. 'The German Expressionists magically extended the vocabulary of architecture, the range of forms, shapes, organisations and the fantastic range of ideas and arrangements. For me the exoticness of encompassed space appealed; not just the surface and only occasionally the shadow.' Peter Cook, interview with Yael Reisner, 11 September 2008.

17. 'It's a way of organising your thoughts. It's what it was about. You're doing architecture, which is "stuff". There's a thing and you use paper because it's quick and there it is, so you draw it. Now whether you call that image, I can't define. It's rather the same with language; to me language is a means of communication and image is a means of putting on paper what you're trying to do. I wanted to have more techniques to make it look good than I initially had.' Peter Cook, interview with Yael Reisner, 11 September 2008.

18. Cook was influenced by the artists Richard Hamilton and Eduardo Paolozzi whom he thought of as observers and consummate 'scramblers' of cultural and commonplace material and references – of particular note were Paolozzi's combinations of aeroplanes/toys/graphics/robots.

19. Colin Rowe discusses the notion of the binary relationship or, as he describes it, infinite 'two-way commerce', between the 'interdependent activities' such as 'establishment attitudes' and 'revolutionary principles'; dogma versus aspects of liberalism; English empiricism, utilitarianism and French Positivism; modern and tradition; 'ordered guarantee' versus 'spontaneity'. 'Does it mean that the normative has a kind of use as a surface or background for the display of the deviant? I think it means that amongst other things. Does it mean that the typical is useful as validating the exceptions? I think it also means that the Ground – if we're talking Gestalt stuff – stimulates the intimate apprehension of the Figure... which is also the balance between Scaffolding and Happening and Grid and Episode.' Colin Rowe, *As I Was Saying: Recollections and Miscellaneous Essays – Volume Two, Cornelliana*, The MIT Press, London, 1996, pp 67–71.

20. Cook's sensibility distinctly departs from the Modernists' pursuit of a metaphor-free architectural language with the exception of 'those drawn from language, and those drawn from science ... a marked tendency to turn particulars into abstract generalities – a path becomes "the route", a house "the dwelling"'. See Adrian Forty, *Words and Buildings: A Vocabulary of Modern Architecture*, Thames & Hudson, London, 2000, p 22.

21. Cook illustrates his metaphorical strategy with a social analogy: 'It's like meeting somebody at a party and if I'm describing him later as "the funny guy with the stomach" rather than the more cumbersome: "It was Professor so-and-so and he's married to so-and-so"' – then you quickly know who I mean. It helps you work ideas around it and keep the narrative moving.' Peter Cook, interview with Yael Reisner, 11 September 2008.

22. Sketching episodic observations as the English comedians – it's all a very quaint combination of irony.

23. 'We were brought up as Modernists and the Victorians were considered too fiddly, but now I've started to realise that the high point of English architecture was the Victorian period. It was highly inventive and imitated by everybody ... It was a brilliant period if you think of the range of ideas, invention, and the degree of pictorialisation, but also the technical aspect was brilliant. If you think of St Pancras, Paddington Station and the Gothic Revival churches – they're extraordinary yet we didn't look at these buildings at the time.' Peter Cook, interview with Yael Reisner, 11 September 2008.

24. The phrase was popular in the 19th century to describe architecture, though it originates from the Roman architect Vitruvius (*c* 80–15 BC) who is famous for asserting in his book *De architectura* that a structure must exhibit the three qualities of *firmitas, utilitas, venustas* – that is, it must be strong or durable, useful and beautiful. As we witness here the meaning was slightly changed in translation to English.

25. He is also unconvinced about a direct impact of his Englishness on the aesthetic of his work, explaining: 'Perhaps aesthetics could be part of my attitude, but they don't drive it. You make an aesthetic out of your position in the same way you might make a character in a play, or a magazine or a drawing out of it. In this way I'm a natural collagist or collector, so anything is potential material. Anything might be relevant and the aesthetic of architecture to me is a way of interestingly and actively combining. It's much more the collagist's view than the compositionist's view.' Peter Cook, interview with Yael Reisner, 11 September 2008.

26. Characteristically, Cook uses an evocative yet accessible example to illustrate his point: 'You could say: "A hat is a hat, is a hat." Some hats are meant to keep the sun off or the rain or conceal bald heads, while some hats are for making short people look taller or are for ceremonial purposes. As long as it sits on the head – and even *that* is questionable – a hat is a hat, is a hat. It all depends what you want to call attention to so, for example, in Venice one wants to keep the sun off yet at the races at Ascot one's attention is drawn to whoever has the most expensive designer hat.' Peter Cook, interview with Yael Reisner, 11 September 2008.

27. Archigram won a major international competition in 1969 to redesign the Entertainments Centre on the waterfront at Monte Carlo. Though the project received much attention and speculation it was never realised. Taking the analogy further, Cook aligns his architectural aesthetic with the sequential process of writing a play: 'As one begins to develop a language for the building in order to play the theatre, so one develops the "look" and "shape" of things. If you take the Archigram Monte Carlo competition project, the proposition plays with theatrical sequence in much the same way that the Kunsthaus Graz does at a much later date. There is a sense of secrecy in both projects, so in Graz you go up, into a hole, towards the roof, while in the Monte Carlo you go into a hole in the ground. In both cases you move into the unknown. It's exactly the same gambit.' Peter Cook, interview with Yael Reisner, 11 September 2008.

28. Artists can interact with the building's skin by downloading a piece of software from www.bix.at to dry-run animations on the computer before they are sent to the facade of the building itself. The Kunsthaus facade becomes a screen that artists can employ as a carrier of art – without commercials – and interact with the building. Moreover, to date artists have programmed applications for the facade that allow 'live' interactivity between viewer and building; that is, the images react to people/situations in real time.

29. Cook's projects such as the Kawasaki project (1987), Trondheim Library (1977), the Veg House (1996) and Super-Houston (2000) all engage with the relationship between vegetation and landscape: 'I mean vegetation as an architectural artefact and landscape as urbanism ... I have to state that my own fascination with vegetation and landscape is a love of that vegetation and landscape with which I am comfortable.' Peter Cook, *Six Conversations*, Architectural Monographs No 28, Academy Editions, London,1993, p 30.

30. Machines include: pumps, motors, bicycles, playground apparatus, old-style cash transporters in drapers' shops, oil refineries, etc.

31. For example, Cook's Arcadia City Tower (1978), Addhox Sequence (1971), Way Out West, Berlin, Germany (1988) and Veg House, Montreal, Canada (1996).

32. Peter Cook, *Six Conversations*, op cit, p 15.

33. Hannes Meyer was the Director of the Bauhaus (1928–30) between Walter Gropius and Mies van der Rohe.

34. Cook states: 'I didn't believe in the prevalent phrase through the 20th century of "ethic is embedded in aesthetics". When I eat calves' liver and two veg, I leave the best part of the tender calves' liver to the end – I want the delight of the flavour to last beyond the end of the meal, to stay with me, and that flavour is our aesthetic pleasure. Because from the point of view of just filling myself the order of what I eat doesn't matter. Is it a moral construct? Yes, it's related to guilt.' Peter Cook, interview with Yael Reisner, 11 September 2008.

35. HS Goodhart-Rendell, *English Architecture Since the Regency: An Interpretation*, Constable, London, 1953.

36. The Frulicht group, Bruno Taut. Berlin 1917 (included work by Karl Krayl, Paul Scheerbart, Mies van der Rohe, etc),

37. As Cook states: 'It's that your chosen area of interest could arouse in recent history such passion ... Not only is the stuff interesting, but my God there were gangs of people and I'm sure that motivated Archigram – the notion of having a rhetorical positional thing. My motivation in Archigram largely came through reading about the "Frulicht" group in Berlin in 1917 and the battle of the styles in England in the 19th century – the idea that architecture could raise passion ... I find that absolutely fascinating.' Peter Cook, interview with Yael Reisner, 11 September 2008.

38. On the topic of beauty, Cook muses: 'I would say the interior of Asplund's Gothenburg law courts is both beautiful and interesting, but it's both of these things together because he understood how to develop some very interesting conditions. But is it beautiful? I think it's beautiful, but I wouldn't say another building using the same parti would necessarily be beautiful at all, even with the same composition. It's a combination of certain phenomena – it happens just to hit the "combo". I'm always on about Clorindo Testa's bank in Buenos Aires. I think that's beautiful, but some people might find it ugly. It's full of ideas and it's an interesting, quirky building, but whether you could quantify its assets, I'm not sure – it's just bloody good.' Peter Cook, interview with Yael Reisner, 11 September 2008.

Juhani Pallasmaa

BEAUTY IS ANCHORED IN HUMAN LIFE

FINNISH ARCHITECT AND ACADEMIC Juhani Pallasmaa explains in a calm and gentle voice that he feels a sublime sense of order and destiny in nature. Residing in Helsinki for over half a century, where craftsmanship and design remain an integral part of the national culture, Pallasmaa is currently looking to relocate permanently to Lapland and experience the challenges of living within an extreme environment. He describes a deep-seated desire to experience the strong causalities and primitiveness in nature, as opposed to modern urban life where things just appear and disappear, without a sense of where they came from or why they appeared.

Pallasmaa's conversation reveals his conviction that beauty is fundamentally rooted in human experience, and his belief that when a culture loses its sense and desire for beauty it is a decaying culture. His texts explore the importance of image in architecture and discern between the notion of the historical 'primal image' derived from our collective memory and the liberating 'poetic image' that opens new horizons to personal experience.[1] He believes that when images effectively communicate their authentic history they echo with memory and meaning.

Pallasmaa views architecture within an existential framework, stating his belief that architecture resides in how one understands one's own life. He advocates that art and architecture should be anchored in our biological past based on the fact that we are biological beings and our collective genetic pool controls human behaviour, metabolic processes and feelings of desire, fear and safety. Therefore, when Pallasmaa talks about tradition, historicity or meaning, he means they all evolve from our biological past and a collective memory that extends back millions of years. He cites Nobel Prize Laureate Joseph Brodsky as an influential mentor, often quoting the poet's belief that 'the purpose of evolution is beauty' within his texts and lectures.

OPPOSITE ALVAR AALTO, VILLA MAIREA, NOORMARKKU, FINLAND, 1939

The entrance hall, living room and main staircase. Citing Villa Mairea as an example of the Finnish attitude to nature, Pallasmaa explains: 'You are not looking at nature as a view – you are inside nature. And I think it's a historical and cultural characteristic that, as Finns, we are the last of the Nordic peoples to come out of the forest – our soul is still there.'

Pallasmaa clearly describes his position on why he believes the topic of aesthetics within architectural discourse is so troubled: 'One part of architecture wants to advance along with scientific thought and technological development, while the other desires to focus on the eternal enigma of human existence.' He explains further: 'The discipline of architecture is "impure" in the sense that it fuses utility and poetics, function and image, rationality and metaphysics, technology and art, economy and symbolisation. Architecture is a muddle of irreconcilable things and categories.'

Like his American contemporary Lebbeus Woods, Pallasmaa is preoccupied with the promise of a better world, although his writings differ from Woods's preoccupation of ethics over aesthetics. Instead, Pallasmaa focuses on the potential for architectural space to affect and evoke the inhabitants through images and emotions: 'Real architecture can only affect our soul if it can touch the stratum of forgotten memories and feelings.'[2] He suggests that 'the primary criteria of architectural quality is existential sincerity. However, in this age of the commercialised and mass-produced image, there is so much architecture that is not based on any existential or personal experience. Rather, it is a manipulation of images on a level of aestheticisation.'

Interestingly, Pallasmaa talks about image manipulation in the height of the 'digital age' where form generating in the computational architectural design process is seen to be threatening the status of the designer's internal imagination and the fluidity of lateral thinking. The mathematical input and accompanying rules of procedure are often more valued than the human mental processes. In stark contrast to this approach, Pallasmaa believes that architects should rely on their encounters with the world, trust their

OPPOSITE ALVAR AALTO, CHURCH OF THE THREE CROSSES, VUOKSENNISKA, FINLAND, 1958

Pallasmaa describes his idea of the 'tactility of light' and believes that our connection to landscape has a vital influence on how we see, think and act.

BELOW ALVAR AALTO, CHURCH OF THE THREE CROSSES, VUOKSENNISKA, FINLAND, 1958

Model built to test the acoustic qualities inside the church. Pallasmaa suggests that the struggle within architectural discourse is a result of the conflict between the discipline wanting to advance along with scientific thought and technological development while paradoxically investigating the 'eternal enigma of human existence'.

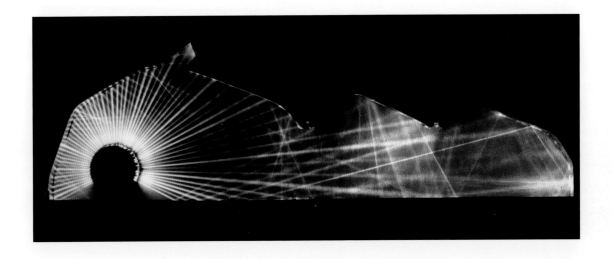

subjective intuition,[3] create from their personal imagination and dwell on mental, emotional and emphatic capacities.

Pallasmaa grounds his criticism with contemporary cultural references, firmly rooting the notion of aestheticisation through architectural manipulation within a wider social and a political realm: 'The Gulf War was an aestheticised war; personal and intimate lives as well as politics are being aestheticised, everything is turning into a manipulation, including human life itself – the kind of lifestyle that the media seems to support today is an aestheticised lifestyle, which is severely detached from existential grounds and personal experience. I support an architecture that seeks to be rooted in tradition and culture.' His texts also explore the importance of the mind–body relationship – the collaboration between the eye, the hand, the body at large, and the mind. Pallasmaa explains that as humans we participate in the creative endeavour through our whole embodied being. He believes that all our senses 'think' in terms of unconsciously processing information, contextual situations and hidden memories into spontaneous physical reactions. As a consequence, Pallasmaa questions the ability to design meaningful and experiential architecture through a 'mind–mouse' relationship.

The relationship between mind, body and design is an area of research that Pallasmaa believes is crucial to architectural and psychological discourse: 'These are not just my prejudices; these are real issues that are yet to be sufficiently discussed. In any creative effort the whole body along with ones sense of being and historicity combine to constitute the site of the work.' He refutes the notion that he is simply of a different school of architectural thought and therefore unable to engage with the digital perspective, and points to the missing presence of 'self' in today's intellectualised design processes, declaring: 'The essence of architecture resides in how you understand your own life: everything that one does profoundly is one's self-portrait, whether he intends it or not.'

Pallasmaa's sense of aesthetic values is tradition-bound, contextual and strongly aligned with ethical concerns. He strives to fuse the aesthetic and the ethical attitude embedded within a deep understanding of our collective culture's historical framework. When this fusion is broken or misrepresented, the result is confronting. For example, Pallasmaa recalls travelling to the Soviet Union by train from Finland early in 1960 and seeing a series of rubbish bins at the railway station, cast in concrete in the form of a Corinthian column. From his Finnish Modernist sensibilities, the architect felt confronted and shocked with what he saw as a misrepresentation of symbolic language and an alienation from the authentic values of culture. He recalls: 'The idea hit me that a society that has lost its judgement in the aesthetic realm is not going to last and, in fact, that's what happened

BELOW JUHANI PALLASMAA, FIREPLACE AT THE ARCHITECT'S ATTIC FLAT, HELSINKI, FINLAND, 1993

The fireplace forms the centre of a residential space, evoking archaic associations and memories. When Pallasmaa references tradition, historicity or meaning, he means they evolve from our biological past and a collective memory that extends back millions of years.

RIGHT PETER ZUMTHOR, KOLUMBA ART MUSEUM OF THE ARCHDIOCESE OF COLOGNE, COLOGNE, GERMANY, 2007

Entrance to the church within the museum complex. Pallasmaa suggests that meaning in the arts arises from life itself rather than an invention. He states: 'In fact, meaning cannot be an invention because it is existential and is bound to echo something that already exists in one's memory, either biological, cultural, collective or individual.'

40 years later in the USSR. Beauty is not an aesthetic or sentimental matter. There is an established interest among philosophers and writers in a dialectic interaction of aesthetics and ethics. The notion of beauty for me is close to the notion of being just and justice, and in that sense the loss of beauty in ordinary landscapes has a rather important message.'

He is resolute in his belief that memory – both the personal and the collective – must form the basis of any meaningful awareness and sensitivity to beauty and aesthetics. He insists: 'In my view, any image that is generated solely by either geometry, a preconceived idea, a theory, or a computational process is bound to be existentially empty, because an existentially meaningful image always echoes with memory and pre-existing meaning. It must always have its ontology in human experience because as individuals and as a species, we are historical beings. My position is to defend the historicity of the human being and advocate that artistic images need to grasp and communicate this historicity. Today's obsession with novelty is based on a shallow understanding of artistic phenomena.'

To illustrate his point, Pallasmaa uses simple yet resonant examples of human connection to a deeper, unified memory: 'Most people enjoy looking at and being next to an open fire, for the reason that mankind has been enjoying the heat and benefits of fire for a couple of million years. The force of that experience comes through a collective memory. That's also why most people want to have an open fire in their house, although it has no real function any longer beyond being a reminder of our forgotten past.' Adding another layer of depth to his discussion, Pallasmaa expands with the words of philosopher Gaston Bachelard and poet Paul Valéry: 'As Bachelard declared, "My oldest memories are a hundred years old," whereas Valéry said, "An artist is worth thousands of years," but I would say that our biological memory extends back millions of years. We have even preserved physiological remnants of our early acquatic life in our bodies.'

However, Pallasmaa quickly rejects the suggestion that his position is one of a retrospective nature and points to the importance of image as a reflection of our society: 'I'm not saying that art and architecture should not be interested in human future, but I think the soil, the ontological ground, is our historical nature and the image that represents our cultural and biological history is one of the most complicated notions there is. In my opinion there are at least two fundamentally different concepts of the image: the first is the "manipulative image" used in advertising and political propaganda; for instance, that aims to catch immediate attention and to seduce, focus, close and fully manipulate arising associations. The second type of image is the "poetic image" that is more layered and slow, and it liberates and emancipates, opening new horizons for personal experience. A special category of the poetic image is the "primal image" – Bachelard's notion – that resonates with the deepest collective and unconscious memories of the human mind. Poetic images usually awaken the archaic layers of the mind.'

When questioned about the notion of the *Zeitgeist* and whether the phenomenon holds any value in representing collective human experience, Pallasmaa explains: 'My understanding is that all of our work is existential, and as historical beings we produce the work at a given moment, and what is included in the mental agglomerate is beyond our choice.' He continues: 'As biological beings we survive because we intensely react to what is around us. It is very interesting, and little studied, why certain things emerge simultaneously in various parts of the world, in different disciplines. I think it is simply creative chemistry or, as Gaston Bachelard describes it, a product of "poetic chemistry", which is a nice way of saying that in poetry unexpected compounds appear. Not simply the use of the words, but arriving at novel conceptual and verbal compounds altogether.'

Returning to reference his mentor, Pallasmaa reveals a deep distrust of the notion of 'currency', quoting Brodsky's famous quip 'No real writer ever wanted to be contemporary'. He says: 'I have never wanted the *Zeitgeist* to be consciously thematised as a motive of creative work. A collective body of work can be thematised afterwards, but not in advance or in the present time. I am against any kind of thematisation of creative work, because the process of categorisation tends to make it sentimental and formalist, or simply naive.'

Pallasmaa's writings on topics such as the 'architecture of the forest', and the 'geometry of the forest' reference the Finnish attitude to aesthetic objects and architecture. He believes that our connection to landscape has a vital influence on how we see, think and act, and he cites anthropological studies that reveal the impact of landscape on human conceptual and perceptual functions: 'Our Finnish sensibilities are strongly conditioned by the forest context and that is obviously different from Holland or the urbanised Mediterranean areas. These mental differences are very difficult to verbalise – what is the difference between Finnish, Swedish, Norwegian and Danish architectures, for example? However, if you show me images of Nordic architecture I can immediately say from which country they are. Perhaps one of the differences is that the Swedish and the Norwegian architectures look *at* nature, whereas in Finnish architecture you are *inside* nature.

Citing Alvar Aalto's Villa Mairea (1939) as an example, Pallasmaa explains: 'You are not looking at nature as a view – you are inside nature. And I think that's a historical, cultural thing, that, as Finns, we are the last of the Nordic peoples to come out of the forest – our soul is still there.' Described as an *opus con amore* by Aalto himself, Villa Mairea is imbued with a combination of intimacy, tactility and a kind of benevolence that feels as though the building comes and takes care of you in a wonderful manner. According to Pallasmaa: 'The combination of intimacy and monumentality is one of the most difficult things to achieve, but it's also one of the finest things to experience in architecture; intimate monumentality or monumental intimacy. A work has its outer face that addresses the world at large with a sense of authority and dignity, but it also has its intimate core: *Weltinnenraum*, to use a wonderful notion of Rilke, that entices and comforts our souls.'

This thematic of identity, resonance and continuity has recently formed the basis of several of the architect's essays that aspire to discuss and dissect this intimacy with the landscape and fusion of the 'outer' and 'inner' worlds, or as Pallasmaa puts it: 'As I inhabit a landscape, it inhabits me. Space and mind form a chiasmatic continuum.' He describes the emotions of nostalgia or melancholia as an essential part of the Finnish mentality as nature and light, and laments the lack of depth in emotional representation in contemporary architecture. 'For me melancholia is a very fine and deep emotion, and I'm impressed by architects who are able to express melancholy, solitude and silence. Today's architectural ideas and values tend to evoke only one part of the spectrum of emotions as appropriate for architectural expression. It's the same spectrum of emotions

LEFT JUHANI PALLASMAA (WITH DAN HOFFMAN AND THE CRANBROOK ARCHITECTURE STUDIO), ARRIVAL PLAZA 'ANALEMMA' (CALENDAR TEACHER), CRANBROOK ACADEMY, BLOOMFIELD HILLS, MICHIGAN, USA, 1994

Describing melancholia as a vital part of the Finnish quality of light and natural environment, Pallasmaa states: 'For me melancholia is a very fine and deep emotion.'

SIGURD LEWERENTZ, ST MARK'S CHURCH, BJÖRKHAGEN, SWEDEN, 1960

Sigurd Lewerentz's St Mark's Church is a resonant example of a healing image of melancholy, time, otherness and death. It is poetic and metaphysical in a similar way that the paintings of Giorgio de Chirico and Giorgio Morandi convey a sense of optimistic sadness.

that our society adores in terms of human character: well built, beautiful, energetic, youthful, and this, of course, is a distortion of human reality.'

Looking towards the future, Pallasmaa suggests that education is the key to empowering a more authentic engagement with our physical, sensorial and emotional environments: 'We no longer trust our senses, emotions or our own sense of being. When I use the word "emotion" I feel a bit uneasy myself because we confront the world as total human beings; we measure the world by being in the world, and the emotional realm is just one aspect of that unity. But we tend not to trust this encounter; we need to analyse it, learn from it and feel we *know* it before we trust ourselves. As far as I'm concerned, education should be as much about teaching young people to trust their own embodied choices and have full confidence in their aesthetic, emotional and sensorial judgements. Beauty is also the promise of a better world, and that is why beauty is such an important element in human experience. It maintains optimism, and that also creates the authentic ground for an interest in the future.'

Interviews
Pallasmaa's office, Helsinki, 13 December 2004
Malmaison Hotel, London, 20 February 2007

Notes

1. Books and writings by Juhani Pallasmaa include: *The Eyes of the Skin: Architecture and the Senses*, John Wiley & Sons Inc., New York, 2005; *The Architecture of Image: Existential Space in Cinema*, Rakennustieto Publishing, Helsinki, 2001; *Encounters: Architectural Essays* (edited by Peter MacKeith), Rakennustieto Publishing, Helsinki, 2005; and *The Thinking Hand: Existential and Embodied Wisdom in Architecture*, John Wiley & Sons Ltd, Chichester, 2009.

2. Juhani Pallasmaa, *The Architecture of Image: Existential Space in Cinema*, Rakennustieto Publishing, Helsinki, 2001.

3. 'I do believe in one's subjective insight, but it is an existential judgement, not an intellectual one.' Juhani Pallasmaa, interview with Yael Reisner, December 2004.

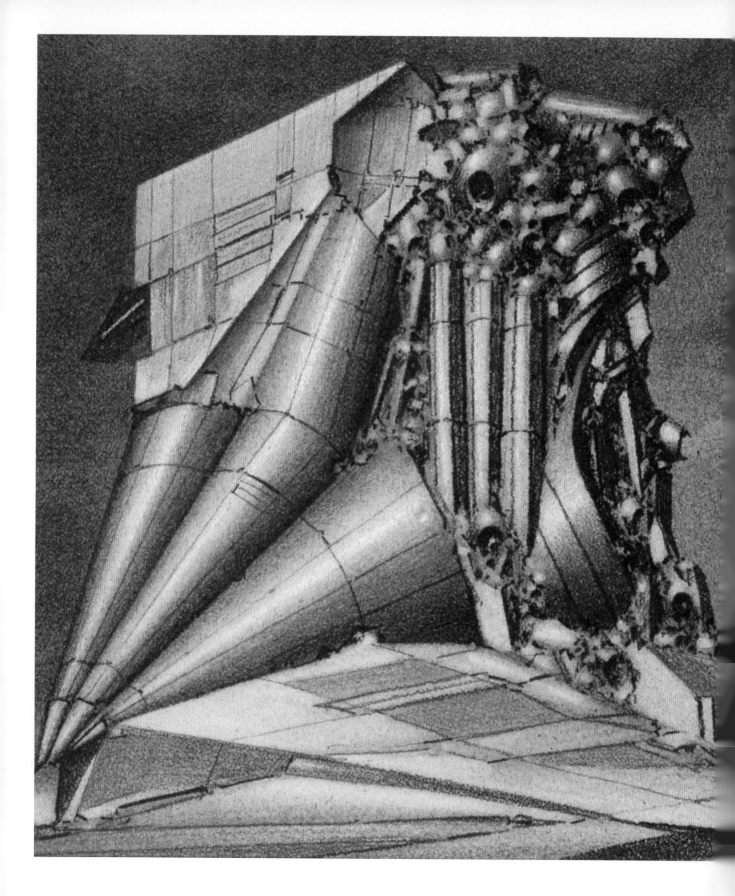

Lebbeus Woods

HEROIC
IMPERFECTION

THE POWERFUL AND EVOCATIVE DRAWINGS AND TEXTS of the American architect Lebbeus Woods are equally engaged with the realms of quantum mechanics, relativity, cybernetics, existentialism, notions of freedom and aspirations for a non-hierarchical society as they are with the practice and discourse of architecture. While Woods's prose is the product of an abstract mind, his poetry and drawings are derived from a sense of creative spontaneity with intuitive drawing at its epicentre.[1]

Talking about his process, Woods emphasises that it is only as he draws the physical worlds he aspires to that the distinctive qualities of his visual ideas start to formalise and pour through his pen. Through his texts the reader gains an intimate view of his intentions, ambitions and ideas. For the architect, the opportunity to connect to the reader within an intellectual framework is vitally important and facilitates his desire to share his vision for a new kind of physical world for inhabitation.

Woods's is a vision of a radically new world from both an ethical and aesthetic perspective. His architectural spaces provide a world of heterarchy consisting of a spontaneous lateral network of autonomous individuals.[2] His work embraces an inevitable sense of angst and anxiety, where individuals take the responsibility to construct their own interpretation of an authentic world of freedom. It is a perceptive and radical proposition that provokes and influences architects, film-makers and directors from around the world – all of whom take inspiration from the visionary world that Woods creates.

OPPOSITE STATIONS, 1989

Woods's visionary ideas are brought to the fore through the dexterity of his hand and pencil. His drawings capture his thoughts while intuitively creating a dynamic three-dimensional world; the ethics and the aesthetics of his architecture are equally important and inseparable.

Lebbeus Woods initially studied engineering at Purdue University in Indiana although he explains that he 'always wanted to be an architect'. After enrolling in the architecture programme at the University of Illinois in 1960, it became increasingly clear that his interest in architecture was from an intellectual rather than a design-based perspective. As Woods recalls: 'I think what attracted me to architecture was the idea that the

Through the 1980s and 1990s, Woods explored concepts for a new heroic architecture. The projects were radical for their unprecedented combination of 'low-tech', grand yet imperfect composition and form, everyday materials, and a dark, brooding, slightly decayed aesthetic.

BELOW STATIONS, 1989

Implicitly an architecture of freedom, Woods's work creates a physical world where individuals can live an authentic life in spaces that enable and symbolise freedom through non-deterministic organisation. He believes the progressive world resides in social and ethical aspects rather than in technological progress.

discipline could be a comprehensive field of knowledge so that all my interests, whether they lay in engineering or literature, could come together. In this respect it wasn't so much the look of things that I was attracted to as much as the realm of ideas.'

Early on in his student life a chance meeting with the Viennese-born cybernetician Heinz von Foerster proved to have a lasting and influential impact on the young architect: 'I met Heinz at the University of Illinois. He wasn't teaching in my field but his son, Andreas, was studying with me. Heinz asked me to illustrate some of his papers because he saw that I could draw and that's how I became involved with his world of cybernetics. He was dealing with the theory of how the brain works through nerve nets, cognition, perception and concepts and questioning: "What is thinking? What is memory?" I realised later that he was considered one of the world's top researchers in this field and his work appealed to my philosophical sensibilities.'

As a European intellectual of Jewish origin who had survived the war and been lured to teach and research in America, von Foerster proved an influential mentor, exposing the young architect to a culture beyond his own experience: 'Heinz would have champagne soirées at his house and I was always the kid hanging around and listening to the conversations taking place. It was an extraordinary experience that introduced me to a

Woods's work advocates an Arte Povera attitude which he uses as a political statement to critique global capitalised forces and the association with high-tech, anonymous architecture. His work suggests a less materialistic world through the utilisation of 'poor' materials with a 'found' or recycled sensibility.

ABOVE RECONSTRUCTION OF LA HABANA VIEJA,
HAVANA RECONSTRUCTION PROJECT, 1995

Woods's architecture is one of big ideas that are
simultaneously democratic for all. He describes the
Havana Reconstruction project as large-scale yet broken
down to smaller tectonic parts that are pieced together
and built of concrete and recycled materials.

new cultural world so it wasn't just being exposed to data. I was very fortunate to encounter him and that whole world, and I think of it as a lucky break in my life.'

Despite the lasting influence of these early experiences, it was not until many years later – during the 1970s and 1980s – that the serendipity of this chance meeting became clear to Woods: 'My work eventually revealed itself as coming from a particularly Heinzian perspective. I continuously questioned throughout my projects "What is thinking? What is architecture?" Cybernetics was an extension of all this, particularly because Heinz's version was called "Radical Constructivism" which suggests that we are in control of constructing our reality. The other element that appealed to me about Heinz's work was the multidisciplinary aspect. I was attracted to architecture for the same reasons as it wasn't a rigidly defined field. Cybernetics brought many people together from different fields.'

As Woods continued to rigorously question and test his ideology through his drawings and texts, his relationship with the output of his student work became increasingly difficult. His early work was conflicted by his deep admiration of Modernist, clear, planar geometric architecture and the forms emerging from his own hand. As he recalls: 'My student work[3] is all sort of Miesien, De-Stijlien and planar but, at some point, something else began to emerge and I would see what I was drawing and I really didn't like it. So then I would go back and try and do drawings that I liked, but they seemed predictable. Eventually, I reached a point in my mid-thirties when I had to say to myself: "This is what is emerging; this work is me. So, whether I like it or not is irrelevant." From that point on I was free of the feeling that I had to *like* what I was doing.'

From these crucial early influences, Woods's position consolidated to be one that continually questioned and reframed the traditional notion of the 'master architect'. He asserts: 'Architects aren't neutral; they're trying to promote something to the world. In my case, I've experienced serious doubts about perceived ideas of what architecture ought to be so I think a lot of my work has been about exploring content. I am asking questions rather than trying to take an established idea of architecture as a particular way of making buildings in the landscape and improving it or evolving it. I want people coming away from my work and asking: "Is that really architecture?" I've never had a preacher-like attitude because I also like other types of architectural approaches than my own. So I've never been able to say definitively: "This is the way to make architecture".'

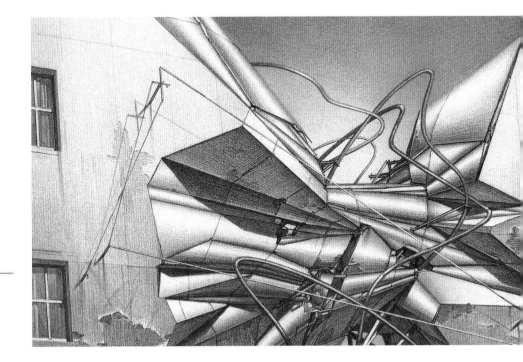

RIGHT SCAR CONSTRUCTION, WAR AND ARCHITECTURE SERIES, 1993

A critique on the values of our society, Woods's architecture is imbued with ethical messages. Scar construction communicates an architecture of heroic imperfection with emotional appeal that rejects the combination of international finance and glittering, glass buildings.

This design proposal for reconstruction in a post-war
environment is led by Woods's ethical approach to
architecture. An introspective quality is tangible within
his metaphorical image that communicates and reflects
on the process of healing and memory and facilitates
an optimistic process of moving forward without
forgetting the past.

While Woods's architecture is heroic in form and meaning, this sensibility is not necessarily expressed through the project's size or materials. In fact, his work suggests a less materialistic world through the utilisation of 'poor' materials such as crude wood and metal sheets that are imbued with a 'found' or recycled sensibility – an architecture of imperfection yet nevertheless grand in its composition. Unlike the Modernists who believed their vision for a progressive society should be expressed through new technologies, radical materials and construction, Woods develops his notion of a new world with 'low-tech'; where grandness is achieved by composition and form, and constructed with everyday materials that are imbued with a dark, brooding and slightly decayed aesthetic, in stark contrast to the Modernist's brightly coloured, shiny new forms.

As Woods explains: 'In my work, I've had a kind of Arte Povera attitude where I'm not driven by hi-tech, therefore highly capitalised forces.[4] I'd rather see what I have offered in my drawings as a kind of hand-made architecture for people who don't have factories driven by computers at their disposal. It's about putting things together in a more primitive or low-tech way.' Woods developed this aesthetic into a form of societal critique manifested in his early work such as the Geomechanical Tower (1987), Solohouse (1988), Stations (1989), and his Berlin Free Zone (1990) and Zagreb Free-Zone (1991). Ultimately, his position and imagery progressed further to become clear political dialogue through the War and Architecture series (1993), Sarajevo Reconstruction and Havana Reconstruction projects (1995).

Woods's natural ability to draw prescribed his chosen medium and provided an early forum to develop his ideas as he learnt to manipulate his inherent abilities in a very clear and decisive way: 'When you draw with ink you put down an ink line and you can't erase it. That decisiveness means that you can't go back in a process where you are inventing. So when I started to look at the limits of the Cartesian, then I knew the basic geometry and I could see how far one can structure it. I like the idea of taking limitations and seeing how far you can push them. That's an architect's mentality not an artist's. The artist feels freer, I believe. I want to take the limitations and see what I can do to maintain some kind of discipline.'

This major shift in Woods's work derived through this new restrictive methodology was documented in his 2004 publication *The Storm and the Fall*. The title for the book is derived primarily from two earlier installations, The Storm at the Cooper Union in New York (December 2001) and The Fall at the Cartier Foundation Gallery in Paris (November 2002), that captured the changes evident from Woods's Terrain series (1999) to the present day. While the installations are still related to Woods's notion of 'heterarchical space,[5] the surprising aspect is the limitation the architect has chosen to impose on his

BELOW RECONSTRUCTION OF THE ELECTRICAL
MANAGEMENT BUILDING, SARAJEVO
RECONSTRUCTION PROJECT, 1995

Woods believes his body of work is primarily addressed
and discussed by other architects and, in recent times,
members of the architectural community have often
filled the function of 'client' as well. Sarajevo-based
architect Ivan Straus designed the Electrical
Management Building before the war, in 1985, and
after its destruction invited Woods to respond with a
proposal for reconstruction.

natural drawing ability[6] by using mostly straight lines to describe and express the spatial
fields and, in effect, design with the purpose of leaving behind the 'tyranny of the object'.[7]

Woods extends the discussion, describing his shift from drawing forms to investigating
spatial fields as one that is intrinsically engaged with an exploration of contemporary
society: 'It is also looking at what is the most effective means of organising the elements
of thought or structure in our society. Obviously the hierarchy is still operating but, the
heterarchy, or this field condition is vibrating and bubbling and the question is: How does
anything emerge from that? If we ask where the authorship and meaning comes from I
think that the principal authority is emerging from a broad field, rather than from a single

force. That is the difference from previous historical efforts. So I believe that this is a condition that needs to be addressed in architecture. Where do forms arise from? I propose they emerge from a broad field, rather than from the head of Zeus, so to speak.'[8]

He continues: 'We obviously live in a volumetric and planar field; however, we also live within other frameworks such as a sociological field of different cultures, different genders, etc. Each generates a particular kind of field and, as an architect, I am interested in the structure of that space. I have discovered that this is a really unique discussion. I realised that most architects have not talked much about space in the past despite there being great discourse about form. For example, when I did the Berlin Free-Zone project in 1990, it was entirely an interior space and there was no exterior form. So I could show it architecturally in section lines, but otherwise it did not have a form, it was only interior space. So that was so much more interesting than external form – the spatial conditions, and how we occupy that space and what meaning we are able to give it by our occupation, by our habitation, by our living. It gives it another dimension.'

While many of his admirers mourned the loss of richness within his earlier drawings, for Woods the restricted framework provided a set of constraints to work within: 'It's a bit like haiku poetry,[9] where you only have 17 Japanese count sounds that you can use to construct the poem. What can you do with 17 count sounds?' Woods explains: 'I like that approach and I think of all the possibilities. As architects, we have to deal with increasingly restricted means and at the same time we need to extend those further. So it's a kind of duality – how far can you push the limit.' When pressed as to whether he felt any sense of loss at restricting his drawing palette to a language of straight lines in space he admits: 'I felt it was a wonderful thing to be able to express an idea that was grand and beautiful by an image and something that was your own creation. So that was an important feature of my work and I always attempted to give form to an idea.' However, he refutes any notion of his drawing ability being valuable within itself: 'I don't draw unless I've got some reason to draw and then I just use it as a tool. Drawing is not an end in itself – it's just a device I use to think things through. You have got to have the idea. And if you don't have an idea, I don't care what you can do visually; it just doesn't matter. If you are just producing graphics, that's not good enough.'

Woods returns to one of his great philosophical references – existentialism – to describe his desire to create meaning within his work, saying: 'We actually inhabit space, not volume; we inhabit the void and emptiness. The existentialism point of view is that this sense of emptiness that we are given needs to be filled. So, in my work, I am exploring the spatial field that is also an empty field in an ontological sense. We have to create meaning and this is an old philosophical problem. Unfortunately within our present

ABOVE TURBULENCE, 1988

In his early work and illustrated here in Turbulence, the viewer sees an intense field of lines and, at times, there is an emergence of a form. However, in his later work Woods rejects and reduces form to focus his interest and concentrate on pure line fields.

building – I think that's a mistake. The draw
else. And I know that there are architects v
autonomous in the sense that it is an imac

However, while Woods is comfortable witl
encourages a crossover of his work from the
he draws the line at his work being referer
example of this conundrum is the powerfu
Twelve Monkeys directed by Terry Gilliam,
carbon of one of Woods's evocative drawinç
the architect. As Woods recalls: 'In *Twel*
production designer. They simply copied my
the chair and the scenes when they're w
Underground Berlin project.'

The controversy and court case erupted into
visionary architecture into a greater public
collaborate within the film-making process

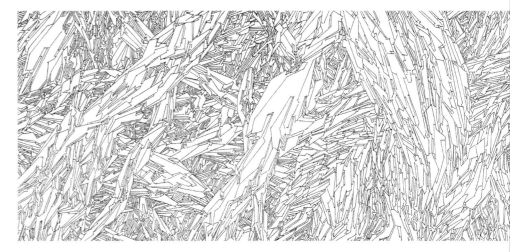

culture it is common to believe that we fill the emptiness simply with a lot of activity and
energy and it will automatically be filled with meaning. However, in fact, it doesn't work
that way. So I think the test for architects is to somehow imagine space as something
that is occupied, filled with ideas and concepts.'

This quest for meaning and the notion of the ethical within Woods's work permeates his
aesthetic within an inseparable duality. However, the architect makes it clear that his
work does not aspire to expressing idealised notions of liberty and freedom. In its
autonomy,[10] it is implicitly an architecture of freedom; creating a physical world where
individuals can live an authentic life in spaces that enable and symbolise freedom
through non-deterministic organisation. Woods expands: 'The ethical is the aesthetic and
vice versa; you can't separate them. What concerns me in my work is both, because I
think the aesthetic carries an ethic: How are things made? For what purpose are they
made? Who's going to see them and who's going to use them? How are they going to
be used? These are all things that one must take into account when one makes
something; you can't just send it off into the world and say "I don't care". I think that my
work tries to frame the answer to these questions: Why am I doing this work? What is
this work? and so on.'

This continual rigorous questioning and setting of boundaries is a self-imposed constraint
that the architect feels is integral to the process of his practice. 'When I work I always try
to make my task difficult. I think the notion of "ethical" has to do with a certain kind of
difficulty with a certain problematic. The ethical is not about some easy flaw; it always

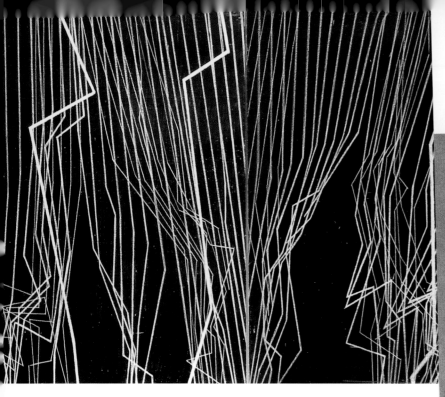

involves decisions and taking a position. You are not just drawing. So, for me,
making the work difficult and somehow problematic.'

Yet in setting these self-imposed boundaries and restrictions, is it possible that
lost something of the natural dexterity and evocative aesthetic of his earlie
'Looking back and reflecting on my own work, I think my earlier projects
colourful and had recognisable elements, but once you got into it you felt "wh
is it?"' he responds. 'So I think the ethical element was the real difficulty. I ha
it what I call the theory of "indigestibility", which means that my work should
digest; you should have a hard time swallowing it. The reason I make it dif
leave you with the hard choices. I like to follow the German philosopher Schop
point of view. He spoke about the idea of "the beautiful", which he called "k
which is pleasurable", then "the sublime", which is the notion that knowl
comes from pain. I always feel that that's neglected in the field of architecture
more interested in the pleasure process and what we can consume with our e

Pressed on the question of his level of comfort with his drawings being referenc
as architectural images, Woods says: 'I gradually came to understand my dra
imagery, but I applied to it a fancy term – "heuristic" images – meaning that t
you something, and that "something" may be able to apply towards the de
building or not. There were exceptions, of course, where I was designing some
was going to be built, but even then I don't think that I try to copy my dr

Woods describes his delight at being able to express an
idea that is grand, beautiful and of one's own creation
through drawing. He considers his contribution to
architecture has always been rooted in giving form to
an idea and strongly believes in the growing
importance of architectural imagery.

BELOW GEOMECHANICAL TOWER, UPPER CHAMBER,
CENTRICITY PROJECT, 1987

Although Woods welcomes interest in his work beyond
the architecture profession, he rejects his intellectual
property being referenced without his permission. A
pivotal scene in the film Twelve Monkeys directed by
Terry Gilliam mirrored an evocative architectural sketch
he created in 1987, resulting in a charge of copyright
infringement.

ultimately unsatisfying: 'After the controversy of *Twelve Monkeys*[12] I was contracted to
work on the film *Aliens 3*, and I was actually involved in the production process. However,
my experience was that Hollywood grinds everything up into a soup of images. So I
decided from that point on I didn't want to be involved in movies.'

Despite his disappointing film experience, Woods agrees that the image is a powerful and
valuable tool for the architectural community to communicate architectural ideas and
discourse to other disciplines and to convey the contribution that architecture can make
to contemporary society. He advocates harnessing the opportunity to communicate
through imagery, yet acknowledges that any discussion of image or aesthetics continues
to be a taboo topic for many architects to address within contemporary discourse,
reflecting: 'I think we have difficulties discussing aesthetics because looking back through
the history of architecture and the tradition of the École des Beaux-Arts, it was very much
about the way things looked prior to the advent of Modernism. If you examine the
evolution of Mies van der Rohe's drawings over the years, you can see that he started
with this incredible, romantic, charcoal rhetoric that later became simply minimal.' He
expands: 'Before Modernism, architects were just decorators with ornaments on
buildings, and for the Modernists that was not "real" architecture; real architecture is
structure, space and form.'

Even within his own teaching curriculum at the Cooper Union School of Architecture in
New York, Woods admits that the relationship of aesthetics within architectural discourse
is also rarely debated with his students. 'I do think it's still a legacy of, we might say, a
Judeo-Christian, Jewish-Protestant ethic, because you know the Protestants are equally
anti-aesthetic. I mean you can take Calvinism as an extreme example, but generally all
Protestant religions are very anti-visual and anti-aesthetic.'

Musing on the future of aesthetics and its enduring yet difficult relationship within an
architectural framework, Woods references one of his very early experiences as an 18-
year-old student in 1958, working in an old and established architectural office. He
remembers coming across the archival drawings of the practice dating back to the mid-
19th century: 'In 1850 there were no methods of reproducing architectural drawings and
so the architect made one set of drawings. But these drawings were for the purposes of
construction; they were instructing craftspeople who knew how to build in brick and
wood, and so on. The craftsmen knew how to do the work, so the architect was there to
say: "Just make it look like this." I thought that was a fantastic concept and the ideal
scenario. I realise that sounds crazy today and yet, on the other hand, with computer
technology I think architects will get back to a point where they'll make a drawing and
say: "Make it look like this."'

Concluding, Woods expands on the theme: 'So, in a sense, the way the thing looks is the real domain of the architect because it's about visual sensibility and culture. It's been around through the centuries, and it's still here although it's treated differently – we have different technology and ways of communicating and developing that culture – but there is an intelligence in the way things look. Whether it's the way a plant or flower or the sky looks, there is something we need to analyse about it and understand rationally. It's not just emotion; the way things look is actually deeply intellectual.'

Interviews
Woods's apartment, New York, 16 November 2004
Chez Gérard restaurant, London, 30 October 2006

ABOVE TRANSFORMATION VECTORS IN A STREET, SYSTEM WIEN, 2005

On the role of architects, Woods says: 'Architecture, we hope, is first of all a field of knowledge, and only then an action. Our hope is rooted in the judgement that actions are most constructive when informed by an idea that fits into a larger understanding of ourselves and the world. When we design and build, we demand that they embody such an idea of human experience and how it is enabled by the conception, design and construction of space ... It remains only for us to see this structure as though it has not been seen before, freshly, as though for the first time. This is, I believe, the task of architects.' From Lebbeus Woods, *System Wien*, Hatje Cantz Publishers, Berlin, 2005, p 16.

LEFT INSTALLATION VIEW, SYSTEM WIEN, 2005

On the responsibility of architects, Woods says: 'Individuals ... are identified ... by what they "do", how they interact with others, including the inanimate systems in their environment ... What architects do seriously impacts networks of interacting human and other energy flows, as well as the energies latent in the city. Their way of thinking and working needs to integrate this reality more than they do at present.' From Lebbeus Woods, *System Wien*, Hatje Cantz Publishers, Berlin, 2005, p 18.

Notes

1. Olive Brown, 'The mind of Lebbeus Woods', in Lebbeus Woods, Olive Brown and Peter Cook, *Origins: Mega II*, Architectural Association Publications, London, 1985.

2. See 'Glossary', in Lebbeus Woods, *Anarchitecture Architecture Is a Political Act*, Architectural Monographs, No 22, John Wiley & Sons, Inc., New York, 1992.

3. Lebbeus Woods was a student from 1958 to 1964.

4. A similarity to Gaetano Pesce's ideological position, although the output of their work varies greatly.

5. See 'Glossary', in Lebbeus Woods, *Anarchitecture Architecture Is a Political Act*, op cit.

Heterarchy: A spontaneous lateral network of autonomous individuals; a system of authority based on the evolving performances of individuals, eg A cybernetic circus.

Individual: Human embodiment of autonomous being; inventor of the world.

Ontogenetics: The study of becoming, dynamic and heterarchical.

Freespace: A construction free of preconceived value, use or meaning; an element in a heterarchy.

Free-Zone: Heterarchy of freespaces; pattern of urban order based on knowledge and performance; a system opposing mass culture; a subversion of hierarchies.

6. Woods's architectural language changed completely; an aesthetical shift that still holds a similar ethics.

7. 'The shift of focus I have made from objects to fields has not been made simply as a rejection of typological thinking, which dominates the design of buildings; nor simply as a rejection of the politics of identity that buildings inevitably work to sustain; nor simply as a rejection of the illusions of authority conjured by buildings – especially innovative buildings, designed and built in the service of private or institutional power. How can I advocate the revelation latent in the process of making things? Without freedom from the tyranny of the object. If I cannot free myself, how can I advocate the freedom of others, in whichever terms they might choose?' Lebbeus Woods, *The Storm and The Fall*, Architectural Press, New York, 2004, p 37.

8. Woods's intellectual exploration requires that he restrict his hand as a designer as part of the consistent drive to lead to a non-deterministic design.

9. Haiku is a form of Japanese poetry with a 17-count sound verse form.

10. 'I need to believe, rightly or wrongly, that my work manifests something autonomous. They're ideas and not expressions or an extension of something else.' Lebbeus Woods, interview with Yael Reisner, November 2004.

'The role of architecture on this landscape is instrumental, not expressive ... Expression is possession, the manifestation of a lust for domination. Any attempt to express in a form an idea external to it is an attempt to arrest the idea in time, to control it beyond its life. I despise all such "expressionism", and none more than that which appropriate ineffable symbols, archetypes – in fact types of any kind. These are the most vain and tyrannical attempts to eternalise the ephemeral.' Lebbeus Woods, *Anarchitecture: Architecture Is A Political Act*, op cit, p 11.

11. Geomechanical Tower, Upper Chamber, Centricity project (1987).

12. Woods's injunction alleged that the set mirrored an architectural sketch he created in 1987 and that Universal Studios did not ask his permission to use it, thereby making it a copyright infringement.

Gaetano Pesce

UNFETTERED MAVERICK

STANDING IN HIS MANHATTAN-BASED STUDIO, Italian architect Gaetano Pesce cuts a striking presence among the accumulated and colourful debris of lamp, chair and table prototypes amid bright exhibition posters, all haphazardly displayed as if an illustration of his enduring and influential 40-something-year career.

Still handsome, well dressed in comfortable clothing and speaking in a distinctive Italian accent with great clarity, Pesce extends a warmth and generosity with his time and conversation that is rare among high-profile architects. At the age of 68, he is as productive now as he was during his emergence, in the late 1960s, as a provocative architect who embraced new technologies and synthetic materials to express socio-political and cultural references through his innovative product designs.

Like many of his contemporaries, Pesce is suspicious of aesthetic values and advocates curbing the instinctive visual ability for design. He delights in the self-described 'badly done' object where a product's individual flaws or inconsistencies in the manufacturing process are accepted and embraced, believing this illustrates his commitment to the importance of individuality and a liberal society. However, while he adamantly rejects the role of 'eye judgment' or the notion of a formal aesthetic within his design process, he does reluctantly concede that without natural intuition or a 'good eye' there is little chance for a designer to develop a valuable product.

OPPOSITE AND PAGE 106 I FELTRI, FELT ARMCHAIRS FOR CASSINA, 1986–7

Marking a new application and innovative technology for wool felt, the wonderful softness of the material is maintained while a structural quality is achieved by adding liquid polyester resin during the manufacturing process. The opposite qualities of the softness of the felt and the rigidity of the form are an intriguing combination, allowing the chair to be both structure and blanket.

Pesce's distinctive body of work is ultimately driven by material and technological experimentation layered with cultural metaphors bound by principles yet without the limitations of rules. The wonderfully whimsical qualities inherent in his objects are imbued with imperfection, softness, accessibility, colour and humour all layered with sociopolitical messages that include and respond to the cultural issues of the world we live within.

Gaetano Pesce

UNFETTERED MAVERICK

STANDING IN HIS MANHATTAN-BASED STUDIO, Italian architect Gaetano Pesce cuts a striking presence among the accumulated and colourful debris of lamp, chair and table prototypes amid bright exhibition posters, all haphazardly displayed as if an illustration of his enduring and influential 40-something-year career.

Still handsome, well dressed in comfortable clothing and speaking in a distinctive Italian accent with great clarity, Pesce extends a warmth and generosity with his time and conversation that is rare among high-profile architects. At the age of 68, he is as productive now as he was during his emergence, in the late 1960s, as a provocative architect who embraced new technologies and synthetic materials to express socio-political and cultural references through his innovative product designs.

Like many of his contemporaries, Pesce is suspicious of aesthetic values and advocates curbing the instinctive visual ability for design. He delights in the self-described 'badly done' object where a product's individual flaws or inconsistencies in the manufacturing process are accepted and embraced, believing this illustrates his commitment to the importance of individuality and a liberal society. However, while he adamantly rejects the role of 'eye judgment' or the notion of a formal aesthetic within his design process, he does reluctantly concede that without natural intuition or a 'good eye' there is little chance for a designer to develop a valuable product.

Pesce's distinctive body of work is ultimately driven by material and technological experimentation layered with cultural metaphors bound by principles yet without the limitations of rules. The wonderfully whimsical qualities inherent in his objects are imbued with imperfection, softness, accessibility, colour and humour all layered with sociopolitical messages that include and respond to the cultural issues of the world we live within.

OPPOSITE AND PAGE 106 | FELTRI, FELT ARMCHAIRS FOR CASSINA, 1986-7

Marking a new application and innovative technology for wool felt, the wonderful softness of the material is maintained while a structural quality is achieved by adding liquid polyester resin during the manufacturing process. The opposite qualities of the softness of the felt and the rigidity of the form are an intriguing combination, allowing the chair to be both structure and blanket.

Notes

1. Olive Brown, 'The mind of Lebbeus Woods', in Lebbeus Woods, Olive Brown and Peter Cook, *Origins: Mega II*, Architectural Association Publications, London, 1985.

2. See 'Glossary', in Lebbeus Woods, *Anarchitecture Architecture Is a Political Act*, Architectural Monographs, No 22, John Wiley & Sons, Inc., New York, 1992.

3. Lebbeus Woods was a student from 1958 to 1964.

4. A similarity to Gaetano Pesce's ideological position, although the output of their work varies greatly.

5. See 'Glossary', in Lebbeus Woods, *Anarchitecture Architecture Is a Political Act*, op cit.

Heterarchy: A spontaneous lateral network of autonomous individuals; a system of authority based on the evolving performances of individuals, eg A cybernetic circus.

Individual: Human embodiment of autonomous being; inventor of the world.

Ontogenetics: The study of becoming, dynamic and heterarchical.

Freespace: A construction free of preconceived value, use or meaning; an element in a heterarchy.

Free-Zone: Heterarchy of freespaces; pattern of urban order based on knowledge and performance; a system opposing mass culture; a subversion of hierarchies.

6. Woods's architectural language changed completely; an aesthetical shift that still holds a similar ethics.

7. 'The shift of focus I have made from objects to fields has not been made simply as a rejection of typological thinking, which dominates the design of buildings; nor simply as a rejection of the politics of identity that buildings inevitably work to sustain; nor simply as a rejection of the illusions of authority conjured by buildings – especially innovative buildings, designed and built in the service of private or institutional power. How can I advocate the revelation latent in the process of making things? Without freedom from the tyranny of the object. If I cannot free myself, how can I advocate the freedom of others, in whichever terms they might choose?' Lebbeus Woods, *The Storm and The Fall*, Architectural Press, New York, 2004, p 37.

8. Woods's intellectual exploration requires that he restrict his hand as a designer as part of the consistent drive to lead to a non-deterministic design.

9. Haiku is a form of Japanese poetry with a 17-count sound verse form.

10. 'I need to believe, rightly or wrongly, that my work manifests something autonomous. They're ideas and not expressions or an extension of something else.' Lebbeus Woods, interview with Yael Reisner, November 2004.

'The role of architecture on this landscape is instrumental, not expressive ... Expression is possession, the manifestation of a lust for domination. Any attempt to express in a form an idea external to it is an attempt to arrest the idea in time, to control it beyond its life. I despise all such "expressionism", and none more than that which appropriate ineffable symbols, archetypes – in fact types of any kind. These are the most vain and tyrannical attempts to eternalise the ephemeral.' Lebbeus Woods, *Anarchitecture: Architecture Is A Political Act*, op cit, p 11.

11. Geomechanical Tower, Upper Chamber, Centricity project (1987).

12. Woods's injunction alleged that the set mirrored an architectural sketch he created in 1987 and that Universal Studios did not ask his permission to use it, thereby making it a copyright infringement.

Concluding, Woods expands on the theme: 'So, in a sense, the way the thing looks is the real domain of the architect because it's about visual sensibility and culture. It's been around through the centuries, and it's still here although it's treated differently – we have different technology and ways of communicating and developing that culture – but there is an intelligence in the way things look. Whether it's the way a plant or flower or the sky looks, there is something we need to analyse about it and understand rationally. It's not just emotion; the way things look is actually deeply intellectual.'

Interviews
Woods's apartment, New York, 16 November 2004
Chez Gérard restaurant, London, 30 October 2006

ABOVE TRANSFORMATION VECTORS IN A STREET, SYSTEM WIEN, 2005

On the role of architects, Woods says: 'Architecture, we hope, is first of all a field of knowledge, and only then an action. Our hope is rooted in the judgement that actions are most constructive when informed by an idea that fits into a larger understanding of ourselves and the world. When we design and build, we demand that they embody such an idea of human experience and how it is enabled by the conception, design and construction of space ... It remains only for us to see this structure as though it has not been seen before, freshly, as though for the first time. This is, I believe, the task of architects.' From Lebbeus Woods, *System Wien*, Hatje Cantz Publishers, Berlin, 2005, p 16.

LEFT INSTALLATION VIEW, SYSTEM WIEN, 2005

On the responsibility of architects, Woods says: 'Individuals ... are identified ... by what they "do", how they interact with others, including the inanimate systems in their environment ... What architects do seriously impacts networks of interacting human and other energy flows, as well as the energies latent in the city. Their way of thinking and working needs to integrate this reality more than they do at present.' From Lebbeus Woods, *System Wien*, Hatje Cantz Publishers, Berlin, 2005, p 18.

ultimately unsatisfying: 'After the controversy of *Twelve Monkeys*[12] I was contracted to
work on the film *Aliens 3*, and I was actually involved in the production process. However,
my experience was that Hollywood grinds everything up into a soup of images. So I
decided from that point on I didn't want to be involved in movies.'

Despite his disappointing film experience, Woods agrees that the image is a powerful and
valuable tool for the architectural community to communicate architectural ideas and
discourse to other disciplines and to convey the contribution that architecture can make
to contemporary society. He advocates harnessing the opportunity to communicate
through imagery, yet acknowledges that any discussion of image or aesthetics continues
to be a taboo topic for many architects to address within contemporary discourse,
reflecting: 'I think we have difficulties discussing aesthetics because looking back through
the history of architecture and the tradition of the École des Beaux-Arts, it was very much
about the way things looked prior to the advent of Modernism. If you examine the
evolution of Mies van der Rohe's drawings over the years, you can see that he started
with this incredible, romantic, charcoal rhetoric that later became simply minimal.' He
expands: 'Before Modernism, architects were just decorators with ornaments on
buildings, and for the Modernists that was not "real" architecture; real architecture is
structure, space and form.'

Even within his own teaching curriculum at the Cooper Union School of Architecture in
New York, Woods admits that the relationship of aesthetics within architectural discourse
is also rarely debated with his students. 'I do think it's still a legacy of, we might say, a
Judeo-Christian, Jewish-Protestant ethic, because you know the Protestants are equally
anti-aesthetic. I mean you can take Calvinism as an extreme example, but generally all
Protestant religions are very anti-visual and anti-aesthetic.'

Musing on the future of aesthetics and its enduring yet difficult relationship within an
architectural framework, Woods references one of his very early experiences as an 18-
year-old student in 1958, working in an old and established architectural office. He
remembers coming across the archival drawings of the practice dating back to the mid-
19th century: 'In 1850 there were no methods of reproducing architectural drawings and
so the architect made one set of drawings. But these drawings were for the purposes of
construction; they were instructing craftspeople who knew how to build in brick and
wood, and so on. The craftsmen knew how to do the work, so the architect was there to
say: "Just make it look like this." I thought that was a fantastic concept and the ideal
scenario. I realise that sounds crazy today and yet, on the other hand, with computer
technology I think architects will get back to a point where they'll make a drawing and
say: "Make it look like this."'

Pesce's distinctive language engaged with innovating new manufacturing technologies for applications of synthetic materials and was further enriched by the communication of cultural messages through recognisable imagery. He employed carriers such as figurative elements, cultural references and energising colours that triggered a primal emotional response in people through their familiarity. The unexpected combination of a facial profile and the shoes re-contextualised within an industrial product, as illustrated here, enhance the impact.

Despite living in New York for the past 27 years, Gaetano Pesce is inherently Italian in his sensibilities, describing his Manhattan base as a 'servicing' office and revealing that much of his work is still derived from his connections in Italy. The longevity of this working connection to his homeland is perhaps partly influenced by his mother – a strong, intelligent woman who proved a pivotal influence on the beginnings of his creative career. As Pesce recalls: 'My mother was a pianist and I have memories of her discussing important composers and why she preferred one artist to another. She was the one who introduced me to the concept of thinking creatively, explaining why Beethoven was innovative and impressing upon me the importance of being original and having a free mind.'

Growing up and playing in the streets of Florence near his grandmother's home, art was very much in the background of Pesce's early experience: 'As children we were very much in contact with art just by being on the streets. For example, I remember playing soccer games in a Florentine portico done by Brunelleschi. We used to throw a ball against the column and the doorframes would get heavily kicked – it seems criminal

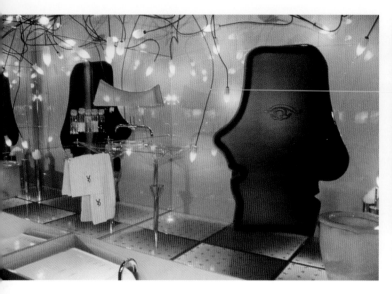
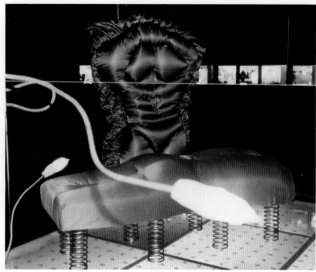

ABOVE GRAND HOTEL SALONE, MOSCOW, RUSSIA, 2002

Pesce credits his mother as a driving influence on his creative career, saying: 'My mother was the one who introduced me to the concept of thinking creatively, explaining why Beethoven was innovative and impressing upon me the importance of being original and having a free mind.'

today! Yet this physical engagement with the building was a way of understanding the art we were surrounded by. It was my milieu, if you like.'

While studying architecture at the University of Venice, it was the chance meeting of two influential figures in his life that resulted in Pesce's introduction to, and subsequent pursuit of, industrial design. Cesare Cassina, an established industrialist whose family business was emerging as one of the world's most innovative furniture manufacturers, became a lifelong collaborator after initially visiting Pesce's studio with the intention of buying some drawings from the young designer. And Pesce's chance encounter with Milena Vettore, a young industrial design student studying at Venice's Institut Superiore di Disegno Industriale, evolved into a long-time collaboration and love affair. Tragically, Milena died as the result of an industrial accident at the height of their creative partnership. Recalling the importance of these relationships, Pesce describes their influence on his subsequent rejection of the elitism of contemporary abstract art: 'Milena and Cassina introduced me to the new world of the factory. I started to slowly realise that art should always be a product. As students we viewed art as a cultural phenomenon and I started to realise this was totally wrong. I came to the conclusion that my job was to be a designer, not an artist.'

The collaboration marked a pivotal point in Pesce's ideology and a commitment to pushing the boundaries of design within a social context. As he suggests: 'Working with

Pesce's products are typically made from synthetic materials and are always saturated in colour from warm reds, oranges, yellows, dark blues and greens. This colourful aspect of his work is influenced by 'living and studying in Venice, where the history of expression carries light. Light is formed by colour. Light and colour are energy. So understanding the power of colour I started using it in my work from the very beginning.'

Milena and Cassina I came to understand that the revolution today is to accept the ideology of our times, and to transform it through expression. Unfortunately I feel that there are very few people engaged with this idea today. Most designers' work is superficial decoration and most architects simply remake what they know.'

These pivotal relationships, coupled with Pesce's politically active environment at Venice's School of Architecture, provided fertile ground for the young architect's developing social ideology. While still a student, he founded the collaborative Gruppo N – a group committed to the idea of exploring the concept of 'programmed art'.[1] Pesce explains: 'We became very critical of the establishment and we realised that there was a lot of immorality in the art world.'

Establishing a gallery, the group organised exhibitions that aspired to demystify art and communicate the idea that the artist's content is more important than the form. The exhibitions were groundbreaking for their conceptual approach and often used symbolic methodologies to express a simple message: 'I remember one exhibition that Milena curated with us in 1959 called "Il Pane". We visited all the local shops collecting bread

and then we exhibited all the different forms of bread we had found. It was a beautiful exhibition because of the simplicity, the smell, and it was all so tasty! Yet, the show's message was that the form of the bread is of little importance; what is important is if the bread is good. This was the kind of conceptual approach that underpinned our work as Gruppo N.'

The Gruppo N collaboration provided an important grounding for Pesce in conceptual expression,[2] yet his growing political convictions were difficult to pursue within the limitations of a collective. At 33, the young architect made the difficult decision to leave the group and embark on a series of travels that he hoped would inspire and refine how he might express such convictions through his creative work.

The architect strongly refutes the notion that visual
judgement or aesthetics have any part in his creative
process. Pesce describes the Samson table, for
example, as the result of the manufacturing process
rather than any kind of preoccupation with form.

ABOVE 'PIECE FOR AN EXECUTION BY SHOOTING',
PADUA, ITALY, 1967

Marking a turning point early on in Pesce's career,
this dramatic multimedia performance illustrates
his conviction that contemporary sociopolitical
themes should be expressed through accessible
contemporary art.

Communism had formed a fundamental underpinning to Gruppo N's theory and process, yet Pesce came to suspect he had little understanding of the full implications of the political reality. As part of his quest for meaning it seemed apt to gravitate towards Russia – a country that the architect viewed idealistically as 'the place of freedom'. However, his direct exposure to the realities of communism soon radically altered his views and manifested in a clearly defined personal strategy. He remembers the definitive experience vividly: 'I clearly understood that communism in Russia was hell, a horrible place with a dictatorship that was very violent. The experience helped me to understand that it's much better to fight and to express your ideas as an individual, and so I came to the self-realisation that this was not the time for uniform artistic movement; it was a time for "solitary birds".'

After returning to Italy in 1959 Pesce set up work as an individual practitioner with a renewed energy and commitment to expressing contemporary political themes through communicative and accessible art forms. The first of these works found form in the startling and provocative performance 'Piece for an Execution by Shooting' (1967). Recalling the seminal work, Pesce describes it as 'an execution by gunshot. The audience literally watches someone bleed to death and there is so much blood that it flows all around their feet so it's very dramatic. The work is communicating the idea that if a very traumatic event happens then the reality is that everybody is involved and we are all responsible and accountable for blame.'

LEFT GOLGOTHA RANGE FOR BRACCIODIFFERO, 1972–3

The images of his products are vitally important to Pesce, who often directs and controls the photography used for marketing and promotion to ensure the themes of the designs are communicative and accessible. To him, 'An image, not writing, is the most important carrier of a culture.'

Broadly speaking, Pesce's work, particularly during the late 1960s to late 1980s, contains a series of highly recognisable elements – warm, primary colours, plastic or 'new' materials and feminine characteristics. Yet, despite his belief that 'image, not writing, is the most important carrier of a culture',[3] the architect strongly refutes the notion that visual judgement or aesthetics have any part in his creative process. He describes the Samson table (1980), for example, as the result of the manufacturing process rather than any kind of preoccupation with form: 'I wanted to do a table using a process that was repeatable, but that also allowed for differences with each individual object. I came up with a drawing to describe the technique of this table to the manufacturers in a very simple way. So instead of focusing on the form, I concentrated on the process – by carrying out the process, the table was realised.'

This is not to say that there is no kind of visual imagery at all – it is simply that Pesce does not accept the notion of the aesthetics being an inspiration of the eventual form. In fact, some of his work references religious iconography drawn from his Catholic upbringing that is then reinterpreted and imbued with a new meaning for a contemporary context. His Samson table interprets the imagery of the final hours of the biblical Samson – the Israelite judge and warrior – who used his enormous strength to fight the Philistines until eventually betrayed by his mistress Delilah. Pesce re-contextualises the well-known legend by recalling the imagery of Samson's final hours[4] to provide a product that holds an easily accessible yet political message: 'I thought of the beautiful image of Samson pushing in and collapsing the temple's columns and his

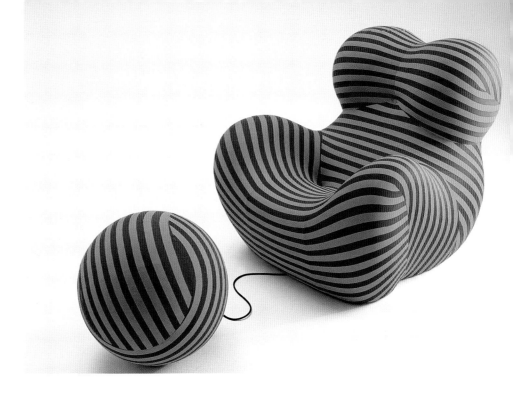

ABOVE LA MAMMA AND THE OTTOMAN BALL, UP
SERIES, 1969

The UP series marked the first time in contemporary
furniture design that a form was created without a
wood or metal structure. The liquid utilised became a
form when coupled with 84 per cent air which, in turn,
enabled flat packaging – another new innovation. The
series is exemplary of Pesce's ambition to express his
cultural message – 'Women have always been victims
of masculine mentality' and 'prisoners of prejudice' –
within the framework of three primary design
principles: innovative materials, experimental
technologies and a new language.

strength in refusing the hypocrisy of the priests. Samson fought the rigidity of common
thought and a scheme he didn't accept. In much the same way that, historically, there's
rigidity in understanding what a table might be – it is usually a surface with four legs, very
rigid and schematic. So the table's legs are in that position in easy reference to the story.'

Pesce's desire to communicate to a wide-ranging public through narrative metaphors and
without intellectual pretence naturally evolved into experimenting with other forms of
'carriers' for his sociopolitical messages. By utilising recognisable figurative elements
coupled with manufacturing experiments using synthetic materials, his work aspired to
trigger an emotional response in people generated by the contrast of a familiar form
within the unexpected framework of a product.

Rather than attempting to create a distinct visual language for his products, the use of
the figurative within Pesce's work was intended as a damning critique of the alienating
effect of abstract art on society. He believed the advent of abstraction had become
'dangerous territory' where creativity has the potential to become useless and
uncommunicative to the wider community: 'With the advent of abstraction the universal
reach of traditional art forms was lost – nobody understood what the art was about. As
an alternative to abstraction, I thought if I want to connect with and communicate to a
wide range of people then I have to express myself through recognisable images. That's
why I made a chair in the recognisable shape of a female body. The shape was supposed
to represent the private side of expression – and the human condition of women.'

The results of this metaphoric protest mark the beginning of a new kind of expression for Pesce's work and one that he fought hard to pursue within the conservative confines of the manufacturing industry. Many companies resisted making products that carried political meaning, and it took courage and determination to convince them to extend their commitment. As the architect recalls: 'Finally they trusted me and the Up 5, 6 series and the La Mama armchair mark the starting point of when I began using the recognisable form of a woman's body in my work. However, if you look at the ottoman ball I designed to connect with the La Mama chair, then I feel there is something interesting there: an image of a prisoner with her ball and chain. Historically, today, and unfortunately possibly in the future, women are still prisoners of prejudice. To express this within an article would have been banal because it's been done so often before, but to express this message with a chair that is supposed to simply sit in a living room seemed quite provocative. From this experience, I understood that a product could carry expression, content, function with a sense of joy in its use; this was the beginning of a lot of the ideas inherent in my work.'

In the early 1970s Pesce began to speak of the importance of the 'Third Industrial Revolution' – a concept borne from his frustration with the lingering influence of the International Style and its doctrine of a Utopian ideal of mass-produced architecture and design. While the architect acknowledged the influential movement's revolutionary nature and its appropriateness for its time, he also harboured doubts about its validity for an increasingly complex society: 'I realised that just as people have the right to think in a different way – address and express themselves in relation to their origin, territory, identity and religion – so did objects.'[5]

His lingering doubts prompted his commitment to developing a manufacturing process that accepted flaws within mass-produced objects, allowing an embracement of similarity over equality. In pushing the boundaries of conventional manufacturing, Pesce describes his delight in discovering a new material language, one that was set free from the notion of perfection and continues to preoccupy his work today: 'I discovered that perfection doesn't exist; it is mistakes that characterise the human capacity. I allowed mistakes to be present in my work because they were capable of doing two things: firstly, they express a human aspect to the work, and secondly, the inherent nature of the mistake avoids repetition. So when I'm working on something, it is never the same because there are new mistakes. The work is "badly done" in the sense that I'm incapable of doing something perfectly.'

Pesce is intensely suspicious of the notions of perfection and beauty and rejects wholeheartedly any suggestion of a recognisable aesthetic or visual language in his

The notions of the 'Third Industrial Revolution' and the 'mass production of originals' have occupied Pesce's design process since the early 1970s. He critiqued the idea of perfection in manufacturing, believing that 'just as people had the right to think in different way so did objects ... the designer should accept flaws and look for similarities but not for equality.' The products are not equal and also, in Pesce's words, are 'badly done' since he does not wish them to be perfect either.

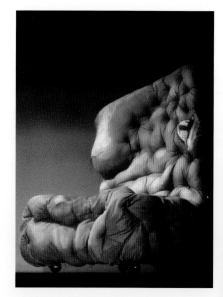

ABOVE PRATT CHAIR NO. 3, 1983

Pesce firmly rejects the notion of 'eye judgement' or aesthetics playing a dominant role in his design process. As he succinctly states: 'Beauty is perfect. The idea of the perfect detail frightens me. Personally I can't accept the idea of beauty; I simply must not.'

work. The balance between the power of the metaphorical techniques that he employs to illustrate his commitment to the importance of individuality within his products, and their ultimate perception as individual 'beautiful objects' by their users, presents a difficult relationship for the architect to reconcile. However, regardless of this dilemma, Pesce's work is imbued with qualities that resonate with the human spirit – softness, accessibility, colour and humour – providing a stark contrast to a Modernist ideal of elegance, transparency, lightness and Utopian perfection. As he succinctly concludes: 'The idea of the perfect detail frightens me. Personally I can't accept the idea of beauty; I simply must not. Ugly may one day be seen as beautiful; however, it's not yet the reality, so for the moment I have to fight for things in our society that are not established. The role of the intellectual is to fight!'

Interviews

Pesce's studio, New York, 15 November 2004

The Royal Garden Hotel in Kensington, London, 19 February 2006

Notes

1. The notion of 'programmatic art' for Gruppo N was a reaction against the expressive improvisation of Art Informel, the European equivalent of Abstract Expressionism in America.

2. Pesce continued, throughout his career, to criticise abstraction in art and architecture. He rejected the interest in the importance of form as a shallow, decorative act, believing that art should tell meaningful stories and carry cultural messages to allow a direct dialogue with the public. This position is reflected in the metaphors and figurative elements demonstrated in his own work.

3. Marisa Bartolucci, *Gaetano Pesce*, Chronicle Books, San Francisco, CA, 2003, p 23.

4. The angle of the Samson table's legs are positioned to recall the legend of Samson's final hours where, blinded by his captors, he collapsed the temple of the Philistine god Dagon upon himself and upon a crowd of the enemy who were taunting him.

5. This notion of 'mass production of originals' precedes and predicts the ambition of 'non-standard design' developed many years later in digital design laboratories. For example, the seminal exhibition 'Non-Standard Architectures' at the Centre Pompidou (December 2003) displayed the work of 12 selected digital design studios that engaged with the notion of the generalisation of singularity in architecture. Pesce may or may not have been aware of the notion of 'non-standard' in mathematics; however, his approach was undoubtedly dictated by innovative technologies in manufacturing products from new synthetic materials and his vehement belief in the importance of individuality in a liberal society.

Wolf D Prix

SELF-CONFIDENT FORMS

THE PROVOCATIVE, EMOTIONALLY CHARGED DRAWINGS AND MODELS produced by COOP HIMMELB(L)AU founders Wolf D Prix, Helmut Swiczinsky[1] and Michael Holzer during the late 1970s through to the early 1980s inspired a generation of young architects all over the world to experiment with form and space through intuitive and spontaneous processes. Yet, COOP HIMMELB(L)AU's visionary architecture[2] was always conceived with the intention of transcending beyond speculative fantasy to large-scale built form and, following 40 years of rigorous conceptual development and a series of powerful yet smaller built works, the practice's most recent projects are being realised and completed at an increasing rate and dramatically evolving scale.

The close of 2007 saw the opening of two major COOP HIMMELB(L)AU buildings to global acclaim: the bold design of the Akron Art Museum in Ohio in July, closely followed in October by the dynamic BMW Welt in Munich. Moreover, in 2012 the Busan Cinema Center in South Korea will open, followed by the intriguing Musée des Confluences Center which is scheduled to open in Lyons in 2014. This culmination of built work moves the influence of the practice – and in particular its remaining founding member, Wolf D Prix – into a global context, and in doing so encourages the next generation of architects to pursue their architectural dreams and resist conforming to a capitalistic world.

Sitting in his busy studio in Vienna, surrounded by a collection of young architects working within an intense yet friendly atmosphere, Prix appears youthful and full of enthusiasm despite a career spanning more than 40 years. Still very much the Viennese man, he is well dressed in dark stylish suits, often smoking cigars, and speaking animatedly in trans-Continental English with a strong Austrian accent. He belongs to a generation that fought intensely for their architectural ideology, and he remains a fighter and a non-conformist even as he moves into the latter stages of his career where he is afforded the luxury of being viewed as an elder statesman. However, he

OPPOSITE ARCHITECTURE IS NOW 'THE PANTHER IN THE CAGE', STUTTGART, GERMANY, 1982

As young architects, Wolf D Prix and Helmut Swiczinsky embraced intuition and spontaneity as the key elements of their design process. By using their first emotive sketches as the primary generator for each project, they believed their work was released from the limits of the conscious mind.

remains engaged with current architectural debate and discourse, the importance of sophisticated architectural forms, the movement of a body in space and what he describes as an 'emotionally intense architecture'.

Prix's enthusiasm for COOP HIMMELB(L)AU's relatively recent transition from a prolific, powerful practice at the forefront of the architectural vanguard to its latest incarnation as a competition-winning global entity is engagingly exuberant and youthful. 'I'm happy, I'm really happy!' he exclaims with a smile. 'Now we are able to build what we dreamed of when we were 26 years old. So I have to admit that I now realise we had to learn. I'm personally very impatient, but I think a young architect has to learn how to be patient, because it takes a long time until you get where you want to be.[3] This is life experience.' He continues: 'However, I'm happy that we have now built such large-scale projects because it's no longer valid for people to dismiss our work as "not possible".'

Yet, despite the fact that building at a significant scale has cemented the practice's reputation among the great architects of our age, the reality is that COOP HIMMELB(L)AU has not changed its intentions or pursuits; its focus is still about creating form and space that draws on emotion and aims at an architecture that is intense and authentic to its time.

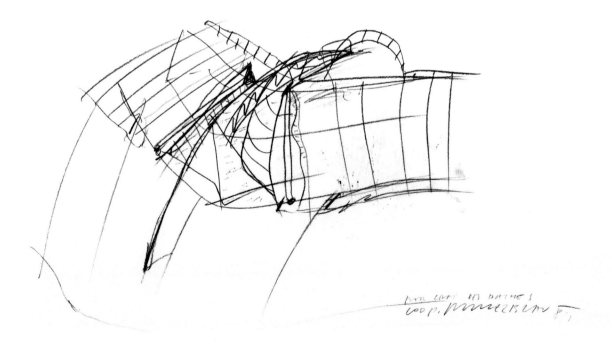

COOP HIMMELB(L)AU's concept of an 'open system' of
architectural design creates a framework for design
freedom with an emphasis on imagination and fluid
decisions rather than on the constraints of
preconceived, prescribed objectives.

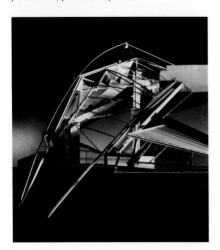

Founded in Vienna in 1968, COOP HIMMELB(L)AU came to international prominence
during the late 1970s and early 1980s through the practice's avant-garde design process
of drawing with their eyes shut and building models as interpretations of the early sketch
to express the generating forces of each project and capture their emotional input. As Prix
describes it: 'I could literally *feel* the building by using this technique. I used my hand as
the seismograph for detecting my feeling,[4] and from this drawing we made the model
and developed the project.[5] We wanted to change architecture immediately and we were
looking for the greatest and best way we could do that.'

He continues: 'We asked ourselves: "What's the most vulnerable point in the architectural
process?" So we pinpointed the moment of beginning a drawing as the start of designing
the building and realised that, if we wanted to create a new language in architecture, we
had to focus on this moment, because this is when the building is decided. This first
moment is both vulnerable and influential because the architect decides by the
subconscious. We believe that in order to liberate space we have to liberate the moment
of conceiving the space.'

Release from the limits of the conscious mind allowed the young architects to focus on
producing architecture where priority was placed on the ability to act spontaneously on
their intuition as a key step within their design process. 'Doing the sketch in a very explosive
and condensed moment enabled us to create a level of complexity which you never get if
you put one part next to the other,'[6] Prix confirms. 'It's kind of a black hole in the moment
of designing. We have to introduce another language into architecture in order to create a
new aesthetic that is much more advanced than the aesthetics of the time; it is an
intellectual point of view – understanding ahead of the time and seeing into the future.'

International recognition for the firm came largely through its inclusion in critical
exhibitions such as the 'Deconstructivist Architecture' show at New York's Museum of
Modern Art (MoMA) in 1988, as well as its long-term commitment to the influential
architectural avant-garde. Prix in particular realised the need to resist separating theory
from built work and invested much of his time in teaching, writing, working and lecturing
both in Europe and America.[7] The practice's built projects between 1980 and 1989[8] –
coupled with their original and innovative conceptual schemes – provided a wealth of
material for international design journals who embraced and celebrated their anti-
establishment values and further cemented their progressive reputation across the
western world.

Throughout the 1990s, COOP HIMMELB(L)AU began to build increasingly large-scale
projects such as the East Pavilion for the Groninger Museum in the Netherlands (1994)

three significant housing projects in Vienna,[9] and the internationally renowned UFA Cinema Centre in Dresden, Germany (1998). Finally, a string of competition wins in 2000 and 2001 firmly propelled the practice to 'star architect' status and provided the opportunity for the office to expand in order to build increasingly complex and cutting-edge architecture for corporate giants such as BMW and the European Central Bank.

Tracing the practice's evolution, it is clear that its success is partly due to what they refer to as their 'open system' approach to architectural design.[10] Prix suggests that this 'open' strategy creates a framework for design freedom with an emphasis on imagination rather than on the limitations of preconceived objectives, and facilitates the architect's artistic authority to create a space and take responsibility for a design. There is a strong affinity

ABOVE ROOFTOP REMODELLING FALKESTRASSE, VIENNA, AUSTRIA, 1983 AND 1987–8

Prix refers to the importance of the cultural context within his work: 'I was born in Vienna, the city of Freud and Schönberg, and their seminal work was very important to us in order to develop a new architectural language.'

LEFT UFA CINEMA CENTRE, DRESDEN, GERMANY, 1998

Addressing the idea of aesthetics and beauty within the architectural design process, Prix declares: 'I want to see what I imagined built and have the opportunity to step into my own brain, so to speak. This is my interpretation of "beauty" ... Intensity and authenticity – these are the issues of architecture.'

From the Guangzhou Opera House project (1983) to the practice's more recently completed BMW Welt (2007), COOP HIMMELB(L)AU's emphasis on roof structure has evolved to become the most distinctive visual feature of their architecture: 'A roof is an expression, a gesture, a symbol for things going on beneath,' explains Prix.

Prix expands on the emotional aspect of the subconscious mind with a reference to existentialism: 'There is something in space which touches your body from behind. It's not only what you see, but also what you feel as your body is walking through time.'

between COOP HIMMELB(L)AU's use of spontaneous sketches and the practice's later 'open system' strategy. Using the first sketch as a design generator captured an emotional impact,[11] inviting an artistic act and a new aesthetic while also freeing the spatial conditions from any constrains of circumstantial needs or causality. Through this, a new language of form emerged which though not dependent on the brief, nevertheless related to it: form no longer followed function. This new language subsequently enabled other spaces to emerge and developed into what became the spatial condition of the practice's projects: the Open System.

Another striking factor evident in the firm's early projects, such as the Open House (1983) and the more recently completed BMW Welt (2007), is the practice's preoccupation with the roof.[12] As Prix declares: 'A roof is an expression, a gesture, a symbol for things going on beneath.' As such, the roof has evolved over 40 years of collective work to become the most distinctive visual feature of COOP HIMMELB(L)AU's architecture.[13]

The practice also continues to strive to maintain the relationship between the desire for form and the necessity of function. 'We now use the term "synergy",' Prix explains. 'We don't say "form follows function" or "function follows form". We're designing synergy between both, so the function becomes a hybrid element of the form.' He expands: 'For example, in our recently completed BMW Welt project, the roof starts to differentiate the space.[14] It doesn't dictate it, but issues an invitation to do things under it. It is the most important element; when you step into the building – which is absolutely enormous[15] – it feels differentiated.'

Prix insists that this differentiation is determined almost entirely by the roof form which controls not only the activities within the space but also the vignettes, the light, the atmosphere and so on – a starkly opposing strategy to functional design where it is the plan that drives the process. He also acknowledges the increasing impact on this process of sophisticated computer software tools that influence and affect the resulting aesthetic. The BMW Welt project, for example, extended the practice's early approach of producing a 'first-hand sketch' by substituting computer-generated wind simulations as 'energy input'. The simulation models were then shaped and recorded under Prix's direction and interpretations produced in the form of physical models, allowing the further investigation of spatial and visual relationships.[16]

Refreshingly, COOP HIMMELB(L)AU continue to push their innovative and speculative principles in built form within the reality of an increasingly commercial environment where the role of the architect is constantly under debate and scrutiny. Prix wholeheartedly believes in the idea of the architect as visionary, and that every good architect should aspire to build extraordinary architecture. 'This is a must! The vision is to finish the Tower of Babel,' he exclaims. 'It is the duty of every architect. If they are not thinking about their vision, then they are a builder, not an architect.'

ABOVE AKRON ART MUSEUM, AKRON, OHIO, USA, 2007

The firm's 'self-confident forms' have evolved through the practice's long commitment to pursuing a spontaneous and artistic design process. Prix suggests that the practice of architecture moves beyond the basic notion of a profession, aligning itself with art and acting as a vital register of culture. He states his belief that architects are inevitably influenced by their cultural context.

Consequently, COOP HIMMELB(L)AU's buildings are dominated by a strong aesthetic that pursues engaging forms and spatial qualities to create a personal architectural language. Their built architecture is equally as challenging as their convention-defying drawings and models with a dynamic sense of composition that continues to be experimental, fresh and bold. Prix delights in describing the aesthetic of the most recently completed work as 'self-confident forms'[17] that have evolved through the practice's long commitment to pursuing a spontaneous and artistic design process. He continues: 'I want to see what I imagined built and have the opportunity to step into my own brain, so to speak. This is my interpretation of "beauty" – the aesthetic value may change very quickly, but the beauty is not one hundred per cent an aesthetic issue; it is in being authentic at the moment of making it. Intensity and authenticity – these are the issues of architecture.'

When pressed on the role of aesthetics within the formal language of his architecture, Prix declares: 'Architects are always denying the place of aesthetics in design and this is because of the notion of the "eye",' he proclaims. 'Those who don't have "an eye" are not concerned with forms, and when you look at the work of many contemporaries who propose to be architects you can see that there is actually no quality at all in the concept

BELOW AKRON ART MUSEUM, AKRON, OHIO, USA, 2007

Prix advocates that architects must engage with academic discourse to break down the division between theory and practice. He believes that architectural theory should move beyond an intellectual discussion into the domain of the practising architect.

itself. In fact, they are not looking for quality – they are talking about numbers, diagrams and statistics.'

Prix is refreshingly direct in his engagement with aesthetics, describing COOP HIMMELB(L)AU's work as 'about form and the changing value of beauty. For me, the three-dimensional language of architecture is form, and architecture will always be judged on its initial appearance.' He continues: 'Of course, if you know the concept, you have a better understanding of what's going on. But it's not necessary to explain everything in architecture. As the film director Roman Polanski said: "If I can tell you the movie, it is not necessary to make it" – and it's the same with architecture. At the moment it becomes three-dimensional; the power that is given to the shape and the form will speak for itself – it's in the subconscious.' In stark contrast to a purely computational preoccupation, Prix expands on the emotional aspect of the subconscious mind and with a reference to existentialism adds: 'There is something in space which touches your body from behind. It's not only what you see, but also what you feel as your body is walking through time – time and emotion are very important for experiencing space.'

A tireless promoter of the importance of a holistic investment in architectural culture, Prix is adamant that good architecture can only succeed when the architect remains in complete control through both the design *and* building process of a project. He is critical of the manner in which other professions such as project managers and engineers are usurping the architect's responsibilities. 'The power of architecture is fading and this is because architects are giving it away,' he complains. 'They easily accept and say to themselves: "I'm doing the function and the diagram but I don't care what it looks like." The result is that the architect is suppressed or is pushed to the background for nothing more than atmospheric renderings. I believe that if we continue and step over this point in the next couple of years, we will risk losing everything.'

However, Prix acknowledges that the power of architecture has limitations and is realistic in his aspirations, suggesting: 'Architecture alone can't effect changes in society's values, but it can encourage and support an appreciation of culture.' Using a simple example to illustrate his point, he says: 'If you give an untalented painter a beautiful studio he will not be able to paint better, but give a talented painter a studio without light and he will still be able to paint.' In the context of COOP HIMMELB(L)AU's own body of work, Prix states: 'Our architecture embodies dynamic shapes and forms and it's because this gives you multiple choice. This is something that we try to "give" to our clients in the process of working through our projects. Of course, it's always a fight to get through planning codes and rules, and maintain the relationship with a client, because this is an accepted

BELOW BMW WELT, MUNICH, GERMANY, 2007

The roof of the BMW World starts to differentiate the space, emphasising the synergies between the building's form and programme. As Prix describes: 'The roof doesn't dictate the space, but issues an invitation to do things under it. It is the most important element; when you step into the building – which is absolutely enormous – it feels differentiated.'

Prix believes that many architects are uncomfortable with discussing aesthetics because of the role of the 'eye' in the design process: 'Those who don't have "an eye" are not concerned with forms, and when you look at the work of many contemporaries who propose to be architects you can see that there is actually no quality at all in the concept itself. In fact, they are not looking for quality – they are talking about numbers, diagrams and statistics.'

and "normal" process of our society. Everyone wants to have control over everything, and people are afraid of our architecture because it can appear uncontrolled. Though this isn't true, it can be perceived that way.'

Prix advocates that architects must engage with architectural discourse to break down the division between architectural academia and practitioners working on built form. To this end, he believes it is only through the ability of architects to 'test' theory through built form that the success of a project can be judged. 'I think that talking about architecture theory is very important,' he says. 'The notion of the concept is vital but, in the end, the building itself is judged on whether it's good or not. A sketch has the power to be much more influential than a big building, but the experience of realising a three-dimensional thought by moving through a constructed space – that is the essential importance of architecture.'

He also firmly believes that the practice of architecture moves beyond the basic notion of a 'profession' to align itself with art; acting as a vital register of culture. As a result, the actions of the architect are deeply personal. 'I have a theory,' he begins, 'that the

The Austrian Baroque architects such as Rudolph Schindler, Frederick Kiesler and Hans Hollein celebrated space as an experience of the human mind and body. This is a concept that resonates within the work of COOP HIMMELB(L)AU, Domenig, Gehry and Moss, who were all interested in Baroque spatial qualities enhanced by further emotional engagement.

background of the architect determines the way he practices. Architecture is not coming from architecture alone, but is influenced by the cultural connection of where the architect is working and where he grew up.' He expands: 'For example, I was born in Vienna – the city of Freud and Schönberg – and their seminal work was very important to us in order to develop a new architectural language. This initial interest in Freud and the notion of subconscious routes personally connected me to Jacques Derrida,[18] who said that in every piece of poetry there is a line, a word, a paragraph which is written by the poet's subconscious and this subconscious rules the whole opus. It's a very private interpretation. The concept resonated with me particularly after the MoMA exhibition because it recalls the moment of designing, of perception and the attempt to erase all circumstantial pressure in order to liberate space. There is a moment of subconscious influence in every work.'[19]

Prix's interest in cultural context and its place within contemporary architecture is not limited to his own work. He maintains an outward vision and does not disguise or mediate his position on the state of European architecture or the work of his contemporaries: 'Architecture is, in my view, a very specific language of culture. For example, there is a big difference between a Jewish architect such as Peter Eisenman, a Calvinist architect like Rem Koolhaas and an Austrian Baroque architect such as Günther Domenig or ourselves who have a Catholic influence on the one hand but are not Jesuit like the Spanish architects.' He continues 'The Austrian Baroque architects are celebrating space as an experience of the human mind and body,[20] Calvinistic architects appreciate diagrams and are "space secretaries", while Jewish architects are ambivalent and less easy to categorise. Many of them reject imagery because of their long tradition of thinking and, therefore, creating intellectual space.[21] Yet on the other hand, other Jewish architects, such as Frank Gehry or Eric Owen Moss, are very emotional and engage with aesthetics and form over programmatic constraints. I think it's interesting to note that Freud invented psychoanalysis in Vienna; that comes out of a historical cultural connection and certainly there is a lot of Jewish influence in our culture, so I feel that ultimately, and because of this tradition, our work is much more related to that of Moss and Gehry.'

Arguably, a commitment to communicating cultural context, subconscious experience and a celebration of emotion and beauty within architectural practice is a challenging agenda to pursue. The constraints that define contemporary architectural language are often overwhelmingly influenced by the complexities of programme, building regulations, construction systems and servicing, yet Prix is not daunted by these realities, believing that the emotive qualities of space will always overcome: 'There is a statement from our collective work at COOP HIMMELB(L)AU that expresses my position clearly: "The feeling of the inside makes the form of the outside."' He continues, declaring: 'It has absolutely nothing to do with content as a response to functional requirements. The content is more than function. The content is the emotion of the space. If you step into a church or a monastery, it's important that you receive an immediate impact; it's not a direct experience like in music, but you get the feeling that comes with the fact that you know you are in an extremely important space.[22] You are tense and relaxed at the same time, which I believe is a very important quality of good architecture. In German, we say "*Schein und Sein*",[23] which means ugliness is the next step in the pursuit of beauty.'

Interviews

Lido Hotel, Venice Architecture Biennale, Venice, 9 September 2004

COOP HIMMELB(L)AU's office, Vienna, 6 June 2007

Notes

1. Prix was responsible for the practice's early sketches and Helmut Swiczinsky for the early interpretational models.

2. 'COOP HIMMELB(L)AU is not a colour but an idea, of creating architecture with fantasy, as buoyant and variable as clouds.' Wolf D Prix, in Martina Kandeler-Fritsch and Thomas Kramer (eds), *Get Off of My Cloud: Wolf D Prix and Coop Himmelb(l)au, Texts, 1968–2005*, Hatje Cantz, Berlin, 2005, p 24. As evidenced by the above quote, Prix and Swiczinsky have described their architecture as one created 'with fantasy' since 1968. It is architecture approached as art, encompassing visually wild dreams and streams of innovative ideas captured by a new aesthetic.

3. Prix recalls that COOP HIMMELB(L)AU battled for years to gain their clients' trust to build larger-scale and more ambitious projects that would introduce a new intense and authentic aesthetic, and not to conform to convention. As he explains: 'There were times when we experienced a chain of arguments such as: "OK, this is your design, this is your project. It cannot be built." Then we'd say: "OK, we can prove it can be built." Then, "OK, it can be built, but it's too expensive." Then we would prove that it wasn't expensive and was within the budget. But then the client's argument would suddenly change direction to be: "But I don't like it." So for us this meant, and it continues to mean, that by pushing the envelope and inventing a new aesthetic, it becomes a political issue because at first sight it will mostly be rejected. So innovation is always on the edge of being highly appreciated or rejected.' Wolf D Prix, interview with Yael Reisner, June 2007.

4. 'Our architecture has no physical ground plan, but a psychic one.' Wolf D Prix, in *Get Off of My Cloud*, op cit, p 25.

5. COOP HIMMELB(L)AU was influenced by the Viennese art scene at the time, which was concerned with emotional painting, and especially works by Austrian painter Arnulf Rainer.

6. Prix explains that the design process focused on 'complex, spatially entangled volumes, transitions, situations, and their possible transformation. As if one could see the building with X-ray eyes, we begin to draw our views and sections on top of one another.' Wolf D Prix, in *Get Off of My Cloud*, op cit, p 47.

7. 'There is the expression that I've heard used in the past that "there's building architecture and there's theoretical architecture". However, I believe that this sentiment is the death of architecture. It's actually cutting off the head from the body; it is the guillotine of architecture.' Wolf D Prix, interview with Yael Reisner, June 2007.

8. Examples include the small yet iconic Red Angel Bar in Vienna (1981), the Merz School, Stuttgart (1981), the Architecture is Now installation, Stuttgart (1982), the Open House project in Malibu (1983 and 1988–9), the infamous Rooftop Remodelling Falkestrasse in Vienna (1983 and 1987–8), the competition-winning scheme for the Ronacher Theatre, Vienna (1987) and the Funder Factory 3 in St Veit/Glan, Austria (1989).

9. COOP HIMMELB(L)AU built three significant large-scale residential projects in Vienna during the 1990s, including two SEG apartment buildings: the SEG Apartment Tower (1998) and the Block Remise (2000); and the challenging Gasometer B (also completed in 2000).

10. '"Open System" is a term for complex, spatially entangled volumes, transitions, situations, and their possible transformation. In the design description for the Merz School (1981) we used the concept "Open System" for the first time.' Wolf D Prix, in *Get Off of My Cloud*, op cit, p 47. A year later the open system was further defined as the following: 'It would be ideal to build architecture without objectives and then release it for free use. There are no longer any enclosed spaces in these interlacing, opening buildings: only vaguely designated areas. Divided and developed, however, the occupants choose. The differentiated spatial situations are no longer – at most, they present the challenge of taking possession of the space.' Ibid, p 49 .

11. 'The drawing is important to us. It is, actually, often forced to replace the building. But we never make a drawing for its own sake. It is much more a "building" of ideas on paper. The first, emotional confrontation with the psychic spaces of the project.' Ibid, p 48.

12. COOP HIMMELB(L)AU's first flying roof was a hovering helium balloon (House with a Flying Roof, London, 1973). The preoccupation with roof structures can be also seen in the Merz School (1981), the Open House, (1983) and the Rooftop Remodelling project (1984), and continues through the firm's projects to the present day.

13. COOP HIMMELB(L)AU were primarily influenced by Le Corbusier and Romanian sculptor Constantin Brâncuşi. Prix suggests that Le Corbusier's 'flying roof' concept coupled with Brâncuşi's 'open system' approach to design provided the most influential seeds for the practice's architectural thinking. Le Corbusier's floating roof, as seen in projects such as La Chapelle de Ronchamp (1954), appears as if detached from the walls it sits on and not to follow the pattern of the ground-floor plan, and proved a seminal influence. The ability to capture an emotional impact within a three-dimensional architectural form was also a quality they observed in Le Corbusier's work, most resonantly in La Tourette monastery in Eveux-sur-Arbresle, near Lyons. As Prix recalls: 'It was my first experience of Le Corbusier. He had the talent to shape space and create an atmosphere which you cannot find in Mies van der Rohe's work.' Wolf D Prix, interview with Yael Reisner, June 2007.

14. Prix enjoys referencing Le Corbusier, using the analogy of the Corbusian roof terrace when describing the BMW Welt roof. He says: 'When I saw the L'Unité d'habitation in Marseille (1952), I realised it was basically an inverse and converse roof landscape, and the BMW roof is just the reverse. Corbusier did it this way [Prix gestures with an inverted hand], and we did it this way.' Wolf D Prix, interview with Yael Reisner, 6 June 2007.

15. It is approximately the same size as the Piazza San Marco in Venice.

16. COOP HIMMELB(L)AU often quote a line from Herman Melville's Moby Dick: 'Would now the wind but had a body.' See Wolf D Prix, in *Get Off of My Cloud*, op cit, p 280. More recently, Prix has extended the metaphor to the dynamic power of a tornado in space. Wolf D Prix, interview with Yael Reisner, 6 June 2007.

17. This is also a term COOP HIMMELB(L)AU used in one of its statements on the idea of the 'open system' in 1982: 'We can't prove it, but we strongly surmise that self-confident forms, made available to use and shape freely – not repressively administered, but run in a friendly way – must have consequences for an occupant's development of a creative self-concept.' Ibid, p 49.

18. From a conversation between Wolf D Prix and Jacques Derrida.

19. At the time of the 'Deconstructivist Architecture' MoMA exhibition (1988), only Peter Eisenman and Bernard Tschumi acknowledged the connection of their work to the theoretical position of Derrida, and only Zaha Hadid to that of Constructivism – in contrast to the more collective interpretation by curator Mark Wigley. However, as witnessed below, Prix eventually embraced the interpretation of his work as connected to Derrida's writings.

Prix has described feeling honoured and flattered when asked to take part in the MoMA 'Deconstructivist Architecture' exhibition in 1988 in New York. The curator, Mark Wigley, chose the work of seven architects to exhibit: Frank Gehry, Coop Himmelb(l)au, Zaha Hadid, Rem Koolhaas, Daniel Libeskind, Bernard Tschumi, and Peter Eisenman. At the time, Coop Himmelb(l)au had no objection to their architecture being identified with the Deconstructivist movement or with the theories of Jacques Derrida. Nevertheless, Prix didn't agree with the theoretical angle of Mark Wigley's collective curatorial strategy or with what he describes as 'the intellectual way Eisenman or Tschumi tried to interpret it.' Instead, Prix felt Coop Himmelb(l)au's work shared more in common with the work of Frank Gehry and Zaha Hadid. Interview with Yael Reisner, 9 September 2004.

20. 'Within the work of the Viennese and Austrian architects in general ... there's a big interest in creating space sequences and also a Surrealist approach to their architecture. So I discovered that the religious background of the Austrian Baroque approach to life is transplanted in our hearts. For example, let's look at it this way: from Fischer von Erlach, I can trace a connection to the work of Schindler, then Kiesler, Hollein, Abraham, Pichler, Domenig and, finally, to our own work. All are concerned with forms, shapes, space and sequences and so, from my point of view, architecture is a very specific language of culture.' Wolf D Prix, interview with Yael Reisner, September 2004.

21. Prix is referring to Jewish architects Peter Eisenman and Daniel Libeskind. He adds his interpretation that 'Daniel Libeskind plays with words and creates shapes that would crumble without words.'

22. Prix is referring here to his experience when visiting Le Corbusier's La Tourette monastery.

23. 'Schein und Sein' is a German saying used to express the appearance of an object/situation when, at first glance, it is different from the actual physical reality.

Thom Mayne

EXQUISITE COMPLEXITY

ARCHITECT THOM MAYNE IS AN INHERENTLY INTENSE PERSON. Although exceptionally tall and commanding, his intensity is not borne from his physical presence, but through the complexity of his conversation. He is surprisingly candid for an internationally respected architect, continually exchanging ideas, questioning, assessing and then reassessing his concepts rather than attempting to smooth his opinions into a marketable 'position'. Although not arrogant, Mayne is certainly not humble and strives to be as transparent as possible about his ideologies while exposing the uncertainties and tensions that underpin his work. His relentless process of inquisition is actively pursued through his public lectures and teaching activities that are legendary among his architectural colleagues. As Lebbeus Woods once remarked: 'A major feature of Mayne's creative trajectory is his scepticism, his incessant questioning of everything, including himself. Anyone who has heard him speak in public knows that he is filled with doubts and uncertainties ... candid, questioning lectures.'[1]

Mayne founded Morphosis[2] with Jim Stafford in Los Angeles in 1972. Shortly afterwards, Michael Rotondi joined the firm and following Stafford's departure in 1974, the pair produced a collection of incredibly complex small projects in the local area, notably the 2-4-6-8 House (1979), the 72 Market Street restaurant (1983) and the Venice III House (1986). In the mid-1980s the practice received international acclaim through the wide publication of their beautifully crafted drawings and exceptional sectional models. Larger projects followed, with schemes such as the Cedars-Sinai Comprehensive Outpatient Cancer Centre (1990) and the enigmatic Kate Mantilini restaurant (1986), both in Los Angeles, continually receiving the attention of the international press. Yet despite their early success, the realities of the economic downturn later in the decade hit LA hard and the practice stagnated. Rotondi decided to leave to pursue other interests in 1991. However Mayne retained the Morphosis moniker, and continued to evolve his practice and focus on his role as a founding director and board member at the renowned Southern California Institute of Architecture (SCI-Arc).

OPPOSITE 72 MARKET STREET RESTAURANT, LOS ANGELES, CALIFORNIA, USA, 1983

Sectional studies and vertical articulations have formed a cornerstone of Morphosis's architectural language for nearly 30 years, while the plan tends to be treated in a conventional manner. In their recent large-scale projects a new kind of verticality appears in which complex programmes are used to create an increased drama and greater contrast.

LEFT KATE MANTILINI RESTAURANT, LOS ANGELES, CALIFORNIA, USA, 1986

Many of Morphosis's projects create a site for connectivity and memory. As a result, the architecture is composed of elements that are both conventional and innovative. As Mayne explains: 'The conventional parts in a project also connect to an economic strategy. We couldn't build it all of unique parts as it would be more expensive. So it's always the two things: the connective tissue of a project and an economic strategy that allows you to decide where to put your muscle and resources.'

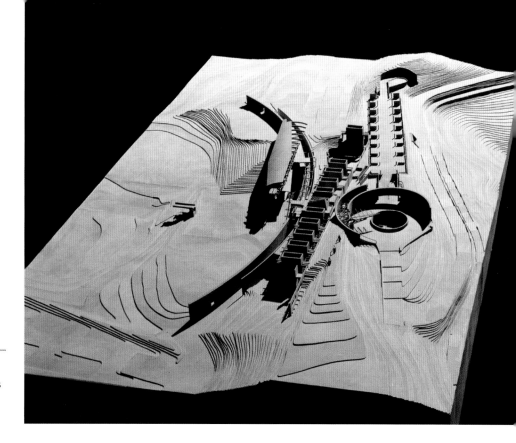

RIGHT LOS ANGELES ARTSPARK PERFORMING ARTS
PAVILION, LOS ANGELES, CALIFORNIA, USA, 1989

For Mayne, one of the key advantages of engaging
with the computer was the release from the
objectification of physical drawings and models: 'I was
building so little, it became apparent that the models
and drawings themselves were the output of my
architecture.'

The advent of the new millennium, however, provided great opportunity for Morphosis
with the completion of a number of significant projects including an elementary school
in Long Beach, California, a high school in Pomona, California, the University of Toronto
graduate student housing project and two elegant and dramatic restaurants in Las
Vegas.[3] From 1999 to 2001, the practice also won a series of prestigious competitions
that propelled the firm into a new phase of large projects with greater layers of
complexity. Far from struggling with the rapid transition, Mayne embraced the
opportunity to build at a greater scale – an attitude that has resulted in a successful and
diverse range of projects that reflect his intense approach to architecture and to life.[4]
In recognition of his outstanding contribution to architecture and education, Mayne
received the Pritzker Prize in March 2005. He continues to work from his office in Santa
Monica and recently expanded the practice's operations to New York. He has remained
committed to education, and currently holds a tenured professorship at the School of
the Arts and Architecture at the University of California, Los Angeles (UCLA).

Thom Mayne's intense, complex architecture is reflected in his adept ability to carry
several conversations simultaneously; pursuing a trajectory of thought and arriving at a
point with insight and clarity only to quickly question his position and shift to a parallel
discussion. His conversation is at once explorative, conflicting and contradictory, all values

that co-exist within the complexity of his architectural process. He is quick to acknowledge the disparate nature of his conversation, explaining: 'I do have this odd kind of wiring that dissects the world in a certain way, although I think that's because I'm also a bit dyslexic. It's always been a joke between my wife and my friends that when I see films or read a book I internalise them completely. When I'm dealing with a particular set of architectural problems, everything around me becomes a resource for that and becomes a component of the strategy to decode the problem and ultimately find a solution. Everything I'm looking at now is working on resolving a particular problem.'

Uncomfortable with being asked to explain the generative process behind his work, Mayne suggests that 'talking about your work is secondary really; it's a precision that does not take place in your visual world'. As a result, he is not interested in the pursuit of a traditional academic rigour, but aspires to 'probe in a speculative manner' – a characteristic that is reflected in his value system: 'Architecture is, in that sense, a metaphor for life.' He argues that it is difficult to identify the specificity of the conditions that provide the influence for or inform the complexity of his architecture: 'You start this process and it's immensely organic and extremely nuanced to every condition that forms the idea.'

ABOVE DIAMOND RANCH HIGH SCHOOL, POMONA, CALIFORNIA, USA, 2000

The Diamond Ranch High School project portrays a shift from typological to morphological issues. As Mayne explains: 'The design process starts with a discourse defining what the values of the project are – that's the source engine. So, for example, a school does not start with architecture, it starts with a discussion of how architecture contributes to educating children and so on.'

BELOW CHIBA GOLF CLUB, CHIBA PREFECTURE, JAPAN, 1991

Morphosis's iconic models were imitated by many worldwide. According to Mayne: 'The initial physical models were never interested in the materiality of the constructed building ... they were a form of painting.'

RIGHT TSUNAMI ASIAN GRILL, LAS VEGAS, NEVADA, USA, 1999

Mayne explains that extracting a fragment from one project may supply the germination for a new whole in the form of a subsequent project. His methodological strategy links large and small projects and informs complexity on a larger scale.

Certainly Mayne has spent many years articulating and refining his position. The work produced by Morphosis in collaboration with his partner in the early days, Michael Rotondi, was celebrated internationally, yet the architects still struggled to make a living. As a result Mayne has no issues with the notion of the architect as artist: 'I totally accept architects as artists. I'm an architect who survived for 15 years by selling my drawings before having the opportunity to build. That's literally how I had to finance myself. The drawings were different forms of my work from the buildings. I'm comfortable with the boundary between architecture and art – or lack thereof. In both disciplines you are dealing with essentially more or less the same issues.'[5]

Mayne's opportunity to build changed with the turn of the century when Morphosis won a number of large-scale and high-profile commissions including the United States Courthouse in Eugene, Oregon (2006); the San Francisco Federal Office Building (2006); the NOAA Satellite Operation Control Facility in Suitland, Maryland (2005); and the Caltrans District 7 Headquarters in Los Angeles (2004). The dramatic change in scale within such a concentrated time frame brought with it some concerns, particularly from his architectural colleagues. He recalls: 'Within a period of two years, I suddenly had more work in my office than I had experienced in my whole career. I remember Lebbeus Woods asking me a series of questions because he was worried that my work would lose its intensity when it increased in scale.' Mayne accepts Woods's concern, explaining: 'I do see that the element of intensity is a key aspect of my work. The difficulty with practising today is that you don't get any serious commissions until you are 55 or 60 and then, all of a sudden, you are offered a huge amount of work and somehow you have to prepare yourself to withstand these new pressures and the radically increased amount of time required for your creative energy.' He continues: 'That concentration in energy absolutely plays a major contributing role within my work and if it starts dissipating, it's part of the process of my obsolescence or, conversely, the beginning of a more vibrant career, so it is really critical. I'm thinking about these issues now in terms of where I'm going and what I'm doing. How do you translate that intensity into your creative world so that you evolve as an architect?'[6]

In the spirit of this evolution, Mayne embraces the opportunity of computational processes, suggesting that Morphosis's beautifully layered drawings and models were part of a different era for the practice: 'I was always aware of the isolation and autonomy of the drawings and models and, because I was building so little, it became apparent that the models and drawings themselves were the output of my architecture. The initial physical models were never interested in the materiality of the constructed building: they had their own world; they were a form of painting.' He continues: 'I have always been focused on the organisational matrix of buildings so it was very clear early on that the

ABOVE 'SILENT COLLISIONS' EXHIBITION, NETHERLANDS ARCHITECTURE INSTITUTE (NAI), ROTTERDAM, THE NETHERLANDS, 1999

The idea for the Morphosis exhibition at the NAI was to make a space that was dynamic and moved at a rate that was outside of perception, transforming the existing interior of the NAI from horizontal to vertical, closed to open, connecting movement and layering time.

computer is the obvious tool to facilitate our work. I accepted that completely, and so it was just about transition. So in 1996, when we started working with computers, we made a very conscious decision to change the way that we were working with physical models.'

For Mayne, one of the key advantages in an engagement with the computer was the release from the objectification of physical drawings and models: 'We thought we would look to more advanced tools that could take us some place that was really about the architecture and where the models don't have an aesthetic sense. Now, instead of an aesthetic object, there is just "stuff", so in a way it's like looking at a chemist's lab or something. You're just going through the process, but the focus now is the end result that leads to architecture.'

BELOW CALTRANS DISTRICT 7 HEADQUARTERS, LOS ANGELES, CALIFORNIA, USA, 2004

The Caltrans project has become a significant landmark in downtown Los Angeles. It brilliantly portrays the expansiveness of Angelino culture, but in doing so it demonstrates the key characteristics of Morphosis's architecture: highly intense, energetic and exquisitely beautiful.

While Mayne is an advocate for the computer, he maintains an open process that allows for personal involvement and intuition, a preoccupation revealed by his admiration for the work of the late Spanish architect Enric Miralles: 'I have always thought of my work as somewhere between that of Peter Eisenman and Miralles.[7] I'm involved in something closer to the behaviour of genetics so I set up abstract organisations like Eisenman, but they are not static. They are open and allow personal involvement as they develop. I can have a position, but my team knows that we can have a discussion on differences in interpretation. The system simply allows me to deal with complicated problems and gives me some sense of coherency.'

Mayne acknowledges the presence of certain consistencies in his work, but refutes the suggestion that they hold any notion of signature form. Conversely, he believes that consistencies are the result of an engagement with personal preoccupations: 'If I think about consistencies in my work, I am interested in a certain type of conflict and that may show up in dark and light, large and small, opaque and clear, etc. I am interested in complex relationships. So the focus is always on the inventions, the potentialities and new possibilities as elements interact, and I have been involved with this preoccupation literally from the beginning of my career.' He expands: 'So if there is consistency in the work then it has to do with an attitude or with first principle ideas that are not yet located in form. Form exists because I am bringing the unique, the contingent, the specific and the idiosyncratic to each project, but the consistency lies in the nature of the dialogue.'

Mayne believes that consistencies are the result of an engagement with personal preoccupations: 'If I think about consistencies in my work, I am interested in a certain type of conflict and that may show up in dark and light, large and small, opaque and clear, etc. I am interested in the complex relationships.'

The elegant monumentality of the building is complemented with exquisitely resolved, open volumes that respond to human scale. Angular, folding elements peel away from the big block defining the entry and provide protective cover for pedestrians on approach. These elements of the architecture converge to create public space without compromising the formal strength of the building.

ABOVE FEDERAL OFFICE BUILDING, SAN FRANCISCO, CALIFORNIA, USA, 2006

The creation of a resonant 'value system' is a vital element of Mayne's process of creating layers with distinctive characteristics – a form of DNA that creates a complex, connectivity between references. He explains: 'For anybody who is interested in creativity – and certainly for architects – it's not an academic or more formalised idea of critique that is important; it is your own ability to extract something that's useful to you and that somehow unlocks, encodes, expands or opens up potentials through an analogy, association or conflict.'

The creation of a resonant 'value system' is a vital element of Mayne's process of creating layers with distinctive characteristics – a form of DNA that creates a complex, connectivity between references: 'For anybody who is interested in creativity – and certainly for architects – it's not an academic or more formalised idea of critique that is important; it is your own ability to extract something that's useful to you and that somehow unlocks, encodes, expands or opens up potentials through an analogy, association or conflict.' He explains: 'As you get older I think the associations – or connective tissue – become much more complicated and less literal so you don't have to be able to identify those relationships in an academic, overt or discursive way. What's important is that they are useful in propelling your own creative energy.'

Mayne's rigorous design process screens out what he views as impurities or contaminating elements: 'When I start working on something and concentrate on the specifics as distinct from any other project, I become focused on this world that surrounds and is connected with the project: site, programme, etc. I shut off everything else. As far

as I know, I am not consciously aware of anything extraneous to the project. Information that creeps in is unconscious and I'm trying to escape, so in times of intense design activity I stop reading and I don't look at anything. I am completely disinterested because external information moves me away from my task and it worries me; it represents contamination. I exclusively and completely focus on what it is. I work on it as material; it's completely real to me, and it's physical.'[8]

Effectively working on two levels, Mayne's process shifts constantly, reassessing and recontextualising as the proposition develops from concept into architecture: 'I am using and relying on a consistency of a methodology or a system to literally keep me from getting lost, because on a complex project you can lose yourself. And two things are happening: there is a sense of order outside of myself and that today would be described as "immersion behaviour". This is outside of my control and remains coherent because the pieces act predictably in a way that parallels natural systems.' He continues: 'On the other hand, the architecture is much more purposeful and has very specific requirements, so I have to negotiate and make discretionary decisions in the system that will give me a basketball court, or a soccer field, or a theatre, or whatever. Personally, it's this continual shift between these two worlds that interests me.'[9]

Sectional studies and vertical articulations have formed a cornerstone of Morphosis's architectural language for nearly 30 years, while a plan is often treated in a conventional manner. 'I was fascinated with the section, and not the plan, as the primary drawing,' Mayne states. 'My preoccupations seemed to preference section over plan, and that led me some place without me even knowing it.' Certainly the dominance of section has traditionally determined the spatial dynamic of Morphosis's projects, and the developmental lineage of this aspect can be traced back to their early buildings such as the Kate Mantilini restaurant in Los Angeles where elaborate mechanisms and devices became part of the architecture, exploring the vertical space.[10] In their large-scale projects, a new kind of verticality appears which uses a complex programme and increased scale to create an even greater contrast and increased drama in the volume, and develops the formal language of the vertical as seen in recent projects such as the San Francisco Federal Office Building and the New Academic Building for the Cooper Union for the Advancement of Science and Art in New York City (2009).[11]

The architectural sensitivity and dexterity evidenced through Morphosis's ability to integrate its avant-garde insertions with conventional built form marks Mayne's point of difference to his European counterparts while echoing the preoccupations of his fellow Californian architects, Eric Owen Moss and Frank Gehry. Mayne views this approach as essentially humanistic, allowing contingencies between the old and the new: 'You can locate history within my work and it seems to be one of the values that separates me from my peers. There is always a vestige of convention and of tradition within the work. There is always a seed of the beginning of a typological structure and it completely separates me from Wolf Prix, Peter Cook, Bernard Tschumi or Daniel Libeskind. The idea is to leave some vestige of DNA matter where I can ground a project mentally and psychologically.'[12]

Expanding, Mayne suggests: 'It seems that architecture requires more connectivity than most of the arts. When a project removes the position of entry for the human being they have no way of accessing the work because there is nothing left that represents any type of connection. We operate from memory, and so if we completely radicalise the process and leave nothing of the "found" history then it is an attack on memory. That's a very brutal attack and an approach that I am clearly not totally comfortable with. So in most of my work I leave pieces that people can enter and all kinds of elements that are absolutely conventional.'[13]

BELOW PHARE TOWER, PARIS, FRANCE, DUE FOR COMPLETION 2012

As Mayne states: 'The uniqueness of architecture allows it to operate in so many modes, including the pragmatic, which is also one of the richest and most complicated precisely because it has to contain so much content. Architecture is so incredibly rich and broad that it needs to absorb intensity ... The first order is the conceptually structured content, but one can also read multiple levels of content at a pragmatic, social, cultural, historical and urbanistic level.'

The strategy also reflects Mayne's ideology and commentary on the situation in Los Angeles: 'From the very beginning we were building our own context within projects, from the Venice III House (1986) onwards. We established our own context so that we operated on the ground through the landscaping and the new built form and tried to find a broader urban connective tissue. A sense of "broader connectivity" doesn't exist in LA; there's no physical public space because it simply doesn't exist as an aspiration. So the fact that there's no desire for public space in the city also makes it interesting in a way.' Continuing, Mayne explains: 'With this lack of broader connectivity comes also a lack of history, and building is seen as an augmented landscape. But these kinds of conflicts and contrasts have been absolutely consistent throughout my life. For example, in the Diamond Ranch High School (2000), we were leaving, or creating, little fragments of history that were also rhythmic events that connected with a more traditional architectural sensibility. The conventional parts in a project also connect to an economic strategy. We couldn't build it all of unique parts as it would be more expensive. So it's always the two things: the connective tissue of a project and an economic strategy that allows you to decide where to put your muscle and resources.

ABOVE PHARE TOWER, PARIS, FRANCE, DUE FOR COMPLETION 2012

Mayne describes how a new visual idea can be evoked by memories: 'I wanted to end the tower in a certain way with the frame disappearing into the sky. At the same time we were looking at a more functional idea of a series of turbines that were going to serve the building ... Suddenly, an image of Moholy-Nagy's Light Modulator (1937) came into my head ... it started to establish the terms by which I would develop this part of the project.'

Mayne is uncomfortable with any attribution of a distinct language within his work, stating: 'I don't worry about the intuitive process; it's the part that I am the most comfortable with. I can draw the line without a lot of discussion; it appears and is a part of me. I don't have to work on that, it just takes place.' Elaborating, he suggests: 'There is leadership within the collective body of my work that is represented by documentation or the ability to articulate particular values and represent some sort of consistency – not a fixed term, but simply a trajectory of values over a long period of time.' He is also quick to refute any suggestion of singular authorship and to point out the collaborative nature of his studio: 'I am not the singular character, the work is not about me finally,' he says. 'In fact, it's quite the opposite. The work is about others.[14] I am the thought leader; I am the one that organises the process. It absolutely has traces of me as I navigate through these processes, but it's produced through a much more complex fabric of circumstances, personalities and characters and conditions.'[15]

BELOW PHARE TOWER, PARIS, FRANCE, DUE FOR COMPLETION 2012

Mayne recalls: 'My study model became the same scale as Moholy-Nagy's original light tower – I think this is what intuition is – synaptic connections. It's like it takes place in dreams that have their own logic and reconnect various realities in your life.'

Mayne maintains that he does not see it as his role as an architect to be interested in beauty: 'I am somewhat ambiguous about the look of something. I really never spend time on what something looks like or what it connects to. In fact, if anything I am quite antagonistic to fixing meanings to things.' Yet when reminded of a personal anecdote where he recalls a car conversation with one of his young sons regarding the attractiveness of an unusually white splatter of mud on a neighbouring car's wheel,[16] he acknowledges: 'So much of our work is derived from this type of spontaneous, non-linear, seemingly non-sequential musing.'[17] Despite the evocative memory, Mayne declares: 'I'm suspicious of the "eye" and over-investing in personality and character. I'm not interested in the philosophical question of beauty. It is the word itself that I find difficult.'

Clearly Mayne is more comfortable with a more oblique interpretation of beauty where, much like his complex architecture, the notion is open for investigation and reinterpretation: 'When I was a young architect, one of the most influential people on my perception of aesthetics within the design process was James Stirling. He was an odd kind of an architect, but I thought of him as a hero and I particularly related to his early work.' He recalls: 'It was later in life when I met him that I realised that one of the reasons I had appreciated the work was that it was not fussy – in fact, it was clumsy.' Continuing, Mayne explains: 'I hadn't really understood this distinction when I was younger, and now I always use this as an example for my students. Stirling's work does not just come from the eye – it's more complicated – and the inherent clumsiness is actually an important part of the essence of the work.'

After a long and reflective investigation, Mayne concludes: 'What I consider to be beautiful would be a sense of "compelling-ness"; what is it that compels you about a

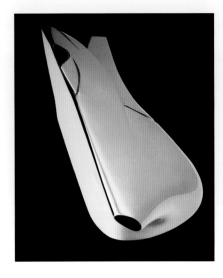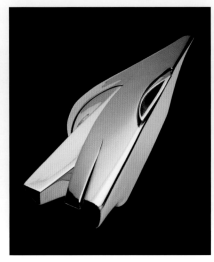

particular type of work and where does it take you? It's about a very particular type of intelligence that takes you some place and allows you to see the world and experience it in an alternative way. Beauty is a by-product of an idea that is under continual evolution.'

Interviews
Centre Pompidou, Paris, 6 March 2006
Morphosis's office, Santa Monica, California, 14 December 2006
Morphosis's office, Santa Monica, California, 15 December 2006

Notes

1. Comment as recalled by author.

2. The name Morphosis is derived from the Greek term meaning to be in constant formation or in a state of continual evolution – the constant sequence or manner of development or change in an organism or any of its parts.

3. The Tsunami Asian Grill and Lutece Restaurant, Las Vegas, Nevada, 1999. The same year Morphosis also produced the powerful retrospective exhibition 'Silent Collisions' at the Netherlands Architecture Institute (NAI) in Rotterdam which included a major installation piece defining a new spatial condition – a moving structural angular form that marked an evolution of the practice's work rather than a reflective position.

4. Many of Mayne's colleagues, as well as the architectural press, have also suggested that the intensity of his work has more power within larger-scale projects.

5. 'If you look at the major period of the 20th century, architects such as Alvar Aalto and Le Corbusier painted objects of all types so clearly there are parallels with the universal characteristics of an artist. In the late 1960s, 1970s and 1980s where all art was becoming more hybridised and the boundaries were totally breaking down, there were artists and architects working across art and architecture practice such as Michael Heizer and Robert Smithson.' Thom Mayne, interview with Yael Reisner, 14 December 2006.

6. Mayne explains: 'That intensity represents a sort of Gestalt which, in turn, brings an enormously focused energy to a singular problem – "singular" meaning that you focus those multiplicities into something that is coherent and able to absorb huge amounts of contingent information. That level of concentration can take a long period of time; possibly two, three or four years on a project.

When you are working on something so intensely you can't sleep, and at night when you dream, at some point you can't distinguish between your dream and real life because you are completely focused and captivated in certain aspects of this problem. Some architects are just not interested or capable of doing that in their practice.' Thom Mayne, interview with Yael Reisner, 14 December 2006.

7. As Mayne recalls: 'I was a huge fan of Enric Miralles and I remember talking with him years ago before he died. I admired him because what I recognised was his sense of relaxation and ease. I think you have to learn how to be at ease sometimes. I had to unlearn my past and my upbringing because my mother was a Christian intellectual and I just said what I read and not what I thought. The consideration of culture within her value system didn't include any of the territory that comes with pleasure, aesthetic or a broader kind of human interest.' Thom Mayne, interview with Yael Reisner, 14 December 2006.

8. 'The relationship of content is directly connected to the relationship with intensity and complexity; the first order is the conceptually structured content, but one can also read multiple levels of content at a pragmatic, social, cultural, historical and urbanistic level, and finally the work is always loaded and layered with multiple readings. The uniqueness of architecture allows it to operate in so many modes, including the pragmatic, which is also one of the richest and most complicated precisely because it has to contain so much content. Architecture is so incredibly rich and broad that it needs to absorb intensity – or to handle a large amount of content within a single frame.' Thom Mayne, interview with Yael Reisner, 15 December 2006.

9. Peter Eisenman references a scientific metaphor when suggesting to Mayne that his design process is parallel to that of 'interference', as in physics, a process where waves are superimposed in such a way that they produce higher peaks, lower troughs or a new wave pattern. The analogy refers to Mayne's methodology of working simultaneously with many design processes that feed from or cancel each other out, eventually resulting in a new idea.

10. Another example can be seen in the Tsunami Asian Grill restaurant where the vertical object becomes a 'frozen moment' that emphasises a vertical shaft directing the way in.

11. Mayne makes references to the British architect James Stirling who, along with his then partner in practice, James Gowan, and the British Architectural Association (established during the late 1950s and early 1960s), believed that a good building should have an interesting and original section. One can thus trace the investigation and development of the use of vertical shafts, cuts and voids in Morphosis's collective body of work.

12. Gehry, Moss and Mayne all use the strategy of including a trace or conventional part of a building within their experimental work – a characteristic they share yet have developed individually for different reasons.

13. Mayne comments: 'If you look at Frank Gehry's own house in Santa Monica, it has an amazing atmosphere – my grandmother would have been comfortable in his house, which I think is fascinating.' Thom Mayne, interview with Yael Reisner, 15 December 2006.

14. 'So if I choose Andrew instead of Chandler, and if I have two young people building the model, I could never recreate what would have taken place if I had chosen Chandler instead of Andrew with another team, or if I was not working in parallel .' Thom Mayne, interview with Yael Reisner, 15 December 2006.

15. Mayne reacts warmly to a reference to contemporary cinema as a metaphor for the architectural process, suggesting: 'A Postmodern film-maker like Robert Altman gives the actors the most minimal kind of directions and just lets it happen; it's a way of continually revitalising his work because he is allowing for contingencies and using matter that has the potential for certain types of synthesis and combustion. I'm not quite as free as Altman, but I like his sense of spontaneous combustion and I find it offers a way to continually revitalise architecture.' Thom Mayne, interview with Yael Reisner, 14 December 2006.

16. Mayne describes the anecdote of the car journey with his son in Thom Mayne, *Morphosis: Buildings and Projects, 1993–1997*, Rizzoli, New York, 1999, Appendix 1.5.

17. Mayne recalls an influential 'contingent' idea during the design process of the competition-winning scheme for the Phare Tower in Paris (due for completion 2012). It is a clear example of how contingent, associative and referential notions can become those that determine the idiosyncratic characteristics and language of one's architecture. 'I wanted to end the tower in a certain way with the frame disappearing into the sky. At the same time we were looking at a more functional idea of a series of turbines that were going to serve the building. Looking at the top, I began to realise that we wanted to fashion our own turbines, and suddenly, an image of Moholy-Nagy's Light Modulator (1937) came into my head. It started to establish the terms by which I would develop this part of the project – the tower and the beacon – as extremely ephemeral, chrome or stainless steel, bouncing light off one another.' Thom Mayne, interview with Yael Reisner, 15th December 2006.

Eric Owen Moss
'THE GNOSTIC VOICE'

RENOWNED AS ONE OF AMERICA'S MOST EXPERIMENTAL and thought-provoking architects, Eric Owen Moss rigorously pursues and communicates his 'Penelope' theory of architecture[1] through his innovative architectural practice, provocative teaching and prolific collection of essays and publications.[2] He discusses his work sharply and logically, often through complicated arguments weighing one idea against the other in a Talmudic manner[3] that strives for authenticity and truth. Moss cherishes individuality[4] and rejects the notion of a 'school of thought', instead embracing and supporting a diversity of approaches to the creation of architecture. His practice has taken him all over the world – most recently to Russia and Kazakhstan. However, his core focus remains the sprawling city of Los Angeles, an environment that continues to provide the stimulus for his thought and drives the character of his innovative architecture.

Born in Los Angeles in 1943, Moss received an arts degree from the University of California, Los Angeles (UCLA) in 1965 before going on to complete a Master of Architecture at the College of Environmental Design at the University of California at Berkeley, in 1968. He then obtained a post-professional Masters of Architecture from Harvard University's Graduate School of Design in 1972 and, returning to Los Angeles a year later, established Eric Owen Moss Architects. During his career, he has accumulated an outstanding and diverse body of both built and theoretical architectural projects, continually testing his methodology and position to allow space for the unexpected. He has won numerous competitions and awards that recognise his emminent status, including the Academy Award in Architecture (1999) from the American Academy of Arts and Letters, which recognised him as 'an American architect whose work is characterised by a strong personal direction', and the Arnold W Brunner Memorial Prize (2007), awarded 'to an architect of any nationality who has made a contribution to architecture as an art'.[5] Additionally, as a director of the influential Southern Californian Institute of Architecture (SCI-Arc),[6] Moss continues to reinforce his reputation as a formidable critic and educator.

OPPOSITE FUN HOUSE, LOS ANGELES, CALIFORNIA, USA, 1980

Early in his career, Moss received international recognition for his distinctive and original drawings, awkward forms and intellectual approach that engaged with cultural and artistic reference points. This original drawing illustrates his instinctive approach, striving for movement and progression to ensure that his architectural language is always fresh and new.

Moss runs his office from Culver City in central Los Angeles, adjacent to a cluster of warehouses in a former manufacturing zone known as the Hayden Tract. Working with visionary developers Frederick and Laurie Samitaur-Smith,[7] Moss saw the potential for a precinct of creative industries and together they transformed the formerly disused industrial landscape, providing a catalyst for the area's growth and rejuvenation and an opportunity for Moss to design site-specific and highly experimental architecture. The result is a collaborative piece of urban renewal with a campus-like cluster of iconic buildings, including film-production and post-production facilities. This unique context and patronage allowed Moss to test and build his ambitious ideas within a concentrated environment for over a decade and, as such, documents the evolution of Moss's ideological and practice-driven development.

The architecture of Eric Owen Moss came to prominence in the early 1980s through the dissemination of his original drawings, awkward forms, experimental use of material and intellectual approach that engaged with cultural and artistic reference points. Unlike his European counterparts, Moss – along with other Los Angeles-based contemporaries such as Morphosis, Franklin D Israel and Frank Gehry – was able to build his designs and, over time, he gained international recognition through the wide publication of his projects.

Moss believes that distinctive architecture is created by individuals who are driven by their personal insights and the manner in which they understand the world around them, rather than being part of a collective trend. He explains: 'For example, I think that Peter Cook is a kind of architect's architect, and Lebbeus Woods could be characterised in that way also, but with a different emphasis. He continues: 'Over the past few generations I think the people who have managed to be successful in terms of implementing their ideas as large-scale manifestations have found an individual approach. It might be "charming/disarming" or "aggressive bad girl/bad boy"; whatever it is doesn't really matter. It's always personal to exchange discourse with people who are fundamentally quite different and have diverse interests and somehow you have to find a way to make what seem to be disparate interests coalesce.'

Although Moss advocates individualism, he is unconvinced about the value of a defined aesthetic or signature within his own body of work. 'I think an architect can make a case for almost any position, so one can say, "I am going to be about today so to hell with yesterday", or "I am going to be about tomorrow",' he exclaims. 'I just don't design like that, I work on things and I am convinced that I don't know what's coming out at the other end of the process. And I am very conscious of resisting producing work which is recognisable or repeatable – a kind of 1 of 15, 1 of 20 series.'

BELOW SAMITAUR COMPLEX PHASE ONE, LOS ANGELES, CALIFORNIA, USA, 1996

Moss's projects strive to retain a connection to their existing fabric to provide a response and counterpoint to the new architecture. Moving beyond the simple creation of tension between old and new, Moss introduces a dialectic tension in his work by confronting two non-conforming forms.

This view is a good example of Moss's dialectical
lyricism, reflecting his aspiration to build up tension
through the overall composition. This potent
combination captures a tension between opposing
ideas that are presented as a unified whole in order to
create an equilibrium between these contrasting forces.

This is a sentiment that underpins Moss's work throughout his career. He strives for movement and progression to ensure that his architectural language is new and unrecognisable from memory,[8] although he does admit that there is 'a kind of admirable dexterity in developing a repertoire and, not so much enlarging it, but increasingly reassociating the pieces.'[9] He continues: 'I think the intellectual process within design has to do with an uncertainty principle, and I think it's useful when conceptual thinking keeps moving. If you look at our Mariinsky Cultural Centre in Russia (2003), the Smithsonian Institution offices in Washington DC (2004), the Guangdong Museum in China (2004), the José Vasconcelos Library in Mexico (2003) or Republic Square in Kazakhstan (2006), then I think you will see my intention and effort not to develop a repeatable repertoire. It's important for me intellectually to keep digging around and to explore new ways.'[10]

Moss is also a vocal critic of the 'non-deterministic' culture within digital architecture and rejects the notion that computational technologies and techniques are anything more than tools for implementing ideas: 'I don't understand the tendency of some digital architects to resist being deterministic or to put themselves within the project ... in fact,

ABOVE STEALTH, CULVER CITY, CALIFORNIA, USA, 2001

Visionary collaborators Frederick and Laurie Samitaur-Smith transcend traditional developer values with their passionate belief in the transformational power of good architectural design and planning. With Moss they transformed this formerly disused industrial landscape, providing a catalyst for the area's rejuvenation and an opportunity for Moss to design site-specific and highly experimental architecture.

LEFT STEALTH, CULVER CITY, CALIFORNIA, USA, 2001

Acting as the entrance to the campus-like cluster of buildings and landscape designed by Moss located in Hayden Tract, Culver City's oldest and largest industrial area, the Stealth office building has a distinctive elegance and powerful presence. For over a decade, Moss has transformed the cluster's existing building stock with his iconic architecture, testing his visionary ideas within a unique and concentrated environment. His work here includes the Umbrella building, the Parking Garage and Pterodactyl.

the digital process is one of the most deterministic and imposing ways to create architecture, despite their claims. One of the durable constants of architecture is that it is absolutely and consciously deterministic.'[11] He continues: 'To have the attitude that "the machine will do it for me" is pointless. What machine ever did anything for anyone? Auschwitz? The technology is always in the service of the ideas that drive it. So to turn architecture over to software is complete idiocy. There is a kind of adolescent arrogance that software or the latest technology is the key to something. It is not the key to anything actually, and it has nothing to do with conservatism or radicalism.'[12]

It was Moss's *Gnostic Architecture* (1999) that marked his significance as a thought-provoking architect unafraid of challenging conventions with new ways of engaging in architectural discourse. The publication eloquently described Moss's distinctive value system and offered an intriguing insight into his diverse influences, from broad literary references to a wide engagement with visual culture. The material presented in the book, however, was widely criticised by the architectural press as being too 'private' and

RIGHT UMBRELLA BUILDING, CULVER CITY, CALIFORNIA, USA, 1999

Moss's book *Gnostic Architecture* (1999) challenges conventions with new ways of engaging in architectural discourse, describing his distinct value system and offering an intriguing insight into his diversity of influences.

RIGHT JEFFERSON TOWERS, LOS ANGELES, CALIFORNIA, USA, 1997–

Moss describes his 'introverted compass' as 'glue': 'The glue is a cerebral underground from which specific conceptual undertakings are generated. The glue is a caricature psyche. It designates a crisscross of emotions and ideas, piled up over many years ... on which the architecture sits.' Eric Owen Moss, *Gnostic Architecture*, Monacelli Press, New York, 1999, p 3.1.

BELOW UMBRELLA BUILDING, CULVER CITY, CALIFORNIA, USA, 1999

Moss cherishes individuality and supports its expression in architecture. He suggests that: 'Language communication is generic and extrinsic when it's inherited. It becomes specific and intrinsic to its user as it becomes personalized.' Eric Owen Moss, *Gnostic Architecture*, Monacelli Press, New York, 1999, p 3.16.

'inaccessible'[13] – a response that clearly frustrates Moss: 'The response was difficult for me, because it was criticised as not being sufficiently accessible, while Rem Koolhaas's *S, M, L, XL* was seen as more engaging.'[14] He expands: 'I feel this attitude limits society as a consequence. And I think that if you view the book as a teaching tool or a discussion piece – which I absolutely think it is – then you have to work on it and care about what's in it, and make a decision about what part of it you choose to care about. I don't think contemporary culture is particularly insistent on working very hard on anything other than the idea of "oneself".'

The book is a fascinating composite full of historical anecdotes, or 'cases' as Moss describes them. Pursuing a trajectory through key moments in history, he recounts personalised concepts that have contributed greatly to society, such as the theories of Marx and Freud, the words of TS Eliot and Joyce, the paintings of Mark Rothko through to Biblical moral anecdotes, Greek mythological legends, Pythagoras's rational thinking, Kant's analogy of human mentality[15] and back to the work of Japanese film-maker

PARKING GARAGE (BUILT) AND PTERODACTYL (UNBUILT), CULVER CITY, CALIFORNIA, USA, 1999–

This mixed-use office building and parking garage was designed with the idea of elevating the former to obviate the presence of the latter. The centre portion of the office building is a three-tiered space that cascades over the front facade of the parking structure, identifying the office and the entry into the garage and serving as the visual and physical terminus of the cluster designed by Moss.

Kurasawa.[16] The core message of the text is that extraordinary things emerge from many different circumstances and reference points, revealing what Moss calls the 'introverted compass'[17] that he believes is the foundation for an architect's integrity. On this he says: 'There is an effort to say that architecture is "everything" in the sense that it folds into itself a colossal amount of experience connected with art, history, prosaic, pragmatics, etc. So it's possible to look at the book as infinitely ambitious, and its aspiration – at least in my view – is in that sense infinite.'

Embedded in Moss's pluralist approach is the notion that all architecture is part of a historic continuum, although not necessarily a linear one. His projects in Los Angeles, in particular, strive to retain a connection with their existing fabric to provide a response and counterpoint to the new architecture. 'This is my sense of what architecture means,' he explains. 'It actually has something to do with a historic continuum, not because it's comforting or reassuring, but because I think reusing means that at some level what preceded you becomes legible as you go forward in time – although it isn't always better.'

ABOVE MARIINSKY CULTURAL CENTRE, NEW
MARIINSKY THEATRE, ST PETERSBURG, RUSSIA, 2003

After years of working almost exclusively in Los
Angeles, Moss, in collaboration with his developer
colleagues, has grasped the opportunity to work
abroad. His scheme for the New Mariinsky Theatre
within the existing urban fabric of St Petersburg was
designed as a dramatic symbol for the future of the
historic Russian city.

He continues: 'So it's kind of a chronology that exists at least in your head or in a history book, and is expressed as a conception within the architecture. This is really the record of people on the planet; so there is a kind of continuum of history, and there is both behind you and in front of you.'[18]

Moss says his personalised and inclusive architectural process was influenced by his father, who encouraged him to look at and understand the world in a non-conventional way: 'Before I ever built anything, my dad, who was a poet and a thinker, encouraged me to look at the world and to try to understand from a different perspective,' he explains. 'He was a New Yorker and wrote for a newspaper, but he also wrote a series of books, one of which, *Holy Holocaust*, is like a poem and discusses the relationship, over many years, between the Christians and the Jews.' Seeing the instinct that his father had for his subject influenced Moss's intellectual position: 'Watching my dad's process confirmed for me that you can have an instinct for certain subjects and, over a period of time, you get to be a little bit more articulate in expressing that instinct. There is something about the history of the Jewish people, both their durability over thousands of years, and the difficulties they had. So I think I am interested both in the differences between people and the continuities, the differences in periods of time, and the continuum over a long period of time.'

Through his non-linear design process, Moss extends his preoccupation with continuum by employing a dialectic tension where, beyond incorporating a tension between the old and

ABOVE MARIINSKY CULTURAL CENTRE, NEW
MARIINSKY THEATRE, ST PETERSBURG, RUSSIA, 2003

The building's 'window' formed by the public lobby
and the performance hall has been transformed into a
21st-century metaphorical opening encompassing
multiple and reflective perspectives: past to future and
future to past; outside to inside, inside to outside; city
to lobby to house, and so on.

ABOVE RIGHT MARIINSKY CULTURAL CENTRE, NEW
MARIINSKY THEATRE, ST PETERSBURG, RUSSIA, 2003

The auditorium's undulating glass surface replicates the
acoustic quality and diffusion within a classical, highly
ornamental opera house. The lobby's curving panels
are supported by a second, faceted plane and reapplied
within the interior.

the new, he also confronts two forms that do not conform to each other but 'share enough
of the congruent aspect to be read as both reinforcing and contradictory: fit and misfit,' he
explains.[19] This potent combination captures a tension between opposing ideas that are
presented as a unified whole in order to create an equilibrium of tension. As he describes
further in *Gnostic Architecture*: 'The dialectic is, or can be, subsumed by the poetry. That
is, the work can contain the dialectic intellectually, and overcome it lyrically. I call this the
dialectical lyric.'[20] Elaborating, he explains: 'Questions are rolling through time, from the
past, to the present and into the future. And what interests me is not so much the answer,
but the emotional or the intellectual, and the tension between possible answers.'[21]

While Moss strives to ensure his architectural language is in a constant state of change
and movement, he is conscious of an aesthetic value in his work: 'Of course, I absolutely
care how my architecture looks. I am actually quite fascinated by that. It needs to look
like something, but the problem is that I don't have any criteria except my own instinct,
in order to say, a little higher, a little thinner, and so on.' He continues: 'I think the term
"ugly" is a little bit disingenuous. In a literal sense, I don't think anybody wants to make
a project that is a kind of architectural Frankenstein. I remember how I used to call up
Wolf Prix on the phone and we'd say to each other about our work, "it's getting ugly, but
it's not ugly enough". I think our comments were made within the context of denying
history and the fact that beauty is already a historic prejudice. In some way we were
trying to averse the historic prejudice by prioritising something that used to be a negation
of architecture and that has now become a positive.'

OPPOSITE MARIINSKY CULTURAL CENTRE, NEW
MARIINSKY THEATRE, ST PETERSBURG, RUSSIA, 2003

Moss questions the 'generic' and advocates a design
process that is embedded in specific and personal life
experiences. He believes that architecture acts as a
public record, explaining: 'There is a continuum of
history, and there is both behind you and in front
of you.'

ABOVE MARIINSKY CULTURAL CENTRE, NEW
MARIINSKY THEATRE, ST PETERSBURG, RUSSIA, 2003

This potent combination captures a tension between
opposing ideas that are presented as a unified whole
in order to create an equilibrium. As Moss says: 'The
dialectic is, or can be, subsumed by the poetry. That is,
the work can contain the dialectic intellectually, and
overcome it lyrically.'

ABOVE RIGHT REPUBLIC SQUARE, ALMATY,
KAZAKHSTAN, 2006

Republic Square is the ceremonial and organisational
centre of Almaty, the largest city in Kazakhstan. Due
to its enormous scale and prominent location, the
competition brief for the project recognised the
square's potential status as a contemporary, constructed
symbol of this newly affluent Central Asian nation.

Ultimately, Moss is ambivalent about the aesthetic communication of his work, at once
delighted when his projects are described as 'awkward' and recalling his early position
of 'the uglier, the better'. However, in keeping with his inclusive approach, he says: 'The
reality is that I am actually very interested in making my work beautiful, but my primary
interest lies with trying to stretch out what I know. What I *am* sure about is that I really
don't know anything. It's an intellectual process between "I don't know and I know". I
think from a personal perspective I could say: "OK, I am going to learn, work on and
master this and it will be Eric Moss architecture." So my idea is that being paradoxically
comfortable with comfort *and* with the tension between possible ideas is ultimately
always more interesting to me than the resolution of the work. The space, the
configuration and the form therefore seem to be, in a sense, ambivalent, and never reach
a sort of equilibrium that results in something that I would define as beauty.'

Interview
Moss's office, Culver City, Los Angeles, California, 14 December 2006

ABOVE REPUBLIC SQUARE, ALMATY, KAZAKHSTAN, 2006

Moss's personal vision for the city of Almaty is communicated through the unity of programme, pragmatism and stability of structure and expressed through the heroic aesthetic of the Republic Square project. The positioning of the primary structure maximises the spectacular views – one looking south to the colossal Tian Shan mountain range and the other north to the vast and austere Central Asian Plateau.

Notes

1. Moss's 'Penelope' theory of architecture takes its name from the legend of the wife of the King of Ithaca, Odysseus, who – while waiting for 20 years for her husband's return – weaves a shroud to distract her suitors, only to undo her work at night. As Moss suggests: 'We pull together; we coalesce; we pull apart – and this metaphysical assembly/disassembly manifests itself daily in lectures, exhibits, building, publishing, teaching and debate.' See Eric Owen Moss, *Who Says What Architecture Is?*, SCI-Arc Press, Los Angeles, CA, 2008.

2. See Eric Owen Moss, *Who Says What Architecture Is?*, SCI-Arc Press, Los Angeles, CA, 2008; Richard Meier, *Eric Owen Moss: Buildings and Projects 3*, Rizzoli, New York, 2002; Eric Owen Moss, *Gnostic Architecture*, Monacelli Press, New York, 1999; Anthony Vidler, *Eric Owen Moss: Buildings and Projects 2*, Rizzoli, New York, 1995; *Eric Owen Moss*, Architectural Monographs, No 29, Academy Editions, London, 1993; Wolf D Prix and Philip Johnson, *Eric Owen Moss: Buildings and Projects 1*, Rizzoli, New York, 1991.

3. Moss's dialectical discussion may have evolved equally in reference to a Talmudic, Socratic or Hegelian manner as they all share the common characteristic of constantly searching for truth. Moss seems familiar with each approach.

4. As Moss suggests in his *Gnostic Architecture*: 'A phonetic or notational language – a form, a way of understanding and communicating – is taught or learned, inherited or internalized by students ... that form of language communication is generic and extrinsic when it's inherited. It becomes specific and intrinsic to its user as it becomes personalized.' Eric Owen Moss, *Gnostic Architecture*, op cit, p 3.16.

5. Other accolades include the AIA/LA Medal in 1998 and the Distinguished Alumni Award from the University of California at Berkeley in 2003.

6. Moss has been involved with SCI-Arc since its foundation in 1972 and was appointed a director in 2002.

7. Collaborators Frederick and Laurie Samitaur-Smith transcend traditional developer values with their passionate belief in the transforming power of good architectural design and planning.

8. As Moss writes: 'What was once fresh becomes a tedious method, no longer an instinct and the light goes out.' Eric Owen Moss, *Gnostic Architecture*, op cit, p 3.6.

9. Moss references COOP HIMMELB(L)AU's BMW Welt in Munich (2007) as an example, suggesting that: 'You could look at Wolf D Prix's work through years and say that their repertoire explores similar parts that have been reinvestigated within different projects. I am not interested in that kind of pursuit.' Eric Owen Moss, interview with Yael Reisner, 14 December 2006.

10. Moss's aim is to create a tension between things that are known and those that are unknown and outside one's memory: 'This effort to create outside the limits of memory is the criterion for the colour at Samitaur, as well as for the nature of the spatial experience, which has the higher priority. The aspiration is always that the building be both known and unknown – that it suggest the world is as it is, and that it suggest the world might be something other than it is.' Eric Owen Moss, *Gnostic Architecture*, op cit, p 5.4.

11. Moss questions the 'generic' and advocates a design process that is embedded in specific life experience and is intrinsic and personalised: 'I'm not interested in the idea that the "masses" need this and "the people" need that. I want to understand life lived singly, one person at a time. Life is personal and private, and not always exchangeable. Yacking about the interest of "the masses" would destroy life, as it's lived, life-by-life. Each person has a story.' Ibid, p 3.6.

12. Rejecting the notion that scientific progress is the most durable for our time, Moss argues: 'In the search for paradigms, it seems to me that the most durable laws involve human behaviour – what you'll do to me, and what I'll do to you, and why. Those patterns seem the most predictable, though not free of exceptions. The least durable models are the so-called scientific laws that, at first glance, seem to the empirical culture to be the most durable, notwithstanding the fact that the scientific priesthood periodically decrees and updates and sometimes inverts the doctrine.' Ibid, p 5.7

13. This is a typical example of the suspicion that arises when an architect's personalised 'black box' is revealed. It is a conservative view within architectural discourse that continues to advocate an impersonal attitude to design – an approach that resurfaced in the late 1990s with a sense of self-righteousness within the digital realm. The debate originated in the early 1930s when a personal expression was regarded as capricious and continued to strengthen as widespread 20th-century democracy raised the importance of 'public opinion' as opposed to the individual. See Wolfgang Pehnt, *Expressionist Architecture*, Thames & Hudson, London, 1973, pp 194-5, and Walter J Ong, SJ, *The Presence of the Word*, Yale University Press, New Haven, 1967, p 5.

14. Office for Metropolitan Architecture (OMA), *S,M,L,XL*, Monacelli Press, New York, 1995.

15. Commenting on the notion of human mentality, Moss notes: 'There is a line from Kant: "from the crooked timber of humanity no straight thing could ever be made." Finally you etch a path even in the biggest swamp; you are already lost in a way and you have forgotten what it was like to make a path. It's like Columbus getting in his boat and sailing to India and Cuba. So you get everything right and the work is not wrong exactly, but different than you had envisaged. I think the only way you can genuinely do that is to continue to try and take apart what you do, and to redo it; it is the best way to capture the uncertainty principle and its result.' Eric Owen Moss, interview with Yael Reisner, 14 December 2006.

16. As Moss writes: 'This relative vantage point is famously portrayed in Akira Kurosawa's Rashomon. I know that some conceptual overlook contributes to the understanding of both "Borodino" (the discussion in Tolstoy's "War and Peace" of the Battle of Borodino – what's real for Tolstoy is what runs through the life of an infinite number of people, person by person) and the "Triumph of Death" (A Brueghel painting) … where the subject of death is not a general matter but specific to each individual. But it would be a mistake to ignore Tolstoy's perception that the history of an event can be told only person by person. Including that hypothesis tends to mitigate the single conclusions requisite to a larger vision.' Eric Owen Moss, *Gnostic Architecture*, op cit, p 3.32.

17. Moss describes his concept of 'the glue': 'The glue is a cerebral underground from which specific conceptual undertakings are generated. The glue is a caricature psyche. It designates a crisscross of emotions and ideas, piled up over many years … on which the architecture sits … Over the years, as I continue to look and draw and travel, and read, numerous disparate items have stuck in my head. Some enter and stay for a while. Some enter and transform.' Ibid, p 3.1.

18. In *Gnostic Architecture*, Moss writes that: 'A building should give back its own history … the psychological construction of a human being, and the collective ethos of a culture, run in both directions: back into memory and forward toward what might reshape memory … Hagia Sophia is a church that becomes a mosque that becomes a church.' Eric Owen Moss, *Gnostic Architecture*, op cit, p 1.6.

19. Ibid, p 1.5.

20. Ibid, p 5.2

21. As Moss writes: 'The Gnostic voice, requires both an intellectual dialectic and a lyrical resolution. The dialectic locates the tension. The lyric subsumes it. The process of making the building is the process of making that cerebral subject tangible as the experience of the building.' Ibid, p 1.4.

Will Alsop
PURSUIT OF PLEASURE

'ARCHITECTURE IS ART!', exclaims British architect Will Alsop. 'It is the most public of arts.' Educated at the renowned Architectural Association (AA) in London during the late 1960s and imbued with the school's commitment to creative process, Alsop is disparaging of the notion of 'objectivism' within architecture. As he suggests: 'The only thing we have is our individuality. That's what we have to give to the world.'[1]

Alsop also believes a fundamental aspect of the architect's role is to improve the quality of people's lives. He explains that the content of his work is embedded in a process of speculation that aspires to create spaces of delight and beauty for the 'man on the street'. To this end, he actively engages the community in the design process for his public projects, inviting them to share their thoughts and desires for the kind of spaces they would like to inhabit.

At the age of 60, Alsop is a jovial, relaxed Englishman who loves his garden and a glass of good wine, is comfortable in his own skin and open to discussing a wide range of topics and ideas. Despite this generosity of spirit, he is also a man with strong convictions who is prepared to fight arduous battles for the acceptance of his architecture. He embodies a strong sense of justice and is not afraid to confront his contemporaries if he feels they are politically conservative and in breech of their positions of power – such is his passion for a diverse and inspiring architectural culture.

OPPOSITE HÔTEL DU DÉPARTEMENT DES BOUCHES-DU-RHÔNE, MARSEILLES, FRANCE, 1994

Alsop is disparaging of the notion of 'objectivism' within architecture. He suggests: 'The only thing we have is our individuality. That's what we have to give to the world ... I think an architect has to have the courage to go wherever their process seems to be going rather than trying to pull it back to something familiar. So I always return to this notion that the unfamiliar is more interesting to me than the familiar. I feel happy not knowing quite where a project is going.'

Will Alsop knew from a very young age that he wanted to become an architect. While still at school, he began working for a local firm and balanced this practical experience by attending art school to gain inspiration and creative skills, and even considered painting as an alternative career. 'I went to art school because I felt I needed "deprogramming" from my early pragmatic architectural experience and so I could begin to put myself somewhere else creatively,' he explains. The experience proved an extremely positive one and propelled him to apply to study at London's prestigious

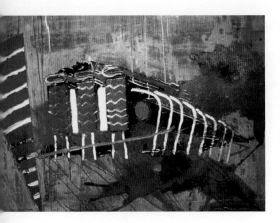

ABOVE HÔTEL DU DÉPARTEMENT DES BOUCHES-DU-RHÔNE, MARSEILLES, FRANCE, 1994

Alsop is well known for the large-scale paintings that inform his work, however he is adamant that they are not an integral part of his process, claiming instead that they influence his work in a more oblique way. 'Painting is a release,' he explains, 'I'm actually making marks on a piece of paper or piece of canvas in order to take myself somewhere new. I'm not trying to confirm anything; I'm trying to open the situation up.'

Architectural Association: 'I only wanted to go to the AA so I never applied for anywhere else. I began studying there in 1968 and, at that time, it was almost completely dominated by Archigram members. I'd seen the absurd magazines Archigram produced which genuinely excited me and it was one of the reasons I wanted to go there – there was a genuine sense that you could do anything.'

Through the 1960s and 1970s, initially under the direction of John Lloyd and then Alvin Boyarsky, the AA encouraged students to pursue their individual talents and take time to pursue a personalised expression through their studies. As Alsop recalls: 'There was a genuine feeling that as an architect you could change the way people lived, or more importantly that you could change the way people *thought* about how they could live; that was interesting to me and it still is today.'

After graduating, Alsop went to work for Cedric Price[2] – an experience that he remembers as concurrently bewildering and rewarding: 'I found Cedric very confusing and it became clear to me early on that he wasn't interested in buildings at all. He was much more engaged in projects that he had invented and so I spent a long time researching such things as how to provide a truck park with security, facilities for the drivers to have a decent night's sleep, and where they could wash and have a good breakfast. But if you were in the right mood you could make a very beautiful truck park!' While Alsop appreciated Price's ethical approach, he felt he lacked a direct engagement with designing buildings. Looking to his other great passion of art to fill the void, he began teaching sculpture after-hours at St Martins College. Eventually, however, it became clear to Alsop that his desire to build architecture meant he needed to move on: 'There was a lot going on in Price's office at the time, but I became frustrated because although the work was interesting I knew that, within myself, there was something deeply missing.'

After establishing his own practice in 1981, Alsop discovered that – like many emerging architects from the UK – it was much easier to gain commissions to build his architecture abroad, and over time he gained a reputation as an internationally significant architect for his vibrant and expressive buildings constructed all over the world. Examples include his first major international commission, Le Grand Bleu, the seat of the regional government of Bouches-du-Rhône in Marseille (1994); the Cardiff Bay Visitor Centre in Wales (1990); Peckham Library, London (1999); the Almere Urban Entertainment Centre, Amsterdam (2004); Alsop Toronto Sales Centre, Toronto (2006); Zhang Jia Bang: Street of Culture, Shanghai (2006) and the Trubnaya office building in Moscow (2007).

Although Alsop embraces technology, he departs from his 'High-Tech' contemporaries[3] with his belief that technology 'helps to get things done' rather than generating the

RIGHT HÔTEL DU DÉPARTEMENT DES BOUCHES-DU-RHÔNE, MARSEILLES, FRANCE, 1994

Alsop studied at the Architectural Association (AA) in London through the 1960s and 1970s, initially under the direction of John Lloyd and then Alvin Boyarsky. The AA encouraged students to pursue their individual talents and take time to craft their personal architectural expression through their studies. As Alsop recalls: 'There was a genuine feeling that as an architect you could change the way people lived, or more importantly that you could change the way people *thought* about how they could live; that was interesting to me and it still is today.'

design itself: 'I'm a big fan of the computer, of course, but I think it has its place. I think that what can be explored with the computer is a limited dialogue.' Instead, his architectural process is embedded in the immediacy of a 'hand-eye' conversation: 'Sketches make things immediately evident and that gives me the confidence that I can draw anything. In my studio cupboard I have a load of sketchbooks. I know that if I'm trying to discover what something might be, it's quicker in a sketchbook than on the computer. And it's not about the expression, it's about moving very quickly through a number of ideas. So if you have a nice quiet hour and you're in the right mood, you can arrive at somewhere that you could never have predicted. An hour on the laptop won't give you the same result because you get locked into the system of the computer.'

The role of beauty[4] within architecture is also not a topic that Alsop shies away from – once again marking out a stark point of difference to many of his contemporaries. 'Is it possible to take things to an extreme and to make something extremely beautiful that has no function at all, but actually has an effect on people?' he ponders. 'After all, we're talking about making life better for people – that's our job – whichever direction you come at, so what's the role of the idea of beauty within that?' He continues: 'We know from experience that people do respond to beauty. For example, if I think of the River Ouse, running through Bedfordshire in May – it's delightful and secure. There are church bells on a Sunday evening echoing down the valley – all is well with the world. Those moments exist, but how could you design those moments? Could you create those moments somewhere else where you weren't expecting them? That interests me a lot.'

It's a thought process that Alsop regularly puts into practice within his public projects, such as the masterplan for the rejuvenation of the centre of Bradford, Barnsley in Yorkshire and New Islington in Manchester. As he explains: 'We have a lot of public clients and that means that we need to engage with the wider community. For example, when you're dealing with the centre of Bradford then essentially all the people who live there are also clients. I'm very interested in tapping into their imagination. Therefore I don't talk with them about design; I speak about discovering what it could be. If you talk about a voyage of discovery then that automatically allows other people to contribute.' He expands: 'So it's about how to disrupt what we've been taught in the past by putting noise into the system. And I've found that if "the man in the street" is given half a chance, he is actually quite imaginative.'

While advocating that this collaborative strategy removes the process from a singular personal vision, Alsop also acknowledges that it is a journey that evolves from a macro to micro scale and is consequently richer for it: 'If I want to broaden the conversation then

LEFT PECKHAM LIBRARY, PECKHAM, LONDON, 1999

Alsop insists a fundamental aspect of the architect's role is to improve the quality of people's lives. He explains that the content of his work is embedded in a process of speculation – a process that aspires to create spaces of delight and beauty for the 'man in the street'. To this end, he actively engages the community in the design process for his public projects, inviting them to share their thoughts and desires for the kinds of spaces they would like to inhabit.

ABOVE SHARP CENTRE FOR DESIGN, ONTARIO COLLEGE
FOR ART AND DESIGN, TORONTO, CANADA, 2004

Alsop rejects the idea that he has a signature style and
states that he finds it hard to understand the need for
a manifesto, as each project requires its own frame of
reference and investigation. He claims that technology
now affords the possibility to design anything, clarifying
that it is only a 'question of budget' that restricts
the process.

Alsop regularly embraces public opinion during the
design process of his work and uses the information
collected within his public projects. As he explains:
'Architects need to engage with the wider community
as essentially all the people who live there are also
clients. I'm very interested in tapping into their
imagination. Therefore, I don't talk with them about
design; I speak about discovering what it could be. If
you talk about a voyage of discovery then that
automatically allows other people to contribute.'

BELOW SHARP CENTRE FOR DESIGN, ONTARIO
COLLEGE FOR ART AND DESIGN, TORONTO, CANADA,
2004

Alsop acknowledges that there is a characteristic thread
through his work, suggesting: 'I can see that there is
something that could be described as "Alsopesque".
But if I said "draw me an Alsop building", you couldn't
really do it. You could draw a building I've done, but
you couldn't draw my next building. I like that because
I don't know what my next building will be and it
continues to challenge me.'

I actually make more noise by talking to more people and then bring it back to the studio,
look at it and think about what I can do with that information. So it goes from the very
public to the very personal.'

'Deprogramming' the obvious line of enquiry is a strategy that can be traced back to the
beginning of Alsop's career when he enrolled in art studies to challenge his practical
training, and it is a technique that he now passes on to his students at Vienna's Technical
University and at London's Royal College of Art. 'I do this exercise with my students, often
in collaboration with Nigel Coates, where you give them a beautiful, large piece of paper
and any materials they want and say that by end of the day they must have drawn a
really ugly building. I say, "don't try to be too clever – the objective is to make it really
ugly. At first they think it's easy, but it's really difficult, and at the end of the day most of
them produce something really beautiful rather than ugly as a speculative building. I think
that's intriguing.'

Alsop rejects the idea that he has a signature style and states that he finds it hard to
understand the need for an overarching philosophy, as each project requires its own
frame of reference and investigation. He claims that technology now affords the
possibility to design anything – it is only a question of budget that restricts the process.
However, he does acknowledge that there is a characteristic thread through his work: 'I

can see that there is something that could be described as "Alsopesque". But if I said "draw me an Alsop building", you couldn't really do it. You could draw a building I've done, but you couldn't draw my next building. I like that because I don't know what my next building will be and it continues to challenge me.'[5]

Alsop's architecture is colourful with a great diversity of materials and a rich palette of forms and colour, yet he resists any notion of an underlying conceptual ideology apart from a desire to do things differently with each new project: 'Why do architects or artists want to write a manifesto? I think there's only one answer to that question – they believe they are right and they want everyone else to do it the same way. I don't want to do that and it is evident in the difference between the way that I teach and the way an architect like David Chipperfield teaches; if you see the work of his students at Düsseldorf, there are 30 David Chipperfield clones – it's like chip shops! That's not very interesting – why would you do that as a teacher? At the Technical University in Vienna I receive a lot

BELOW FOURTH GRACE, LIVERPOOL, 2002

Alsop promotes a collaborative design strategy that removes the process from a personal vision and places design decisions in the public realm, empowering the architect's role as facilitator. He says: 'If I want to broaden the conversation then I actually make more noise by talking to more people and then bring it back to the studio, look at it and think about what I can do with that information. So it goes from the very public to the very personal.'

ABOVE THAMES GATEWAY MASTERPLAN, LONDON, 2003

Referring to his painting for the Thames Gateway masterplan project, Alsop states: 'It's another form of sketching, to see things in another way. By simply saying, "OK, to try and work out what Thames Gateway could be, let's give ourselves 10 days to think about 14 square kilometres and each square kilometre should be different". It's an absurd thing to set yourself as a task, yet wonderful!'

of bad work from the students, but I think that's great because while they might be failing, at least they're trying something new.'

A legacy of being a graduate of the AA lies in the philosophy that architectural design evolves through free thinking with no need for rules or rigid frameworks. Alsop is also quick to reject the need to establish an overriding set of 'rules' within his architecture, explaining that 'the parameters of a project are very ill-defined at the beginning and they become more established as you work through the process, as you involve more people in the conversation and, eventually, it develops its own sort of sensibility'. He continues: 'I think an architect has to have the courage to go with wherever it seems to be going – rather than trying to put it back to something familiar. So I always return to this notion that the unfamiliar[6] is more interesting to me than the familiar. I feel happy not knowing quite where a project is heading.'

Art also continues to provide an important framework for Alsop, and the architect is well known for the large-scale paintings that inform his work. However, he is adamant that they are not an integral part of his process, instead influencing his work in a more oblique way. 'Painting is a release,' he says, 'I'm actually making marks on a piece of paper or a canvas in order to take myself somewhere new. I'm not trying to confirm anything; I'm trying to open the situation up.' He suggests that rather than a methodology, his painting allows him to gain a new perspective and to include other creative influences in his process, such as his ongoing collaboration with artist Bruce McLean:[7] When I'm working with Bruce on large 3-D paintings such as *Malagarba Works*,[8] we're not thinking about a project at all, we're just working on the painting and that process can feed elements of the architecture. We might have done something for one reason, but then say to each other: "See the way that shadow falls? Now that's interesting", and then translate that into the architectural work.'

Alsop gestures to a series of large paintings hanging in his studio as an example of how his artwork can inform a project – in this case his scheme for the Thames Gateway masterplan project (2004). He explains: 'It's another form of sketching, to see things in another way. By simply saying, "OK, to try and work out what Thames Gateway could be, let's give ourselves 10 days to think about 14 square kilometres and each square kilometre should be different". It's an absurd thing to set yourself as a task, yet wonderful! And out of it we discovered some things which allowed us to tell a different story about that part of London.'

From large public projects such as the Thames Gateway or Bradford masterplans to commissions for small objects such as his tea set for Alessi, Alsop finds little difficulty in adjusting his process for dramatic changes of scale. 'To me it's all the same work. I didn't design the table in my studio, but I'd be very happy to design a place to sit because I think you need the right things to support the act of talking. Conversely, a beautiful spoon that's very nice to use isn't an aid to conversation. You might notice the spoon, but you don't have to say anything – it's there nonetheless and it makes you feel comfortable or excited or calm. And I think buildings are formed the same way, so it doesn't matter what the scale of the project is.'

Although Alsop easily embraces the notion of beauty within his work, he is less comfortable with the proposition that the development of his ideas might evolve directly from a consideration of aesthetics. He believes that the content and form of his projects are embedded in a process of speculation rather than visual considerations: 'Whatever the project, I like to start off from somewhere else rather than it being generated by what it looks like. For example, I've recently designed a set of cutlery for Alessi called 'Vertical Cutlery', but the idea started with my observation that people in London live in increasingly smaller apartments. So if you have guests for supper then you don't want all this crap on the table; you want to make it simple so that you've got some space to sit and have a drink and the cutlery can be easily added when it's time to eat. So it was an idea derived from my observations and not generated from an idea about what it should look like.'

Alsop believes that the content and form of his projects are embedded in a process of speculation rather than in visual considerations: 'Whatever the project I like to start off from somewhere else rather than it being generated by what it looks like. For example, I've recently designed a set of cutlery for Alessi ... but the idea started from my observation that people in London live in increasingly smaller apartments ... and was not generated from an idea about what it should look like.'

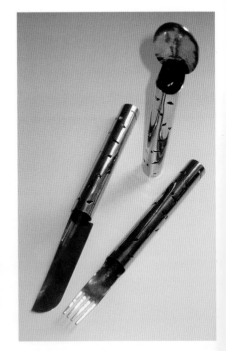

RIGHT BLIZARD BUILDING, SCHOOL OF MEDICINE AND DENTISTRY FOR QUEEN MARY, UNIVERSITY OF LONDON, WHITECHAPEL, LONDON, 2005

Despite his generosity of spirit, Alsop is also a man with strong convictions who is prepared to fight arduous battles for the acceptance of his architecture. He pursues a strong sense of justice and is not afraid to confront his contemporaries if he feels they are politically conservative and in breach of their positions of power and the potential influence of the architect in politics – such is his passion for a diverse and inspiring architectural culture.

Summing up, Alsop credits his inherent curiosity and willingness to collaborate with others as the major driver for the nexus between content, form and aesthetics within his architecture. 'I think that the content of my work is intrinsically linked to the idea of speculation.[9] When you allow other people into the process and they ask difficult questions, then you can learn something. So I believe that if you always employ that sort of openness then everything that you do will be beautiful. How could you disagree with that?', he exclaims. 'If you take a fairly prosaic building like the Peckham Library, for example, then the interesting thing is that three times as many people use the building than it was designed for. It's not conventionally beautiful, but it must have some quality that attracts people – they enjoy it, they find it comfortable and agreeable. I'm not sure that I really want to understand the essence of why that's the case, but I'm happy to know I can do it. The building is successful because it captures people's imagination, and that sounds like such a simple thing to say, but if you can achieve this then you've done the job!'

Interviews
Alsop's studio, Battersea, London, 23 April 2004
Alsop's studio, Battersea, London, 23 April 2007

ABOVE THE PUBLIC ARTS BUILDING, WEST BROMWICH, WEST MIDLANDS, 2008

As Alsop eloquently articulates: 'We know from experience that people do respond to beauty ... For example, if I think of the River Ouse running through Bedfordshire in May, it's delightful and secure. There are church bells on a Sunday evening echoing down the valley – all is well with the world. Those moments exist, but how could you design those moments? Could you create those moments somewhere else where you weren't expecting them? That interests me a lot.'

ABOVE LEFT THE PUBLIC ARTS BUILDING, WEST BROMWICH, WEST MIDLANDS, 2008

The role of beauty within architecture is not a topic that Alsop shies away from, marking a stark point of difference to many of his colleagues within architectural discourse. 'Is it possible to take things to an extreme and to make something extremely beautiful that has no function at all, but actually has an effect on people?' Alsop wonders. 'After all, we're talking about making life better for people – that's our job – whichever direction you come at, so what's the role of the idea of beauty within that?'

Notes

1. Interview in *The Guardian*, 8 December 2003.

2. Will Alsop worked for Cedric Price for three and a half years (1973–1977), immediately after graduating from the Architectural Association.

3. High-Tech embraces industrialised systems to create a pragmatic and aesthetic language within architecture. Examples of architects who made their name as part of the High-Tech movement are UK-based architects Richard Rogers, Norman Foster and Richard Horden.

4. 'My studio has a motto which is "no style, no beauty", which doesn't prevent the production being either stylish or beautiful but recognises that these are values imposed on the project by others. The real purpose of such a dictum is to prevent the architect being seduced by beauty, or indeed encouraging others to fall in love with a drawing through some aesthetic deceit.' Will Alsop, 'Can the architect's art afford to be about beauty and style', column for the *Architects' Journal*, 6 November 2003, p 32.

5. 'The quality of surprise is often underestimated. The strength of Pollock or Rauschenberg came from the peculiarity of their product initially.' Will Alsop, column in the *Architects' Journal*, 2 October 2003.

6. Alsop on the 'no-man's land' situation during the design process: 'An architect free of the necessity to produce beauty or fashion is able to see things in a different way – which will always result in a sense of solitude. Although lonely, it is the only tenable position to take on.' Will Alsop, 'Can the architect's art afford to be about beauty and style', column for the *Architects' Journal*, 6 November 2003, p 32.

7. Alsop has collaborated with artist Bruce McLean on large-scale paintings within his architecture, such as Tottenham Hale railway station, London, 1991.

8. Malagarba Works, Menorca, Spain (2002–07) is an intermittent and accidental series of forms, paintings and ephemeral environments undertaken by Alsop and McLean on holiday in Menorca. At other times, their collaborative work might take place within a studio environment.

9. 'The word "speculation" implies that the process of architecture is sort of a game and also accepts that no one is right. On the other hand, no one is wrong, either.' Will Alsop, interview with Yael Reisner, 23 April 2007.

Zaha Hadid

PLANETARY ARCHITECTURE

A TRULY VISIONARY ARCHITECT has many converging, complementary yet, at times, conflicting characteristics – they must be intellectually sharp, original and highly imaginative, with a strong sense of history and a high level of critique. They must be independent and tough, stubbornly refusing to accept impossibilities yet diplomatic and optimistic in the face of adversity. Most importantly, they must have an unshakable confidence in their talent and ability. Iraqi-born British architect Zaha Hadid embodies all these characteristics and more.

Professionally uncompromising and rigorous when dealing with clients, collaborators and the media yet fiercely protective of her dedicated staff, Hadid is one of the most recognised and powerful characters within international architecture. Her larger-than-life persona also translates into the private realm where she is paradoxically impatient, loud, affectionate, chatty, humorous and nostalgic – generously cooking and sharing traditional Iraqi food with her friends at home.

Hadid's personality infiltrates every part of her working and personal life, from her extensive collection of garments, such as the Issey Miyake-designed pieces that she famously layers and appropriates to her own interpretation, often wearing them upside down, to her East London loft. The space is filled with pieces of her own design, including a large-scale Aqua dining table[1] and a tea and coffee set designed for Alessi. Providing a dramatic backdrop to the space is a huge painting, an enlarged version of her infamous Malevich's Tectonik bridge over the Thames that she produced for her diploma thesis project in 1976/77 while at London's Architectural Association (AA). But despite the avant-garde overtones, Hadid's home environment remains one for comfort and relaxation with personal touches such as an extensive collection of glass art including curvaceous Murano pieces that reflect her love of colour, form and elegant exuberance.

OPPOSITE THE PEAK, HONG KONG, 1983

This image is still breathtaking more than 25 years after winning the international competition for this leisure club on top of the mountain overlooking Hong Kong Island. The work marked a radically new approach to spatial design communicated through large-scale architectural paintings – as Hadid describes it is a vision for a 'Suprematist geology'.

Zaha Hadid won the Pritzker Prize, known as the 'Nobel of Architecture',[2] in 2004 when she was just 54 years old – the first woman and certainly one of the youngest recipients to be awarded the ultimate accolade in her profession. The win was particularly significant because it recognised Hadid's work beyond her few built projects at that time,[3] acclaiming her drawings, large-scale paintings, competition wins and publications for their outstanding clarity, presence, originality of approach and radically new spatial articulation. The attention generated by the award established a growing sense of trust and confidence in her compelling work and translated into a phenomenal period of commissions ensuring Hadid effortlessly transcended the label of 'paper architect' to build her visionary projects.

After more than 30 years of practising architecture, Hadid has unquestionably consolidated her position as a prolific, influential and powerful presence within the architectural landscape. After initially developing her architectural reputation through teaching and competition, it was almost 20 years before she built her first project – the Monsoon restaurant in Sapporo, Japan (1990) – prior to being invited by architecture patron and Vitra Furniture Chairman Rolf Fehlbaum to design a fire station in the factory's grounds to house a collection of innovative pieces of architecture.[4]

BELOW VICTORIA CITY AREAL, BERLIN, 1988

This painting illustrates a horizontal intensification of the urban density in the fortified context of West Berlin. A new spatial organisation, programme and architectural language emerge through Hadid's condensed architectural paintings. In these studies, three-dimensional projective drawing techniques are explored and exploited with numerous horizon lines and vanishing points through layers of abstraction. This characteristic adds to their enigmatic visual appeal yet also attracted hostility among her peers.

ABOVE VITRA FIRE STATION, WEIL AM RHEIN, GERMANY, 1993

Hadid's consistent ambition to radicalise two-dimensional compositional ideas into architecture can be traced throughout the design process of her dynamic projects. Referencing the Suprematists, the fragmented spatial qualities of the Vitra Fire Station demonstrate a frozen motion, a non-linear field of forces with angular and fluid forms suspending tension.

RIGHT MONSOON RESTAURANT, SAPPORO, JAPAN, 1990

It is not surprising that Hadid built her first project in Japan, where aesthetics and visual qualities are entrenched within the culture. This restaurant interior featured an exceptionally dynamic space where exuberant oranges, yellows and reds curled up from the floor 'like a furnace of fire' to a dome like a 'fiery tornado bursting through a pressure vessel', capturing Hadid's love of rich colour.

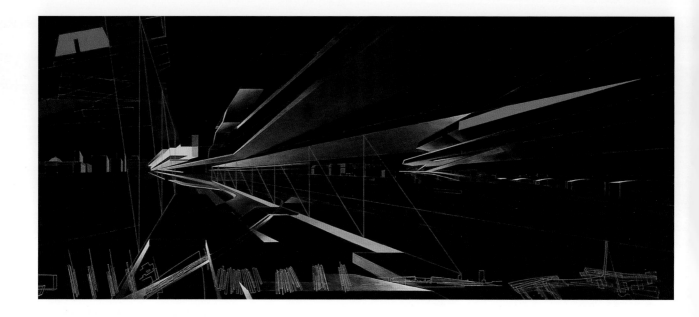

ABOVE HABITABLE BRIDGE, LONDON, 1996

The Habitable Bridge project proposes the metropolis of London as a 'horizontal skyscraper' over the River Thames in order to facilitate a free flow of public services over the bridge while mixed commercial and cultural spaces lie above and below. With this project, Hadid returned to the site of her infamous student thesis project 'Malevich's Tectonik'. To this day, she continues to reference Russian Suprematist ideals that inspire her unique language and architectural expression.

Born in 1950 in Baghdad, Iraq, Hadid went to school in Switzerland and England before studying a mathematics degree at the American University in Beirut. She recalls that her first contact with the architectural process was as a young girl when she became involved in designing a new family house. On completion of her degree in Beirut, she rejoined her family in London and embarked on her architectural studies at the Architectural Association in 1972. A committed and curious student, her work, along with that of others at the time, marked a critical and highly successful period in the school's history where many of the alumni and tutors later emerged as architects of international acclaim.[5]

Through her student years, Hadid's affinity with Persian/Arabic calligraphy provided her early examples of abstract expression[6] and were an inspiration for her evolving aesthetic. 'In my third year I researched geometry, particularly the geometry of Islamic patterns and their connection to mathematics because I'd previously trained in the discipline,' she explains. 'In the Arab world, and especially in Iraq, there is a great culture of teaching algebra, trigonometry and geometry, so the training was always very good. Abstraction was always a big part of that process and I was always interested in maths, logic and abstraction.' Hadid expands: 'At the time, as a student of the AA you were exposed to many different agendas, and not just Modernist theories. Many positions were passionately pursued, so when you put them together after three or four years of study they came into focus.'[7]

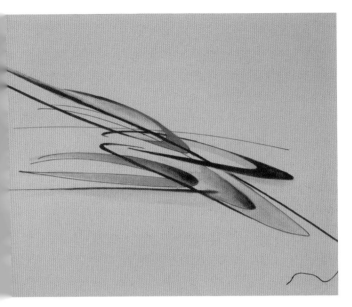

Hadid's abstract compositional sketches resemble Islamic calligraphy. Her architectural language emerges as she initiates the work with lines on paper that form the first external contours of a project's conception. After hundreds of abstract sketches and physical models that rigorously test and interpret contours to locate programme, Hadid begins to consolidate her vision.

Hadid's critics claimed that her architecture was not architectural enough and difficult to build. Ironically, the transition of her dynamic work into built reality has made her paintings more credible and easier to understand.

Her AA diploma project for a bridge over London's River Thames became the catalyst for Hadid's future direction. She recalls: 'In the fourth year, with Elia and Rem[8] as my tutors, everything kind of connected for me. Prior to that I was unfocused; there was some interest here and there, but nothing completely connected so it was definitely through my diploma project – Malevich's Tectonik – that my influences all came together in terms of geometry, abstraction and organisation with an inherent Suprematist ideology.'[9]

The project[10] took its inspiration from the paintings of Suprematist Kazimir Malevich, and more specifically his Alpha Architecton models from 1920. As Hadid explains: 'They weren't inspired by the painterly aspect of Malevich's work, although I was interested in how to represent drawings through paintings, the idea of the form, repertoire and the image. For me, the inspiration lay in looking at the Russian avant-garde movement as a whole and Constructivist art, architecture and photography; it seemed that everything had a trajectory that was connected. The functional and organisational diagrams were very interesting and radical.

Upon graduation from the AA in 1978, Hadid became a partner at the Office of Metropolitan Architecture (OMA) at the invitation of her AA diploma tutors Koolhaas and Zenghelis. It was, however, a short-lived partnership, with Koolhaas once affectionately describing Hadid's presence in the OMA office as 'focused on her own orbit'. In 1979 she

LEFT LANDESGARTENSCHAU, WEIL AM RHEIN,
GERMANY, 1999

Hadid commissioned photographer Hélène Binet to
shoot her first built projects – a collaboration that
continues to this day. Binet's photographs magically
capture the works' elegance of line, composition and
their luminous qualities by night. In her public lectures,
Hadid has suggested that the audience often cannot
tell the difference between some of the photographs
of her built work and her architectural paintings –
evidence that the architecture portrayed in her
paintings was, in fact, always highly achievable.

followed her mentors in taking up a position at the AA,[11] and set up her fledgling practice. While teaching, she continued to pursue her concepts through international competitions,[12] and in 1982 won an open architecture competition with The Peak, a leisure club on the top of the mountain overlooking Hong Kong Island. Her radically new approach to spatial design and sophisticated, original drawing technique were compelling, visually exciting and beautifully illustrated. The scheme won instant acclaim and, in turn, received the attention of avant-garde architectural discourse and the international press, propelling Hadid's work into public consciousness.

Although it was never realised as a building, The Peak presented Hadid's powerful conceptual manner of referencing Suprematist geometry with floating, horizontal planes to create a gravity-free illusion of form and space represented through a dramatic, large-scale painting that super-imposed plan, perspective and axonometric drawing. As Hadid describes the concept: 'A Suprematist geology – materials that are impacted vertically and horizontally ... like the mountain the building is stratified, with each layer defining a function. Platforms are suspended like planets ... the Peak's beams and voids are a gentle seismic shift on an immovable mass.'[13]

While many of her contemporaries in the 1970s were looking back in history, Hadid, though she referenced the Russian Constructivists, pursued a different agenda.[14] Instead she suggested that the 'great Modern project' had been halted by the impact of two World Wars while still in the early days of the diverse experimental attitudes of De Stijl, Russian Constructivism and German Expressionism. As she described in an interview with Alvin Boyarsky in 1983: 'The experiment of the Modernist project was never finished. There was no conclusion as they tried to stretch the limits. They were my point of departure. What interested me most about the Suprematists was that they painted things that were implied as architecture, but which were never injected into architecture, except perhaps in the work of Leonidov. He was really inventive programmatically and the most innovative of all the Russians. His work was very simple but he pushed the limits of all the things that the Constructivists and Suprematists had invented – how you actually correlate between the formed image, the presence on a particular site, its programmatic content, its assembly and so on. That was the principal lesson I learned from the avant-garde of Russia.'[15]

Hadid was also committed to continuing and building upon an early Modernist line of enquiry: 'I think the early Modernists were very connected to the idea of an intimate relationship between art and architecture in the sense that they were interested in similar things. The difference was that from a "painterly" perspective they were simply beautiful compositions, yet I think in terms of organisation they pursued a similar investigation as

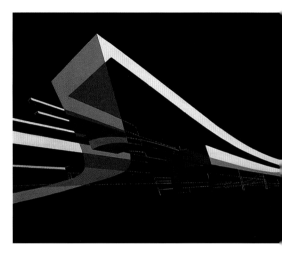

ABOVE LANDESGARTENSCHAU, WEIL AM RHEIN, GERMANY, 1999

In the first 20 years of Hadid's career she envisaged, contemplated and investigated future possibilities of a new spatial organisation, programme manipulation and architectural language. Her ideology was captured in her architectural paintings presenting a new and original way of communicating architecture. This worm's-eye view portrays light projecting from a curved wall to emphasise the dynamic space, and evokes the building's transformation at night.

in architecture.' Expanding, Hadid states: 'If you study the architectural plans of Leonidov,[16] although they were abstract they also included composition and that was the connection back to art. But they were radical beyond an aesthetic composition because as functional and organisational diagrams they were very interesting. I think what is still often misunderstood is the radicalisation of these ideas into architecture.'[17]

With little opportunity to build in her early career, Hadid's large-scale architectural paintings drove her theoretical position, powerfully communicating her radical manifestations. Equally confronting for their layered and dense complexity were her drawings. Her dexterity in employing a multitude of drawing techniques – plan, section, isometric, axonometric, bird's-eye and worm's-eye perspectives with multiple horizons and vanishing points to communicate alternative views – added to their enigmatic and visual appeal yet also attracted hostility from her peers who viewed them as a pursuit of shallow, formal Expressionism.[18]

Reflecting on this criticism, Hadid says: 'I think there was a hostility[19] about me being engaged with a predictive life[20] and about the way I communicated that element in my work, because when I was a student, in the mid-1970s, the architectural discourse of the time was about the social project or alternative life. Besides the different agenda of my investigation, I think there were also many people at the time who simply could not read complex architectural drawings and the implication of navigating through a space, or inventing space; they didn't understand when it appeared on paper or canvas.[21] It was very bizarre and I think they couldn't comprehend my architecture, so anything they didn't understand they dismissed. So I think that there was a degree of stubbornness in the early days to just push ahead and investigate aspects of work which were very important for me.'

RIGHT BMW PLANT, LEIPZIG, GERMANY, 2005

Each angle of the building's interior reveals a different
kind of complexity and an elegance of architectural
resolution. The daily life of the workers inhabiting
the space is enriched by the quality of design
embedded within Hadid's clear ideology and
strong theoretical base.

She goes on to suggest that a latent hostility towards her work still remains within some quarters of the architectural community. 'I think the hostility is still there because they simply can't read my work,' she declares. 'It has become clear to me some critics just do not know how to read drawings and don't have any feeling for architecture. I think they undervalue architecture over what they think is urban design. I think that people misunderstand ideology. They think ideology only exists when it relates to some sort of existing theoretical framework.[22] But they don't understand that sometimes work that has a formal, organisational and functional aspect can also have a theoretical base and not an esoteric one.'

It is perhaps the intensity and determination evident in Hadid's work that some commentators find confronting. The commitment to line and unconventional drawing projection is implicit in her design process and begins with sketching abstract, flat, two-dimensional line compositions that form the first external contours of a project's conception. She continues to develop the sketch as she interprets these early contours further into the programme and layout, and after hundreds of sketches, physical models and rigorous testing she begins to consolidate her vision for the architecture.[23] Like her paintings, Hadid's compositional sketches are used as organisational tools that, in turn, assist in analysing the vision for the building – its layouts, plans and sections, programme and practical aspects. 'I think that the culture that was in place where we designed by doing many models and drawings led to a more rigorous reinvestigation of the diagram,' she suggests. 'I think it's very different now where the current generation of young architects are into the computer and they don't really understand the implication of the

ABOVE PHAENO SCIENCE CENTRE, WOLFSBURG, GERMANY, 2005

In this project Hadid employs a large mass as a horizontal, heavy slab that has seemingly landed on its conical feet to allow people and traffic to continue through the building in different directions. As she describes in the catalogue text to her exhibition at the MAK in Vienna (2003): 'The project is based on an unusual volumetric structural logic; a big volume is supported and also structured by funnel-shaped cones turned inside and out of the box above it.' Zaha Hadid, in *Zaha Hadid: Architecture*, MAK/Hatje Cantz, Vienna, 2003, p 107.

sketch. They're not used to doing things by trial and error – like we used to do 10 or 15 years ago.' Continuing, Hadid explains: 'We'd do a project a hundred times until it was right; now young architects are used to you handing over a diagram and they will go and do it on computer. They don't really understand the layering that's involved.'

Experimental, rich use of colour[24] and manipulations of light and shadow[25] form an integral part of Hadid's architectural vision, and within her intense coloured studies she depicts these qualities as envisaged within the completed buildings.[26] Describing the process of discovering and working with a multitude of grey hues in the process of developing The Peak, she suggests that 'colour is not necessarily used as decoration. It shows the temper, in a way. It also unveils the quality of the architecture ... and it can be muted ... monochromatic ... with The Peak we really had no idea about how it should be finished. By the use of drawings and painting slowly but surely we developed a confirmed opinion. The paintings were like tests.'[27]

Hadid's visual sense and good 'eye' are undisputable, as is her sharp analytical and original intellectual position. However, she refutes any aesthetic aligned with a particular school of thought, explaining that her training at the AA opened up enormous possibilities: 'The aesthetics of the work produced at the AA was very disconnected. I think it was very exciting to be there because through the early 1980s there was such

BELOW ICE-STORM, MAK EXHIBITION HALL, VIENNA, AUSTRIA, 2003

Exhibitions, set design and installations form many of Hadid's earliest built projects and continue to be a field of experimentation for her practice today. Exhibitions such as 'The Great Utopia: The Russian & Soviet Avant-Garde 1915–1932' at the Museum of Modern Art (MoMA) in New York (1992), the 'Mind Zone' at the Millennium Dome, London (1999) and the Summer Pavilion for the Serpentine Gallery in Kensington Gardens, London (2000) are strong examples.

RIGHT PHAENO SCIENCE CENTRE, WOLFSBURG, GERMANY, 2005

'The use of darkness will be a key to the unique experience ... light and shadow offer the opportunity to provide a visual guiding system through the building by creating paths of light and focal points. The overall brightness of the interior should be minimized in order to achieve a more dynamic contrast to the highlighted exhibits, thus creating the moments of astonishment and discovery.' Zaha Hadid, in *Zaha Hadid: Architecture*, MAK/Hatje Cantz, Vienna, 2003, p 111.

an energy and buzz that it felt as though everybody was on the verge of discovering something individual and new.'

Hadid's rise to prominence took on an added dimension in 1988 with her inclusion in the seminal 'Deconstructivist Architecture' exhibition at the Museum of Modern Art (MoMA) in New York, curated by Mark Wigley and Philip Johnson. Despite the exhibition's success, Hadid resents the association drawn between Derrida's philosophy and the architecture of Deconstruction. She explains, though, that the architects in the exhibition shared a historical impulse through their specific output and a diversity of approach: 'What connected the work was a break from historicism. It was about collaging, collapsing things or crashing things into each other, or superimposition, and all these things were coming to the same conclusion, though the architects exhibiting were very different from each other. I think the layering side is when things are dropping into each other, and breaking up was something that came after the dogma of Modernism and after historicism. It was inevitable in a way. I think everyone was trying to break away from the past and it was literally a physical break.'

Hadid's architectural agenda remains committed to challenging convention in pursuit of an exuberant and sensual architectural landscape. The dynamic lightness of her work tears away the tradition of the heavy building that is dumbly grounded to the street and searches for a sense of democracy in the way architecture might hover and open the

ABOVE PHAENO SCIENCE CENTRE, WOLFSBURG, GERMANY, 2005

The Phaeno Science Centre illustrates the culmination of Hadid's major architectural ambitions initially explored through her design for The Peak competition in Hong Kong and in many of her subsequent architectural paintings. The project's heavy yet dynamic concrete volumetric slab appears to be magically suspended due to its innovative form and structure, and playfully conveys natural and artificial light.

PHAENO SCIENCE CENTRE, WOLFSBURG, GERMANY, 2005

The centre illustrates Hadid's philosophy of breaking down the ubiquitous blank bulk of a building to create a generous and democratic entry-level presence while creating a dramatic new spatial experience through the building's expressive form.

NORDPARK CABLE RAILWAY, ALPENZOO STATION, INNSBRUCK, AUSTRIA, 2007

Hadid's fluid compositions suit materials that can be casted, such as concrete or plastics, as we can see through her built projects. Casted plastic was used for the Ice-Storm installation at the MAK in Vienna as well as in the cable railway terminal shown here with the white cladding system that captures the organic elegance of the overall form.

ground floor for public activities in the spirit of the great early Modernists, yet more radical[28] – the result being a panorama of spaces that are exuberant, beautiful, elegant, generous and accessible for all.

Hadid's celebration of colour, rich materiality and dexterity of form attracts intense media attention and she seems to understand and accept the inevitability of her work being oversimplified by the press. 'There are journalists who want to describe my aesthetic by imposing an easily identifiable and recognisable image, and I feel that can work either way for my architecture,' she explains. 'I can't change their views and I think it has its pros and cons in terms of clients. The pros are that they understand a little of what you do; the cons are that they will want you to repeat yourself.' She continues: 'Right now, it seems there's a worldwide shift where most clients think that when they commission a piece of architecture, what they buy is the right to the architect's image and aesthetic.' Pausing to give a characteristically dry smile, Hadid concludes: 'Although the architect might think otherwise and pursue something completely brave and new.'

Interview
Hadid's studio, East London, 20 December 2006

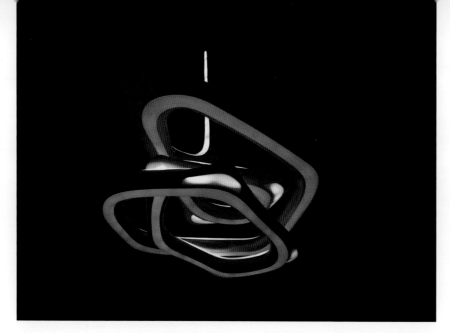

Notes

1. A limited-edition Aqua dining table for London manufacturers Established & Sons.

2. The Pritzker Prize ceremony took place in St Petersburg, Russia, in 2004 – by pure coincidence the city where Soviet artist Malevich lived and worked.

3. Her completed projects in Europe include a fire station for the Vitra Furniture company in Weil am Rhein, Germany (1993), Landesgartenschau, an exhibition building to mark the 1999 garden festival in the same city; the Hoenheim North car park and terminus on the outskirts of Strasbourg, France (2001); and a ski jump situated on the Bergisel Mountain overlooking Innsbruck in Austria (2002). In 2004, the year in which Hadid won the Pritzker Prize, she also had numerous other projects in various stages of development, including a building for BMW in Leipzig, and the Phaeno Science Center in Wolfsburg, both in Germany; a National Center of Contemporary Arts in Rome; a masterplan for Bilbao, Spain; a Guggenheim Museum for Taichung, Taiwan; a high-speed train station outside Naples; and a new public archive, library and sports centre in Montpellier, France.

4. The main Vitra factory building was designed by Nicholas Grimshaw (1954), the Design Museum by Frank Gehry (1989), the Fire Station by Hadid (1993), a conference pavilion by Tadao Ando (1993), and a design shop and additional factory building with a passage by Álvaro Siza (1994). A Buckminster Fuller dome of 1978–9 and a Jean Prouvé petrol station of 1953 were also salvaged, restored and installed on the site.

5. Including Peter Cook, Ron Heron, Jan Kaplický, John Frazer, Peter Wilson, Peter Salter, Christine Hawley, Bernard Tschumi, Nigel Coates, Elia Zenghelis, Rem Koolhaas, Raoul Bunschoten and Don Bates.

6. As a result of the Islamic tradition that forbids figurative drawings, Islamic calligraphy is an aspect of Islamic art that has coevolved alongside the Islamic religion and the Arabic language.

7. 'The series of seminars included one on Russian Constructivism by Elia Zenghelis, for first-year students, which I found particularly interesting.' Zaha Hadid, interview with Yael Reisner, 20 December 2006.

8. During the 1970s, Rem Koolhaas and Elia Zenghelis were interested in extending the Modernist project and were looking at the Russian avant-garde. Zenghelis was Koolhaas's teacher at the time, and the pair would later teach together in Hadid's fourth year.

9. Suprematism is the art movement formed in Russia in 1913 by Kazimir Malevich. Malevich created a Suprematist 'grammar' based on fundamental geometric forms – the square and the circle – that were introduced as superior forms. Though he did not train as an architect, he engaged with architectural concerns through his Alpha Architecton (1920) paintings and models known as 'Malevich's Tectonik'.

10. In which Hadid placed a hotel on the Hungerford Bridge on the River Thames, drawing from Suprematist forms to meet the demands of both programme and site.

11. Hadid began teaching at the AA in 1979 and was a Diploma Unit Master until 1987.

12. Including the Irish Prime Minister's Residence, Dublin (1980) and Parc de la Villette, Paris (1983).

13. Hadid's description of the project in *Zaha Hadid: The Complete Buildings and Projects,* Thames & Hudson, London, 1998, p 20.

14. In her urban projects, Hadid attempts to intensify the urban density horizontally, suspending slabs above ground, often to open the podium under the horizontal slabs or the vertical shafts for the public at street level. The strategy references the Suprematists but without their mysticism, fragmented spatial qualities, non-linear fields of forces, angular and fluid forms. Hadid 's formal repertoire in relation to the complexity of programme continues to expand.

15. Zaha Hadid, Interview with Alvin Boyarsky, then head of the Architectural Association, published in her exhibition catalogue, *Zaha Hadid, Planetary Architecture Two,* Architectural Association Publications, London, 1983.

16. Ivan Leonidov was part of the Suprematist movement and although he built very little, he was incredibly influential, his projects regarded as some of the greatest achievements of Suprematist architecture. His work extended the idea of an architecture composed of masses and lines into layers of spatial complexity in landscape, for example in the Lenin Institute, Moscow (1927), or in his competition projects such as the Sovkino Film Studios, Moscow (1927) or Tsentrosoiuz Building, Moscow (1928).

17. Hadid continues: 'In the early period the Russian avant-garde was more interested in composition. I think the idea of Modernism became more political and became more to do with generic Modernist projects, Functionalism and ideas of mass-production, repetition and exclusion. I think that these ideas became more clinical than in the early period, with architects such as Mart Stam and Bruno Taut, where the idea of colour and compositional value was critical.' Zaha Hadid, interview with Yael Reisner, 20 December 2006.

18. Most of Hadid's early architectural studies were done in acrylic colours on canvas utilising three-dimensional projective drawing techniques – the axonometric, isometric projections used by the Suprematists. However Hadid's would alter conventional methods by changing the projection angle to distort the perspective.

19. 'An atmosphere of total hostility, where looking forward has been, and still is, seen as almost criminal, makes one more adamant that there is only one way and that is to go forward along the path paved by the experiments of the early Modernists.' Zaha Hadid, Introduction 'The Eighty-Nine Degrees', in *Planetary Architecture Two*, op cit.

20. Hadid uses this term in relation to her visionary approach to architecture; how she envisages, contemplates and investigates future possibilities of new spatial organisation, new programmes and new architectural language, all of which emanated from her unique sketches and models and were captured in her architectural paintings that were presented in an utterly new and original way.

21. Non-architects generally struggle to read architectural drawings, but in Hadid's case her non-conventional and original technique means that even some architects, urban designers or town planners find her drawings difficult to follow.

22. During the 1970s the hostility came from those who believed in the 'social project' ideology as a source for generating projects. Later on, in the 1990s, hostility flowed from those who embraced Derrida's philosophy, followed by Deleuze's, where both were considered a valuable authority for initiating and generating architectural thought.

23. Patrik Schumacher, Hadid's collaborator since 1988, a director of Zaha Hadid Architects since 1999 and partner in the company since 2003, argues that Hadid's body of work on paper actually 'constitutes a form of research; an unorthodox research in as much as its methods include intuitive grouping, randomization. Hadid reconstitutes the functions of territorialization, enclosure and interfacing etc by means of boundaries, fields, planes, volumes, cuts, ribbons etc, the open-ended ness of the compositional configurations.' Patrik Schumacher, 'Mechanism of radical innovation', in the MAK (Vienna) exhibition catalogue *Zaha Hadid: Architecture,* MAK/Hatje Cantz, Vienna, 2003, pp 23–5.

24. Hadid recalls that as a young girl in Iraq she would watch local women walking in the marshlands wearing colourful dresses, and attributes her love of using exotic colour in her work to this experience.

25. A good demonstration of Hadid's consideration of light in her built work can be seen in the Landesgartenschau project, Weil am Rhein (1999), where the photographs of the building bear an uncanny resemblance to her perspective paintings. Hadid enjoys telling anecdotes of audiences in her lectures believing that the paintings she shows are actually the photos of her buildings; a little satisfaction after years of being misunderstood.

26. One can see this use of layered colour in the few built works of Hadid's early career, such as her six pieces of furniture for the 24 Cathcart Road Residence, London (1986) or bright, serpentine forms of the Monsoon Restaurant in Sapporo, Japan (1990). A particularly good example is her Swoosh Sofa, designed and produced for Cathcart Road in which the woven upholstery material, in white with black and green dots, gives the expression of diffused colours. Expression of colour was a direct output of Hadid's experimentation with colour in her elaborate studies and tests for her paintings.

27. Zaha Hadid, Interview with Alvin Boyarsky, in Zaha Hadid, *Planetary Architecture Two*, op cit, 1983.

28. Hadid has developed her own unique language to describe her radicalisation of early Modernism, which includes terms and phrases such as: 'programme mutations', 'structures as large-scale landscape relief', 'mirroring and settling into the land's contours', 'intensifying the urban density horizontally', 'suspending tension', 'fluidity of space', 'emancipating the wall from the floor', 'turning conceivable constraints into new possibilities for space', 'creating new metropolitan scenarios', 'celebrating dynamic possibilities of urban landscape by extending the public realm' and 'displaying new Suprematist geology'. Collection of quotes from *Zaha Hadid: The Complete Buildings and Projects*, Thames & Hudson, London,1988.

Odile Decq
BLACK AS A COUNTERPOINT

RENOWNED FOR THEIR PUNK AESTHETIC and their innovative 'diagnostic' approach to design, French architects Odile Decq and Benoît Cornette imprinted their position in the late 1980s as an influential part of the international architectural avant-garde. After meeting at the ages of 18 and 20 respectively, Decq studied architecture and urban design before establishing her own studio in 1980, while Cornette completed his medical degree before retraining as an architect. Together, they made a formidable team – one that resulted in early success when they won a national competition for their administrative and social buildings for the Banque Populaire de l'Ouest in Rennes, France, in 1990 – five years after establishing their collaborative studio.

The Banque Populaire de l'Ouest won 10 major awards, nationally and internationally, generating worldwide interest in their work. They continued to build at a great pace, with projects such as their social housing schemes for Paris (1995), a masterplan for Paris's Port de Gennevilliers industrial harbour and docks (1995–), a motorway operations centre and motorway bridge for Nanterre (1996), and culminating in their 1996 commission for the French Pavilion at the Venice Architecture Biennale where they were also awarded a Golden Lion for their collective architectural projects.[1]

OPPOSITE HYPER-TENSION, LE MAGASIN NATIONAL CENTRE OF CONTEMPORARY ART, GRENOBLE, FRANCE, 1989

The Hyper-Tension Installation at Grenoble eloquently captured the qualities of displacement, movement and tension that Decq and Cornette were exploring within their work. They were influenced by the work of artist Richard Serra – particularly his sculptures of the late 1980s and early 1990s – that explored and juxtaposed tension and balance.

Tragically, Cornette was killed in a car accident in 1998 while driving home to the couple's house in Brittany. Decq survived the accident and continues their visionary approach to architecture, expanding on their desire to reject the notion of neutrality in architecture and engage with the human and social context of design – a preoccupation that continues to drive her to the present day. Working out of her studio in central Paris, Decq balances a busy practice with being Head of the École Speciale d'Architecture.[2] Projects currently in progress include a contemporary art museum in Rome and an urban housing scheme in Florence, the Rolling Stones houses in Nanjing, office headquarters and a 'floating' restaurant for Archipel in Lyons, a sea passengers terminal in Tangier and offices in Rabat in Morocco, a large resort in Istanbul, and various exhibitions of her architectural and enigmatic 'black' art work.

Odile Decq and Benoît Cornette possessed a rebellious attitude to the inherent conservatism in French architectural, social and political circles. Beyond their architecture and conceptual framework, the couple expressed their radicalism through their personal appearance, engaging with a punk aesthetic and dressing continually in top-to-toe black. Decq appeared as the more radical of the pair, maintaining over-scaled black lioness locks with vibrant extension pieces in red and blue hues, portraying a dramatic and intense energy. In recent years her expression has evolved to take on 'Gothic' overtones with black lips, nails, hair and black, layered, garments.

Decq describes this outward aesthetic expression through clothes and appearance as a rejection of her oppressive Catholic heritage: 'Catholicism prohibited an emphasis on making things beautiful because beauty was seen as something superficial and not important. What was important was content.' She continues: 'Yet I was always interested in the question of appearance. So when I was only eight I learnt to sew and I was very good at it. It was during the time of the optical art movement and I would make something outrageous to wear to school and my parents were always reproaching me and saying that I was pushing things too far. So, I think these early battles marked the beginning of my fight for the appearance of things, and for the aesthetical way.'

Decq and Cornette advocated an 'open' design process
for this administrative and social centre where their
unique 'diagnostic' strategy – a term referenced from
Cornette's medical background – formed the starting
point of each project and supported their explorative
research and creative journey.

RIGHT BANQUE POPULAIRE DE L'OUEST, RENNES,
FRANCE, 1990

By reinterpreting Functionalism as a 'functional
performance', Decq and Cornette played with
qualities of spatial tension within their buildings.
Radically altering the conventional location of
architectural elements, they introduced new ways
of moving through spaces, and extended thresholds
to create ambiguous boundaries between the exterior
and interior.

While Decq rallied against her parents as a young woman, Cornette also battled a conservative family context. After meeting as 20- and 18-year-olds respectively, Cornette initially wanted to join Decq in studying architecture at the École des Beaux-Arts, but bowed to his father's pressure to study a more traditional profession. As Decq recalls: 'Benoît's father wanted to protect him from the unpredictability of the arts and so he compromised and agreed to do medicine. After passing his exams he did one year within a hospital and then decided "this is not my life; this is not what I want".'

After returning to study and completing his training in architecture, Cornette joined Decq in her Parisian studio and their combined expertise – Decq from a literary influence borne out of her initial studies, and Cornette from a scientific perspective – proved a potent combination and one that continued to drive their unique diagnostic approach to the design process.

While Decq is open to the role that aesthetics played within the early success of their collaborative practice, she maintains that process rather than form drives the work: 'Form was the last question that Benoît and I considered – it was always the result of the design process.[3] However, if the form was my first idea then we would still go through our process and, as a result, we usually ended up with a different form from the one I had first envisaged. So even if it started with a notion of form, the idea always evolved, changed and was open to experimentation.'

LEFT FRENCH PAVILION, VENICE ARCHITECTURE BIENNALE, VENICE, ITALY, 1996

As a reaction to the intellectualised systems, abstraction and literary conceptual ideas that dominated architectural discourse in Paris in the early 1980s, Decq and Cornette pursued a visual identity by capturing their intentions in models with no words. In the French Pavilion for the 1996 Venice Architecture Biennale they employed their signature aesthetic of 'darkness' and 'blackness' in juxtaposition with colour and light.

ABOVE MOTORWAY OPERATIONS CENTRE AND
MOTORWAY BRIDGE, NANTERRE, FRANCE, 1996

While Decq is open to the role that aesthetics played
within the early success of her and Cornette's
collaborative practice, she maintains that process drives
the work rather than form: 'Form was the last question
that Benoît and I considered – it was always the result
of the design process. However, if the form was my
first idea then we would still go through our process
and, as a result, we usually ended up with a different
form than the one I had first envisaged.'

BELOW ZENITH SAINT ÉTIENNE, SAINT ÉTIENNE,
FRANCE, 2005

Decq continued to explore the dark thematic with this
competition scheme for a concert hall in Saint Étienne.
The dark exterior marks a stark contrast to the brightly lit
glazed foyers, surrounded by an artificial landscape. The
wide, open concrete walkways wind alongside an
expanse of car parking lots, lit with scattered, flickering
points of light – much like stars within a darkened night.

Decq and Cornette believed in an open process of arriving at architecture through explorative research. They marked the starting point of their creative journey with a 'diagnosis' – a term from Cornette's medical background – that considered meaning within a particular context. Decq references her upbringing in Brittany to describe this constant search for meaning and compares it to sailing in the waters of Northern France: 'When I'm sailing, I can see that the horizon is far ahead and even though you're moving forward, it always lies in front of you. Of course, you can't move straight towards the horizon because of the wind so you have to negotiate and navigate through the sea. So there are different conditions and a process that you must manage to reach something, which is clearly seen, but which you never actually reach.' She continues: 'Benoît and I were always experiencing this notion of having a perspective and a focus but not moving directly towards it. We always followed an objective to keep moving. And to this day, my design process is about going somewhere, creating movement and never being static.'

This fundamental engagement with the concept of constant movement within space extended to studying the human body – a factor that proved a crucial design generator in their award-winning Banque Populaire de l'Ouest in Rennes: 'When Benoît and I designed the main hall of the bank we started to think about dynamic space and the way the body moves through it. Entering the building, the main wall confronts the visitor and forces the body to turn and start to move along the curve. So the space is organised to create an awareness of the body's movements.'

Although the project was immensely successful, Decq and Cornette's discussion of the body seemed out of step with their contemporaries of the time. Decq recalls: 'We were surrounded by architects who were concerned by intellectual discourse and any discussion of the body was not considered to be the purpose of architecture. Architecture was supposedly a question of abstraction, conceptual ideas and intellectual systems. Benoît was a doctor so we were really interested in the relationship of the body and architecture. Our projects investigated questions relating to the body: the broken arm, the skin, the flesh and the muscles. Although we were discussing this aspect, we were also reserved because it was too much for many people, and not the official language of architecture at the time.'

In 1989, Decq and Cornette exhibited a series of coloured models, entitled The Model is the Message, at Artemide's Parisian showroom with the intention of expressing their discontentment with architectural discourse in Paris at the time, which revolved around intellectualised systems, abstraction and conceptual ideas.[4] As Decq explains: 'We felt that if we reduced a model to express only one main idea, then it would force us to try to express the idea within a simpler framework – they were models without an intellectual explanation.' The models expressed the couple's preoccupation with the body and questioned Functionalism in France's architectural culture. Instead they introduced the concept of 'functional performance', creating spatial tension by introducing new ways of moving through their buildings, while creating ambiguous boundaries between exterior and interior.

ABOVE LEFT WALLY 143, FANO, ITALY, 2006

Referencing her native Brittany, Decq compares the constant search for meaning in architecture to sailing in the northern waters of France: 'The horizon ... is always in front of you and although you navigate towards it, you never actually reach it. It's a reminder that you must always follow an objective and keep moving.'

ABOVE RIGHT MACRO MUSEUM OF CONTEMPORARY ART, ROME, ITALY, 2001–

Decq and Cornette's work explored how the human body responds to a particular environment or dynamic space. After Cornette's death, Decq has continued to question these relationships as a commentary and investigation of the increasingly sedentary lifestyle within contemporary culture among both the poor and the affluent.

Decq's interest in the relationship between body, space and time was further encouraged by her friend and academic colleague Paul Virilio – an influential French philosopher – who acted as provocateur for many of their discussions on a wide range of subjects. Decq recalls Virilio's comments just prior to the Venice Architecture Biennale in 2000, where she was preparing the exhibition design for the French Pavilion: 'Virilio suggested that the question of the human body was disappearing for two main reasons. The first was because of social conditions – when people become increasingly poor they don't care about their body because their ambition is just to survive. And, conversely in the affluent world, where people are obsessed with technology, they don't care about their body either because they are immersed in a virtual world. So he suggested that the body is in danger and the architect's role must be to take care of the body.'

Decq uses everyday yet evocative analogies to describe the kinds of spaces she strives for within her work – she takes a sensorial rather than a cerebral approach and likens the question of ambiguity within her architecture to the pleasures of drinking whisky: 'I like it when you have to spend time to understand something – it's a question of ambiguity. It's much like drinking Scotch whisky. You smell it first and your imagination starts to work. Then you put the whisky in your mouth and the first shock on your tongue is spicy and strong – a little bit like an explosion with volume. Then you swallow and the sensation reveals an experience of many layers.'

She extends her analogies to cinematic references, drawing parallels between architecture and the moving image. She explains: 'When Benoît and I first saw *Pulp Fiction* we understood that it was a strategy that could be applied to architecture so that it could be

broken and much more informal.' She continues: 'The younger generation of architecture students are completely comfortable with moving images and non-linear narratives. When they think about the space within a film and the way that characters move between a series of changing spaces – jump, cut, etc – they understand that the construction is a series of non-linear operations and try to reinterpret these operations in their architecture. The traditional way of viewing architecture can change dramatically because we know if it's possible in a movie, then why is it not possible in reality?'

However, while film references influenced Decq and Cornette, they also looked to contemporary art as an avenue of provocation. 'We were very impressed and touched by Richard Serra's work and the elements of tension that he managed to organise as you pass inside his steel structures. Simply standing in front of his sculptures, we felt a great attraction.' Decq credits Serra's Clara-Clara work (1983), which was exhibited in the Square de Choisy, Paris, in 1988, as a pivotal influence[5] for their seminal Banque Populaire de l'Ouest: 'The main hall of that project was absolutely in reference to Serra's sculpture. We thought that if we played with creating tension between the two main walls and had a very high, narrow passage then we could induce people to experience the space differently.'

OPPOSITE RED LACE APARTMENTS AND COMMERCIAL
BUILDING, FLORENCE, ITALY, 2004–

Decq's preoccupation with human context within the
design process continues to drive her to the present
day. She embraces aesthetics and self-expression as
elements that contribute to the creation of a
pleasurable architectural experience.

The strategy was one the pair also employed for their renowned Hyper-Tension
installation in Grenoble (1993), which further explored the question of creating tension
between two walls within their work: 'Hyper–Tension allowed us to further explore this
idea. The tension is created by the space between two walls, the composition of the
compression of the space and the movement in-between. This is as in the electricity
between two opposite polls – fields of forces are created in between the two.'

This desire to create spatial tension is a thematic that Decq continues to explore in her
work, such as the Sensual Hyper-Tension installation at the Artists Space gallery in New
York (2004), which built upon the ideas of Hyper-Tension by introducing a sensorial
preoccupation. She describes the experience as one where you are organised to move
through the space in a similar way to Hyper–Tension, but you can fill your body with the
different senses, so that the experience is sensual rather than extreme. These qualities
of displacement, movement and tension have most recently been explored in her MACRO
Museum of Contemporary Art in Rome (2001–) where the design is generated by the
perception of the body through motion.

Decq does not believe in cultivating an expertise for a specific building type, preferring
instead the architect's great tradition of working in any scale that is required: urban
planning, commercial or civic buildings, housing, furniture, boats, or objects: 'I don't want
to be an expert in only one area such as designing museums or schools or restaurants;
my expertise is architecture, that's all! I don't like to be overly influenced by a specific
pole in architecture or you risk restraining your field of work.'

RIGHT RED LACE APARTMENTS AND COMMERCIAL
BUILDING, FLORENCE, ITALY, 2004–

Decq compares the question of ambiguity within her
architecture to the pleasures of drinking whisky: 'I like
it when you have to spend time to understand
something – it's a question of ambiguity. It's much like
drinking Scotch whisky. You smell it first and your
imagination starts to work. Then you put the whisky in
your mouth and the first shock on your tongue is spicy
and strong – a little bit like an explosion with volume.
Then you swallow and the sensation reveals an
experience of many layers.'

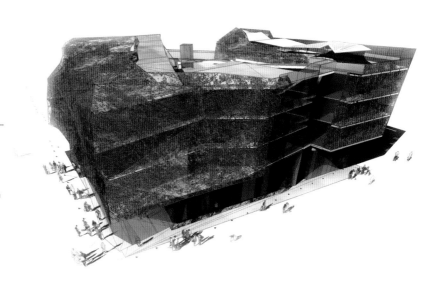

Fighting against 'neutrality' in architecture continues to be a passionate battle for Decq, who aligns the notion with the French values of morality, Catholicism and socialism. 'There is no neutral architecture',[6] she declares, insisting that form and aesthetics are an integral part of the architectural process. 'During the late 1990s, architects in France such as Lacaton and Vassal, were advocating the notion of neutrality claiming they were not interested in aesthetics or form. I remember a discussion with Anne Lacaton who suggested that the main difference between our approaches to architecture was that she didn't care about the form. I responded very strongly, saying "No! Because even if you simply draw a square or a rectangle, you still take care about the proportions and, therefore, you are still mindful of the aesthetic".'

'I think that the discussion of aesthetics within architecture is often equated with a question of moralisation. So if you want to escape this oppressive doctrine of moralisation then you have to be brave.' Decq recalls a discussion with Massimiliano Fuksas prior to him curating the Venice Architecture Biennale in 2000 that challenged the notion that aesthetics and ethics could not coexist: 'I said to him that he couldn't set the theme of "Less Aesthetics, More Ethics" because you can't disregard aesthetics completely.[7] It's just not possible because all human beings appreciate beauty – we are used to admiring, caring and being engaged by aesthetics in nature.' Expanding on this, Decq suggests that architects are often in denial of this basic reality of human nature: 'It's very strange the way that architects talk about beauty or aesthetics and I feel that it is an attitude of pretence – they pretend not to care about how things look. Yet as soon as they regulate proportions, then they are dealing with aesthetics.'

In recent years Decq has returned to art within her own work and as a passionate collector. She describes the thematic of 'black' as the collection's overarching provocation: 'When I began I decided to collect only black art. As I went on collecting I discovered that an artwork that falls within my "black" categorisation does not necessarily mean that it's all black in colour. It's something that evokes "black" – a subject, environment or a feeling. It is dark, strong and often violent in terms of its impact and never neutral.' She continues: 'I feel I have a dual aspiration within my work to create tension and violence and yet, at the same time, imbue spaces with a sense of kindness for the people using them.' The 'black' strategy helps Decq to reduce her process to its essence and eliminate any distraction: 'When you add colour to this dark environment, the colour is actually intensified and is seen at its maximum brightness; equally the addition of light or form becomes very intense and expresses strength. This is the sense of violence that I'm striving for.'

Returning to an earlier pivotal influence Decq is also a great admirer of Richard Serra's asphalt paintings: 'They are just geometrical two-dimensional forms on paper, but

because the material is asphalt it's never dry so the painting is in a process of very slow movement all of the time. The tension is not within space in this instance, but within the material itself, and the paper actually changes form because it contracts and retracts – they're incredibly beautiful.'

The ability to revel in the aesthetic value of art is clearly a freedom that Decq relishes, asking: 'What is beauty? It's subjective, personal and impossible to explain. So it's a very frightening notion for people who need to rationalise every part of their design process.' She remains unwavering in her belief in the aesthetic capacity of architecture and in the power of the architect to add value to people's everyday lives: 'Personally, I feel this is the role of an architect. So even if it's a very minimal project, then the architect has a duty to ensure it is well designed, organised and has an aesthetic value. I think we must offer people the opportunity to think beyond their current context and to be uplifted by something beautiful because without this, we are not really architects.'

Reflecting on her collective body of work – with Cornette and with her own practice – Decq is animated with her plans for the future: 'When I look back at the work Benoît and I did together, I feel that sometimes there were restrictions that we placed upon ourselves. And now, for the first time since I lost Benoît, I have started to discover that I am absolutely free. Because I don't have anything or anyone else, I've realised it's ok to push harder and explore the darker, more sensorial aspects of my work – the violence, seduction and beauty. So now I am committed to an exploration of this notion of "black" – it's what I feel is important to express and it holds many possibilities for the future.'

Interviews
ODBC office, Paris, 7 October 2005
International Design Symposium, University of Oslo, 4 December 2005

Notes

1. Decq and Cornette were also committed teachers both in Paris and at architectural schools internationally. They were both awarded the French Chevalier de l'Ordre des Arts et Lettres and Odile Decq is a Chevalier de la Légion d'Honneur.

2. Decq has been a Professor at the School of Architecture in Paris since 1992.

3. 'Space is no longer defined in terms of a laid-out plan, an elevation, or something that exists in parts; it is instead a coextension to elements which find an organization of their own, hence "form" in Decq and Cornette's terms is substituted by an extensive series of links ... Architecture becomes an act, creating and unfolding itself in the process of its use ... Using the form of a "diagnosis" which the architects arrive at after cutting into the meaning of the work and which exposes the decision-making behind the project ... a long process in order ... to radically displace the question of functionalism and arrive at a redefinition of elements that can articulate afresh all the traditional relations of architecture.' Frederic Migayrou, 'Preface' in Clare Melhuish, *Odile Decq, Benoît Cornette*, Phaidon Press, London, 1996, pp 4–5.

4. The Model is the Message provided provocative commentary within the architectural discourse at the time. However, it has since been supported through the research of Al Miller, a Professor of History and Philosophy of Science at University College London. Miller's research investigates scientific imagery and portrays how creative thinkers – particularly scientists and artists – see visual images first during the creative process prior to putting their concepts into writing or equations. Miller cites that Albert Einstein sketched diagrams prior to his scientific breakthrough: 'This masterstroke led to one of the most beautiful theories ever conceived of – the general theory of relativity, which Einstein completed in 1915.' Arthur I Miller, *Insights of Genius, Imagery and Creativity in Science and Art*, The MIT Press, Cambridge, Mass, 2000, p 314.

5. Serra's sculptural work of the late 1980s dealt with tension versus balance.

6. Decq has spoken out in various interviews against the notion of neutrality. She also references a meeting with city planners during the process of working on a small housing scheme in Paris: 'The planners asked me to design the building so that it was passed in the street, so it would not be perceived as being designed by an architect. It was the worst requirement I have ever received.' Odile Decq, interview with Yael Reisner, 7 October 2005.

7. 'Less Aesthetics, More Ethics' was the title theme of the Venice Architecture Biennale in 2000, curated by Massimiliano Fuksas. In his introduction to the exhibition's catalogue, Fuksas references the theme to Bruno Zevi, the Italian architectural historian.

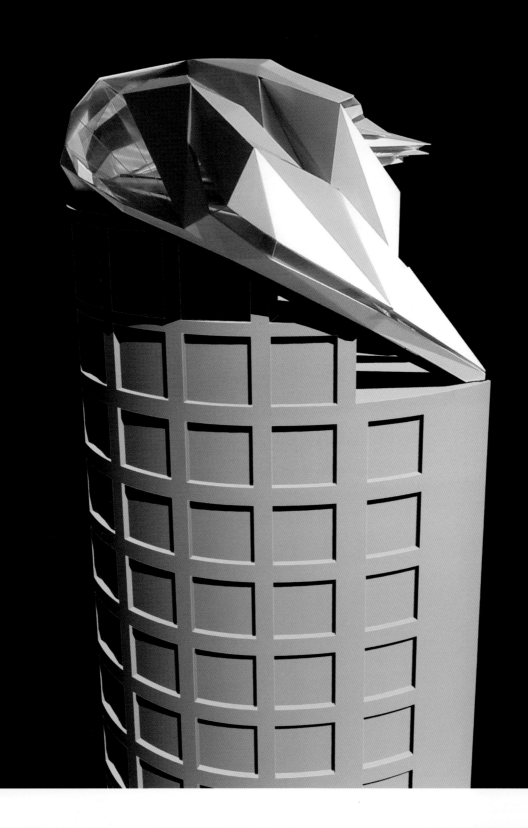

Mark Goulthorpe
INDIFFERENT BEAUTY

THE RISE OF A COMPUTATIONAL CULTURE WITHIN ARCHITECTURE and the diverse range of rapid prototyping technologies have enabled a prolific accumulation of projects created directly from computer models and translated into 3-D physical products. Simultaneously, this culture has resourced a sophisticated exploration of formal and industrial applications that are both economic and evocative, and of increasing public fascination through the dissemination of powerful and seductive architectural imagery produced by computer technologies.

The evolution of digital architecture gathered pace through the late 1990s and is now in a period of consolidation, firmly embraced by the architectural community and emerging beyond pure speculation as built reality all over the world. Further driven into mainstream consciousness by Frederic Migayrou's seminal exhibition 'Non-Standard Architecture'[1] at the Centre Pompidou in Paris in 2003, the much-lauded survey marked and highlighted the work of leading 'digital' protagonists such as Mark Goulthorpe of dECOi architects.

Goulthorpe, an Englishman in his early 40s, has worked and lived in London, New York, Malaysia and Paris, and is currently based in Boston, at the Massachusetts Institute of Technology (MIT) where he is Associate Professor in Advanced Digital Design. On first meeting, he appears bright, sharp and extremely well read, speaking quickly and almost whispering throughout conversations while maintaining a controlled and measured tone during his public lectures. He routinely uses evocative language when discussing his architecture,[2] and borrows terminology from the disciplines of philosophy, sociology, psychology and art history, which he creatively manipulates to explain his designs.

Goulthorpe initially came to international prominence through the beguiling imagery of the Pallas House project in Kuala Lumpur (1997), which was produced in collaboration with fellow architect, programmer and mathematician Bernard Cache.[3] Since this high-profile, collaborative project, Goulthorpe's methodology has evolved from a 'non-deterministic' to what he describes as a 'precisely indeterminate' process of working. Yet he does not merely engage with the semantics of these other disciplines to create his architecture; he genuinely collaborates with programmers, roboticists, mathematicians, architects and clients through an intense and rich generative computerised process that absorbs multiple influences and traces different threads throughout the work. The result is an unpredictable outcome that attempts to transcend any notion of 'signatory architecture', while still providing the architect with the opportunity to 'edit the output along the design process'. As Goulthorpe explains: 'The methodology for the Pallas House lay outside of any kind of determinate image-making and worked within the interior of architectural form and representation, emerging as a mathematical manner rather than through deployment of lines and points.'

There is no doubt in the creative and original nature of the research and subsequent projects produced by many leading architectural studios that employ digital processes and techniques. However, Goulthorpe's engagement, as expressed in his article on poetics in 'evolutionary architecture',[4] tests the notion of yielding 'poetic images'[5] within a procedural and rationalistic design process, but also exposes his doubts[6] about the potential of many digital processes to be 'poetic' in a Bachelardian sense.[7] As he succinctly sums up: 'dECOi deliberately develops multiple creative threads that weave into a final architectural form, frequently allowing the process to lead where it will, and to exceed, in some manner, our rational preconception ... Such images are then seemingly legitimised by Bachelard's *The Poetics of Space*.'[8]

Since the 1950s, architects seem to have struggled with the relationship of beauty and aesthetics to architectural discourse and the generation of ideas, and Mark Goulthorpe is no exception. 'The word "beauty" is a very difficult term to handle,' he says. 'Personally, the notion of beauty has resonated with me through the writings of philosophers such as Friedrich Nietzsche, whose book *The Birth of Tragedy* really moved me as a student for its breaching of formal aesthetics. Most recently, I've read Gianni Vattimo's *The Transparent Society* that describes the need for a new *social* aesthetic rather than a formal one, perhaps marking a closure of the breach.'

The terms 'social' and 'aesthetic' may sound contradictory, but Goulthorpe elaborates on the theme: 'Aesthetics has been a dirty word for architects throughout the 20th century, but in other fields, such as philosophy, Jürgen Habermas and Herbert Marcuse have continued the tradition by reframing aesthetics as a socially formative notion – as an act or an event that allows people to identify within a group rather than as simply the formal

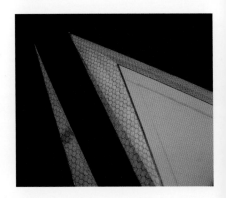

Goulthorpe affirms his belief that the end result of the parametric design process is one where there is no obvious connection to its content. He suggests: 'How do you talk about it? It's like a telegram or calligraphy – something that is just deployed on a rooftop, and it's just what it is.' He believes that content and form are fused, as his design work fuses structure with surface, formal expression, aesthetics and economical production to produce one design with a unified logic to support it.

Goulthorpe's introduction to programmer and mathematician Bernard Cache and the pair's subsequent collaboration on the Pallas House provided an essential underpinning to Goulthorpe's conceptual framework. As he explains: 'I saw that Cache was creating architecture that was entirely implicit through a mathematical process, all the way from inception to manufacture ... The pursuit of an internal interrogational process and an exploration of mathematically driven design is fascinated only with itself. There is no metaphoric or image-based logic.'

quality of something. A good example is the Paris Music Festival, where musicians are allowed to set up in the street for one night. Then the moment that the band begins to play, there is a flicker of judgement that goes round the ring, a momentary social cohesion. It seems like a trivial case study, but it's one where a group of people are clearly brought into a social collective by an artistic act. Evidently most aesthetics operate less explicitly, particularly within the "slow" realm of architecture, yet it's that social identity that seems to be the lure in a digital age.'

Returning to Vattimo's *The Transparent Society*, Goulthorpe suggests that the book describes and speculates what might constitute 'a contemporary social aesthetic that articulates the social cohesion offered by objects, clothes and images to create multiple identity within a digital global condition; an aesthetic not based on formal beauty'. He expands on this: 'How such social aesthetic translates into architecture is a difficult question given architecture's "formal" presence. To a certain extent, every town has a Frank Gehry or Norman Foster building, but I think architecture has the potential to create identity in a far subtler and complex way than the obvious representative bravado of these projects. The identity that develops in and around an architecture of process would unfold differently – it's slower.'

The notion of aesthetics being integrally linked with identity, and architecture's role within a cultural collective identity, intrigues Goulthorpe, who finds the architect's role within society increasingly difficult to reconcile: 'The other day someone said to me that the reason architects are under appreciated and are paid poorly is because of the fact that there's no proximity of the process of architecture to the consumption of the end result – the closer the process and consumption relationship, then the more immediate the result.' Recalling the devastation of 9/11 and the collapse of the World Trade Towers, he continues: 'Nobody realised the towers were important until they were destroyed. In fact, they were grudgingly tolerated, yet once they were destroyed it's amazing how powerful the sentiment is. I believe this is a fundamental form of identity. When the attack was described as "the greatest artwork of the 20th century", it was no glib commentary – it was an attack on the base cultural psyche.'

The pursuit of an internal, interrogational generative process and an exploration of mathematically driven design through interdisciplinary collaborations informs the output of Goulthorpe's work, which essentially strives for no 'style' and no characteristic form. In this respect, Goulthorpe's introduction to, and subsequent collaboration with, Bernard Cache on the Pallas House in Kuala Lumpur (1997) provided an essential underpinning to his creative conceptual framework: 'I'd been trying to create architecture through a process that somehow detached itself from any sense of style. Even though Western culture has drawn on construed known forms and images throughout history, it seemed insufficient to the complexity of our current cognition. When I met Cache I saw that he was creating architecture that was entirely implicit through a mathematical process, all the way from inception to manufacture, and I found his approach aesthetically resonant and conceptually sufficient to our time.'

However, while working with Cache on the project, Goulthorpe found himself confronted by his own sensitivity to resolution despite Cache's rejection of any discussion of 'eye judgement' or aesthetic value: 'We managed to tease out a very beautiful form for the Pallas House despite the fact that Cache doesn't have a sensibility for scale and nuance. He's a mathematician-programmer and he hesitates to make aesthetic judgements. Yet his system certainly woke me up to the fact that generative systems exceed my own ability and hold an incredible potential.'

Despite Goulthorpe's developing personal commitment to generative methodologies, the Pallas House challenged the architect's process when the aesthetic interpretation of the client was introduced into the equation. As Goulthorpe recalls: 'The Pallas House was a mathematically driven design that we worked through to give multiple formal options for the decorative screen. The client was Chinese, and the first time he saw the work, his reaction was: "I'm not going to live in the Koran!" He saw it as a form of Arabic calligraphy; more culturally specific than the abstract "arabesque" we'd imagined it as. So we reworked the mathematics and the motifs as several different "glyphics", to the point where he finally said: "Oh, they're dragons!"'

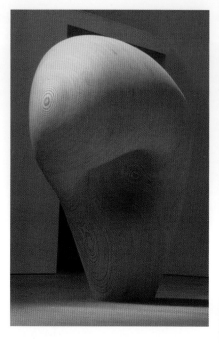

ABOVE IN THE SHADOW OF LEDOUX, GRENOBLE, FRANCE, 1993

Goulthorpe's design process is predominantly procedural and rationalistic although he also embraces a Bachelardian sense of the poetic. He states: 'At dECOi we deliberately develop multiple creative threads that weave into a final architectural form, frequently allowing the process to lead where it will to exceed ... our rational preconception.'

RIGHT AEGIS HYPOSURFACE, HYPO KIDS 1, 2000

Goulthorpe's dynamic interactive installation is an interpretation of Gianni Vattimo's 'social aesthetic' at work; a phenomenon Goulthorpe aspires to bring into his architecture.

The client's instinctive reaction reminded the architects of a description by Viennese-born Ernst Gombrich of the 'dragon force'[9] – a term used by Swedish sinologist Bernhard Karlgren to describe the numinous power of ancient Chinese vessels and their elaborate surfaces, in which hundreds of motifs engender a vertiginous effect. 'The client loved the reference and it became very personal, consolidating his minority identity in Malaysia,' Goulthorpe explains. 'The analogy was suggestive of the possibility of non-representative yet associative cultural memory – a kind of algorithmic equivalent notion to the search for the emperor's new clothes.'

Since completion of the Pallas House, Goulthorpe's position has consolidated to pursue a line of research that he describes as 'investigating how one creates a form with sufficient internal intensity that is left in space with cultural resonance'. He explains further: 'It's certainly not in the image of previous architecture; it's an interrogation and re-interrogation of itself, its internal logic, and you look to put it out in space with the hope that it attains a charged material intensity. It doesn't attempt to communicate in any way beyond a fascination with and in itself – and one hopes that, in its moment, this may produce identity, if not a sense of community. It's not a formal beauty that I'm particularly looking for, although we work very hard to achieve a certain level of formal resolution, to attain a conviction of form. Indeed, I'm convinced that many people would look at certain examples of our "art" objects and say they're ugly. Yet, most interesting is the fact that beauty *is* ugly – the first moment of the beautiful.'

While the singular pursuit of beauty or formal aestheticism holds no interest for Goulthorpe, he agrees that the advent of computer technology has allowed spatial complexity to become increasingly economical. However, he does not seek to exploit this potential per se. Instead his strategy is to challenge existing systems of construction as an industrial collage to further examine the relationship between form and content. He explains: 'A drastic separation of things from each other has occurred in the Modern era, sponsored by the "specialism" of industrial processes, like the separation of structure and surface. So, for example, you separate columns from cladding, mullion from wall, railing from stair. Architecture is separated into its industrially produced components, as a literal collage of pre-made things, and I think that has probably instigated notions of separation within architecture.'

Warming to the topic, Goulthorpe describes the rationale for what he terms a 'new Minimalism' within his work: 'As you begin to deploy these digital, seamless, technologies, what seems to be happening is a fusion of things like structure and surface. Certainly all of our work refolds one thing back within another – the surface becomes the structure, which becomes the formal expression, which becomes the aesthetic. Form and content seem to be fused once again.'

Intriguingly, Goulthorpe peppers his discussion with references to other creative disciplines rather than embedding his references firmly within an architectural framework. However, unlike many of his contemporaries, he deflects a direct analogy between architects and film directors, stating his distrust of the 'director' as someone who is all-powerful and directive, who *determines* form. He expands on this theme: 'I don't think it's an accident that I'm looking at people practising in the kinetic arts – ballet and music, for example. I think that they're ahead of architecture in terms of using and understanding current "technology". In the early 1990s a few composers and choreographers were quick to thoroughly explore what the notion of computation could do for music, and now you're beginning to see the first really profound works from that generation. Within architecture, I think we're still exploring what can be done in a very limited way.'

In the context of dECOi's work, Goulthorpe believes that most of the practice's projects are singular experiments in design fabrication; for example, the Miran Galerie, which was a singular process of milling plywood, and the Glaphyros House, an experiment in plastically redefining elements (both Paris, 2003). 'I'm looking forward to the moment

OPPOSITE AEGIS HYPOSURFACE, HYPO INTERIOR, 2000

The Aegis installation was originally installed in the foyer of the Birmingham Hippodrome Theatre where it worked as a mechanical surface, activated by the presence of human movement via parametric software. Its inclusion in the 2000 Venice Architecture Biennale resulted in the project becoming Goulthorpe's most high-profile work.

when one can deploy a compounded range of techniques that make it possible to create an architecture that is equivalent to the "traumatic" complexity of the art forms emerging in other domains,' he explains. Indeed, he credits American dancer and choreographer Bill Forsythe[10] as one the most resonant and recurring influences on his work: 'Forsythe's no longer the person that controls movement. He's instigated the intellectual environment, the generative rules, on which the performance is based. With the dancers' bodies algorithmically calculating real-time on stage, the result is a bewildering intensity often exquisitely beautiful in its breaching of an art form. I feel that dECOi's projects are striving to work in a similar way, via the expanded formal possibilities of generative rule-sets.'[11]

Forsythe certainly influenced dECOi's most high-profile and acclaimed project to date – the Aegis[12] Hyposurface interactive wall installation exhibited at the Venice Architecture Biennale in 2000, in which a mechanical surface is activated by the presence of human movement via parametric software. 'Forsythe is working parametrically by setting processes in motion and inviting the company to rearticulate them. The Hyposurface is the extension of that ideology, unfolding continually as *and* in an aesthetic, a social "aegis,"' says Goulthorpe. 'Personally, following this project through has been fascinating for a glimpse of social mirroring. Mechanically, it's a grotesque machine, but that's what I love about it. It's so visceral and dumb physically, but the fascination was putting its mechanical power out in the public arena. To hope for a literally malleable or "alloplastic" reciprocity of people and form was really quite a daunting thing. Yet I imagine that there are few architects who have ever witnessed such an immediate engagement and interactive response with their work, literally a real-time mirror for people. Here, the public *were* the work. The experience took me right back to thinking about the early relationships I had with clients that motivated my desire for a parametric search.'[13]

Undoubtedly, Goulthorpe's parametric methodology developed over time through the pivotal influences of Cache, Mark Burry[14] and Forsythe,[15] in addition to the recognition that the position of the architect is politically unpalatable to most clients: 'It seems to me that everybody is so well informed in a digital age that most clients feel they are aesthetic experts. So if you presume to determine their environment they'll tolerate the process for the first few weeks of sketch design but inevitably you get into a debate and struggle. I could recognise the vulgarity of the architect's position and yet I couldn't escape it because I was within it. That discomfort was the first motivation to try to generate things through parameters that explained and allowed some client involvement in the generative process, with flexibility in the shared aesthetic output.'

To illustrate his methodology, Goulthorpe recalls an experience with a particularly difficult yet architecturally literate client, and the successful deployment of a parametric generative strategy: 'We created a rule-based distorted box and we embedded parameters to allow it to be differentially distorted. It offered the potential for a plastic definition of space where the client felt part of the emergent aesthetic. It seemed a significant shift to a rule-based generative process that could be shared, yet it breached the inherited assumptions of architect as simple form-giver. It was remarkable to witness the client's softening attitude, and it told me that if the aesthetic is imposed, then it is resisted, but if people are participating in the formative process, then the result might be quite different.'

Goulthorpe adamantly refutes the notion that his parametric methodology could be viewed as manipulating the client to believe they have an engagement with the design when in reality they have little control through the process. He argues: 'The 20th-century example of the egotistical, precocious, client-architect relationship is a very curious one and a reality that I find unhealthy. If you look back through all the canonical Modernists' houses there's a kind of acid capriciousness that's embedded in the notion of the signatory architect. One of my students, Brenda Galvez, said that you couldn't make love in Le Corbusier's Heidi Weber House because it's an icon to a man's intellect! I thought that was just a fantastic and insightful comment.'

Returning to the difficult topic of aesthetics, Goulthorpe declares: 'I really don't give a damn about the look of the thing itself, but I think there's a beauty that comes from a coherence found in an internal system which you recognise as it emerges. That's what I find interesting.' Yet he does concede that he hopes his architecture 'is an expression of its moment and the processes of "now" and that it creates some kind of identity through a community of people who find the result aesthetically current. I'm not trying to surrender the notion of "aesthetic";[16] I'm actively pursuing it through setting up a generative system that is sufficiently rich that it can absorb multiple influences. It's definitely my goal to involve a wider "community" in the aesthetic act, such as client, engineers and fabricators in each project. I love getting a mathematician or a programmer involved in the development of an aesthetic because it exceeds my own ability.'

Interviews
myhotel café Bloomsbury, London, 19 February 2004
myhotel café Bloomsbury, London, 11 September 2005

Notes

1. 'Non-Standard Architectures', Centre Pompidou, Paris, France, 10 December 2003 to 1 March 2004. The exhibition questioned a new typology of industrialisation within architecture based on non-standard procedures and tools, which allowed for serial and singular production. It took its name from non-standard mathematics and advocated a re-engagement with material and industrial logics of production that accompany and redefine form-making processes. The exhibition confronted non-standardisation to the Modernist notions of type and standard in order to place contemporary digital production in a historical continuity. See www.cnac-gp.fr.

2. Examples of Goulthorpe's evocative language include: 'voluptuous inscrutability', 'imaginary dementia' and 'indifferent beauty', or phrases like: 'emergent forms that slide expansively in/out of the curvaceous yet inexpressive void'. See Mark Goulthorpe, 'Notes on Digital Nesting: A Poetics of Evolutionary Form', *AD Poetics in Architecture*, March/April 2002, p 19.

3. Bernard Cache and Patrick Beauce [Objectile] fight against an author's status for architects. Their position is that the architect is an intellectual worker whose mode of production is increasingly governed by digital technologies. Hostile to random, fluid, moving or virtual architecture, and to all approaches that perpetuate the age-old myth of the architect-artist. 'Liberty in chains', *L'Architecture d'Aujourd'hui*, 349 , Nov/Dec 2003, p 96.

4. 'Evolutionary architecture' is a term coined by John Frazer, the forefather of the evolutionary design process, who was at the Architectural Association in London from the early 1970s to the mid-1990s. Frazer applied the computerised simulation of the evolutionary process to the architectural design process – a well-established technique in biology – using computer programmes known as 'genetic algorithms'. Mark Goulthorpe, 'Notes on Digital Nesting: A Poetics of Evolutionary Form', *AD Poetics in Architecture*, March/April 2002.

5. 'The poetic image is a sudden salience on the surface of the psyche.' Gaston Bachelard, 'Introduction', in *The Poetics of Space*, Beacon Press, Boston, Mass, 1958, 1994, p xv.

6. This reminds one of the historical 'perception' battles between the Romantics and the Enlightenment philosophers in the 18th century who believed in the individual's personal significance. However, the Romantics blamed the philosophers for separating people from their feelings, and for crushing their spontaneity and individuality in order to fit all life into a mechanical framework. See Marvin Perry, *An Intellectual History of Modern Europe*, Houghton Mifflin Company, Boston, 1993, p 174.

7. 'If we were to follow Bachelard precisely, we would talk not of forms but of images, the Poetics focusing on the effect of a poem rather than its specific form, for which he uses, carefully, the term 'image'. It is not just the emergence of an image, but its capacity to exert an influence on other minds, that captivates Bachelard as the essential cultural moment.' Mark Goulthorpe, in *AD Poetics in Architecture*, op cit, p 19.

8. Ibid, p 20.

9. Ernst Gombrich, 'The edge of chaos', in *The Sense of Order, A Study in the Psychology of Decorative Art*, Phaidon, Oxford, 1979, 2nd edn 1984, p 262.

10. American William Forsythe is recognised as one of the world's foremost choreographers. His reputation was developed through his work with the Frankfurt Ballet, which closed in 2004. Since then he has established an independent ensemble, the Forsythe Company, based in Dresden and Frankfurt am Main.

11. Goulthorpe's design preoccupation includes the ambition to get an immediate response to architecture; speeding up the collective social identity that develops around architecture which to date has been a relatively slow process.

12. In Greek mythology, the aegis is the shield of Zeus or Athena.

13. 'For technological change becomes interesting only insofar as it infiltrates cultural psychology and suggests new patterns of behaviour and expectation.' Mark Goulthorpe, 'Misericord to a Grotesque Reification', *AD Architecture + Animation*, Vol 71, No 2, March/April 2001, p 57.

14. Mark Burry is Innovation Professor at the Spatial Information Architecture Laboratory (SIAL) at RMIT University, Melbourne, Australia. He has published internationally on two main themes: the life and work of the architect Antonio Gaudi, and putting design theory into practice, especially in terms of construction and the use of computers.

15. However, as with many digital architects, Goulthorpe's work also takes inspiration from the precedent set by the architect John Frazer. See note 4.

16. 'You set up a system of rules that are highly tuned but do not determine the form. I'm not sitting, drawing it and fixing it. I'm letting the system run, I'm watching it and then I'm inviting the client to participate in that process so that between the mathematician, the client and myself we select something.' Mark Goulthorpe, interview with Yael Reisner, September 2005.

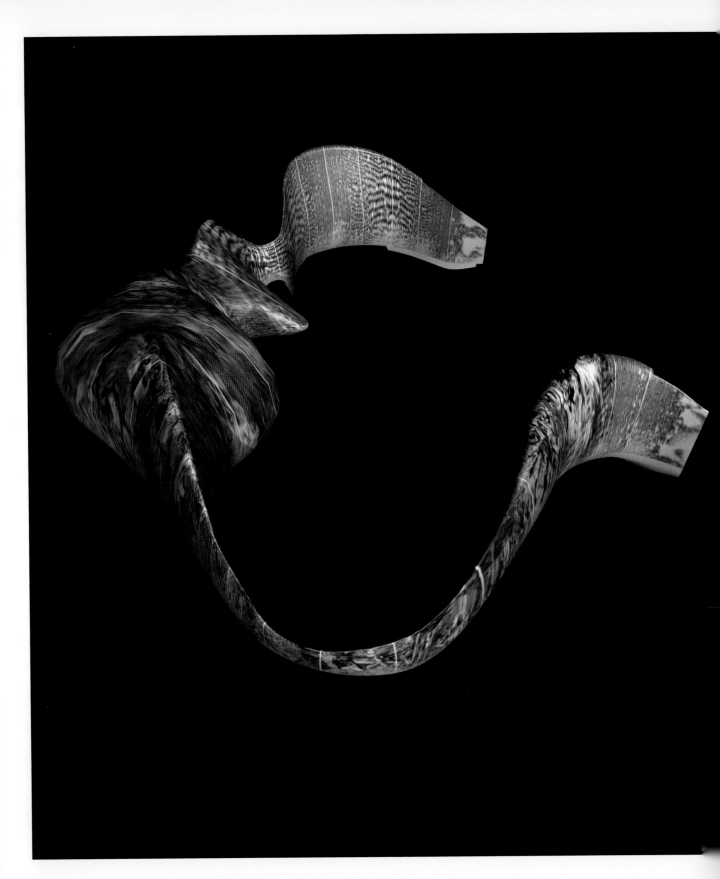

Greg Lynn
TECHNIQUE, LANGUAGE AND FORM

TRANSCENDING THE BOUNDARIES OF ARCHITECTURE, PHILOSOPHY AND MATHEMATICS, American architect Greg Lynn is one of the pioneers in computational technique to generate form. He expertly combines the fundamental principles of calculus with the intellectual philosophical theories of Gilles Deleuze, Gottfried Leibniz and Henri Bergson. By referencing philosophical and mathematical terminology Lynn has developed a unique architectural vocabulary[1] that describes his aesthetic ambitions and rejects any notion that his design process is generated by 'lateral thinking' or the quality of the architect's 'eye'.

With a friendly and patient persona, Lynn articulates his intellectual approach to design and architecture with depth while simultaneously using clear and accessible language. It is this investment in generative ideas and language that Lynn has pursued through his work as a respected writer and educator at Columbia University in New York, and currently at the University of California, Los Angeles (UCLA) and the University of Applied Arts, Vienna.[2] His texts include a commissioned issue of *AD* magazine: *Folding in Architecture* (1993, 2004), his first book *Folds, Bodies & Blobs: Collected Essays* (1998) and *Animate Form* (1999).

The wide publication and success of Lynn's writings coupled with his early competition entries and speculative projects rapidly propelled him to prominence within the international design community. He was also one of the first architects to invest in his own computer numerically controlled (CNC) routers and laser-cutters as well as rapid prototyping technology and 3-D printers that allowed him to continuously experiment with software that could translate complex computer drawings into manufactured

OPPOSITE THE PREDATOR (WITH FABIAN MARCACCIO), WEXNER CENTER FOR THE ARTS, COLUMBUS, OHIO, USA, 1999

The Predator was a digital painting printed and formed onto a free standing three-dimensional plastic panel structure; a result of a three-year collaboration with the New York-based Argentinean painter Fabian Marcaccio. It was a key project for Lynn. As he says: 'My research of decoration, detail and surface were all launched with the Predator.'

models. This progressive strategy fuelled Lynn's ambition to move beyond abstraction and grasp the opportunity of digital material production that quickly marked his importance as an architectural visionary.

After studying philosophy and architecture concurrently at Miami University in Ohio,[3] Greg Lynn graduated with honours and went on to complete a Masters of Architecture at Princeton University in New Jersey. In 1988, he went to work for Peter Eisenman in New York and recalls being attracted by the luminary architect's cerebral approach and lack of reliance on intuition within the design process: 'I went to work for Eisenman because I believed that I'd finally found someone who was using systems to generate architecture and not being subjective.' It was also within Eisenman's office – the most influential

For the Predator, Lynn continuously experimented with translating computational drawings, through software, into manufactured models, and quickly recognised the importance of investing in rapid prototyping machines within his office to further investigate this process. As a result, his concept of 'surface' developed into the notion of modulated 'skin' as a relief surface, as in an animal's skin where the pattern and relief are intricate with the form.

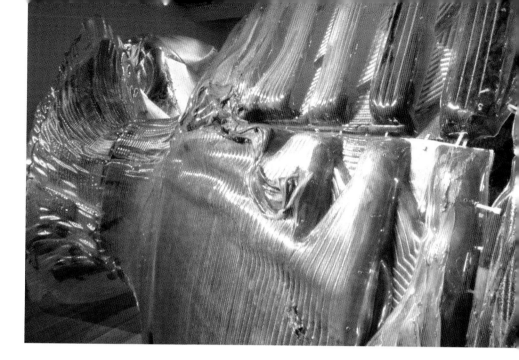

ABOVE THE PREDATOR (WITH FABIAN MARCACCIO), WEXNER CENTER FOR THE ARTS, COLUMBUS, OHIO, USA, 1999

Lynn recalls a key reference for the project: 'The Schwarzenegger film Predator was an inspiration for the project because the geometry of the lenses and the geometry of the jungle mingle with each other and produce an amazing effect. Fabian agreed, saying: "I saw it and I've been all jungle paintings since." So, by coincidence, we both were recognising this look and reproducing it in our work separately.'

practice in New York at the time – that the young architect extended his knowledge of the theories of French philosopher Gilles Deleuze and mastered their application within an architectural context.

Much like the relationship between father and son, Lynn initially shared many of Eisenman's opinions, but quickly grew to aspire to a different architectural agenda. Striking out on his own, as Greg Lynn FORM, in 1992, marked his deliberate attempt to delineate his work from his mentor and to develop his own conceptual and aesthetic language. As he explains: 'Eisenman has a problem with aesthetics – you can see it in how he dresses and how he builds. He doesn't indulge his aesthetic sensibilities. He's uncomfortable with anything except abstraction so he builds out of cardboard.' However, while Lynn has gone on to pursue a starkly different agenda, the architects maintain a close and mutually respectful relationship with Lynn quick to credit Eisenman as an important influence on shaping his theoretical position: 'In terms of form, Eisenman's desire to produce a new kind of expression by looking at new ways of designing and new tools is something I have always found inspiring.'

Lynn's progression through Eisenman's office exposed him to new ways of expressing architectural ideas and clearly influenced the development of his cross-disciplinary terminology – derived, in Lynn's case, from the fundamental principles of differential geometry and topology[4] with customised philosophical references for design strategies[5] – creating a resonant language to describe his computational preferences for continuity as expressed in his form-making. As Lynn expands: 'For example, the notion of "intricacy"[6] is ultimately just like "folding" or any of these other terms I've been

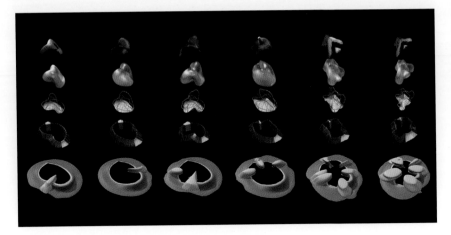

interested in for some time – it's a philosophical result of the invention of calculus, it comes out of physical tools and models[7] and from a 300-year-old tradition of thinking about the relationship of things in a calculus world rather than in a reducible world of pure forms. Aesthetically, the language also hooks up with all these predilections I've had for curvaceous forms since I was a student.'

Indeed, Lynn recalls being engaged by spatial soft curvatures early on in his student days: 'One of the reasons I went to Princeton to study architecture is that I had been inspired by the publication of the work of the New York Five architects.[8] I took Michael Graves's studio just so that I could ask him to describe to me how to build these compound curves. He looked at how I was trying to draw the complex geometries and said: "This is ridiculous – but if you're going to do it, let me show you how to do it rigorously," and I vividly remember him describing his technique over the afternoon.'

While Lynn felt he lacked an intuitive ability to draw the forms he desired by hand, the increasing sophistication of computer technologies enabled the young architect to move beyond a dependency on an Expressionist sensibility and develop his trademark 'calculus sensibility':[9] 'I just gravitated towards the computer because it gave me the power to have an intuitive understanding of calculus which I didn't have without it, and therefore enabled me to work with curves as a completely rigorous[10] ordering system.' He continues: 'The more I understood the principles of the mathematics – the calculus behind these complex curved shapes – the more I understood the medium of the computer. Then I began to understand how you could make the shapes and produce them through the medium of a mill or a stereolithography machine and, therefore, translate the mathematics into

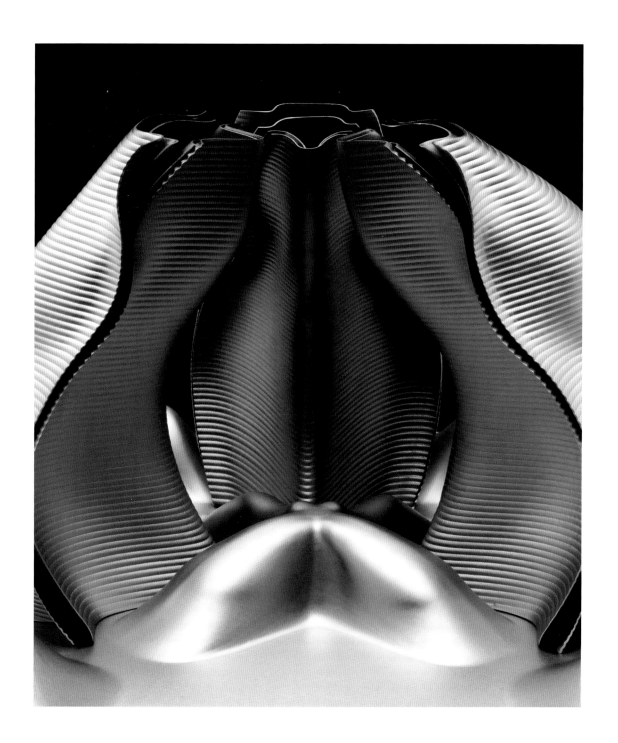

construction. So through this process I could see that I was drawing a line and anticipating the consequences in a way that I felt was intuitive in the Bergson sense.'[11]

Lynn references the English philosopher Henri Bergson's definition of 'intuition' as a seminal text (see 'Intuition as Method' in Gilles Deleuze, *Bergsonism*, trans Hugh Tomlinson and Barbara Habberjam, Zone Books (New York), 1991) in refining his pursuit of technique within his work: 'The students I respected when I was in college were the ones with the best technique. So I would always gravitate towards the student who could draw beautifully, rather than a student who didn't have skills, but had strong opinions. I wanted to be skilled and to have technique first, believing that through technique I could progress.' He expands: 'I also studied philosophy and I recall reading Bergson's text which basically says, "intuition is when you have a technique and you can envision the evolution of that technique at another level, and intuition is seeing that kind of extrapolation of something into the future before you've mastered it." This seemed to say it all and greatly resonated for me.'

Lynn's Predator installation,[12] a three-dimensional physically spatial painting first exhibited in the Wexner Center for the Arts, Columbus, Ohio, in 1999, was a significant project that was an important prelude to his following body of work. As he describes: 'My research of decoration, detail and surface were all really launched in the Predator. The project's surface texture,[13] the relationship of the image mapping the shapes, the way that it supports itself as a shell and the sculptural quality of it as a surface were all ideas first explored in this project.'

For small-scale products such as this, Lynn attempts to derive a distilled image of his formal preoccupations: 'It really is what you believe in and what you value. Frank Gehry produced his cardboard furniture and the world understood that he was a person working with new forms and off-the-shelf materials in a fresh and unconventional way – and those qualities were embodied in the products in a more visible and distilled way than were later expressed in his buildings.'

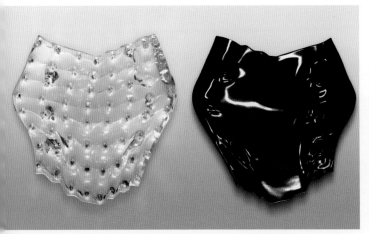

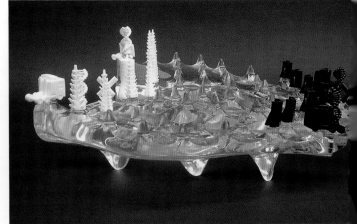

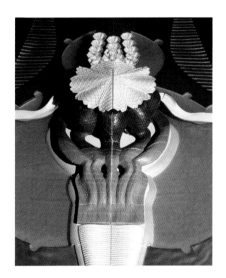

The project instigated Lynn's research around the notion of intricacy[14] that was to shape and influence his design process and aesthetic discourse: 'We bought this mill to make the Predator, and it was really noisy and dusty. It was going from modelling on a computer, tooling it, physically painting it, then digitising the result – a continual process of back and forth, and that's how we figured out the concept. It was after working on the Predator that I started to write the *Intricacy* text.' [15]

Along with his eloquent words, the imagery Lynn produces to describe his work is provocative and seductive. However, unlike many of his digital contemporaries he resists a preoccupation with image making: 'I was never interested in using the computer to make pictures. I was more interested in its mathematics and form. I could see that architects such as Office dA[16] and Bernard Cache[17] were all producing decorative or tectonic effects with computational processes and so – although influenced by their work – I decided to take a different perspective and think about the problem of the detail and the surface, with the details integral to the surface such as windows and apertures.' Lynn expands: 'I decided that if the details were derived from outside the logic of the geometry, it had the potential to be a problem, and so I felt it was important to have all of the parts in communication with one another – as a kind of biological model of holism.'

While Lynn continued to refine his ideas, he became increasingly frustrated with his inability to find an appropriate language that described the architectural qualities of the synthesised environments he was pursuing: 'This was before I had developed the term "intricacy", but as I started to think about how you could describe these qualities, I began to develop a new language, to describe my process.'

Certainly Lynn's natural inclination is to conceptualise and make rigorous and reproducible his design concepts via language in order to evolve and expand the influence of his design techniques. A glance at his website reveals that his projects are categorised in terms of their formal, architectural characteristics or embodied technique: 'lattice', 'branch', 'strand', 'skin', 'shred', 'fold', 'blob', 'bleb', 'flower' and so on[18] are all figurative metaphors that are descriptive, accessible and evoke powerful imagery and associations – a strategy that supports Lynn's ambition to communicate beyond the design community to a wider public arena.[19]

As also evidenced in the Predator project, Lynn's work includes mainstream references along with more complex ideologies and a high-end aesthetic discourse in order to reach the wider community: 'I would never start the design process from popular culture, but the fact that you can start from these authority disciplines, like philosophy and geometry, which have a special place in architecture but then lead them, through to a popular audience basically so that someone can connect with the idea is very appealing. For me, it's all one thing; I really don't make those distinctions.'

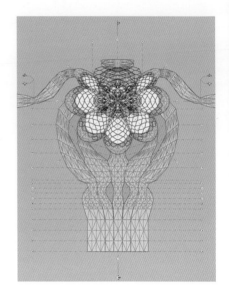

Lynn takes a different point of view from the 'anti-subjectivity' inherent among many 'digital' architects. 'I see computer-aided design tools as well as digital fabrication techniques as a medium rather than as a pseudo-scientific method of optimisation of material or structure, or as a proof of some optimal functional or contextual solution ... It's a new medium, not for expression per se, but for design and an extension of design thinking.'

ABOVE SOCIOPOLIS APARTMENTS, PHASE 1,
VALENCIA, SPAIN, DUE FOR COMPLETION 2009

The early design phase of the Sociopolis project revealed Lynn's exploration of the concept of 'nearly symmetrical', as explored in the Ark of the World museum project for Costa Rica.

Lynn's desire to identify with local, popular culture is underwritten by his engagement with California's preoccupation with the ocean: 'Where I live all my friends and their kids surf. So I decided: "OK, I can ride a skateboard and ski, so I can learn how to surf." But after I'd been doing it for a while, I was still really struggling. An architect friend who works in Gehry's office explained to me that the hardest part was mastering the paddling technique so that you can actually catch the waves. So he described the wave to me in terms of architectural spline modelling, and once I had that concept I was suddenly surfing. It was a great joke, but the reality was that once I had connected with surfing as a surface-modelling problem, then I could do it.'

The notion of 'symmetry' also forms a cornerstone of Lynn's research – a preoccupation that was initially borne out of a rebellion against the unspoken taboo among avant-garde architects of using symmetrical forms, and then further expanded with reference to Deleuzian theory and Lynn's burgeoning interest in the work of geneticist William Bateson[20] through the development of the Embryological House (1997–2001). As Lynn recalls: 'I showed the Embryological project at a conference and explained Bateson's theory of symmetry with variations. I said that even though it might seem scandalous, it's important to see that they all start out symmetrical and they follow the rules of symmetry breaking. Yet for me, what was beautiful about them is that some had a quality of being nearly symmetrical – where you would look at them and they'd look symmetrical, but then you'd look at them more and you'd see that they weren't really symmetrical – and so I was convinced this was a quality that I wanted to flirt with.'[21]

Responding to the relationship between aesthetics, form and content within his work, Lynn declares: 'Aesthetics are not an overarching preoccupation within my work, but integral to the concept of "intricacy" is the relationship between detail and surface. It's a relationship made up of parts and a whole, where you see an array of parts that make a volume so that you get this kind of hierarchy of scale that merges with a geometry – I feel that the combination of these things produces beautiful work.'

Characteristically, Lynn becomes more animated as he describes a personalised strategy: 'I could also take a more systematic approach and outline the 10 things you need for beauty and, in my opinion, they are pretty consistent: voluptuous curvature and surface, modulation of detail and components across the surface, a scale shift of a large interior out of components, or a large scheme out of components or gradient colour. I can see these elements in many disciplines such as architecture, automobile design and others. However, they are all qualitative effects that make things beautiful and I don't think it's totally subjective – I believe there is an inherent aesthetic that an audience understands.'

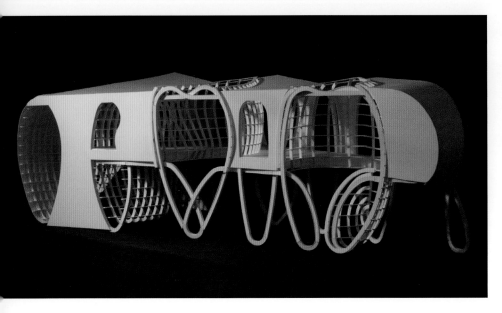

Greg Lynn shares a preoccupation with Frank Gehry, Thom Mayne and Eric Owen Moss to include traces of the old along with the new, as he reveals when describing the Slavin House process: 'It started off as an addition to a bungalow. Zaha Hadid was visiting my office at the time and she said to me: "It's ridiculous, tear the house down." I responded: "What's the matter, I'm really fond of it." She came to look at the site and said: "It's a sweet house, but you've got to tear it down!"'

Lynn also takes a different point of view from the 'anti-subjectivity' inherent within digital discourse,[22] believing that computational processes offer more than simply a logical, rational procedure: 'I see computer-aided design tools as well as digital fabrication techniques as a medium rather than as a pseudo-scientific method of optimisation of material or structure, or as a proof of some optimal functional or contextual solution.' Expanding, he explains: 'Now I understand that there is a new medium, not for expression per se, but for design. I feel that the digital tools are an extension of design thinking in the same way that I thought, and still think, of drafting tools and hand-built models. It is not a set of tools or proofs, but a design medium that has changed and expanded in the last couple of decades to include new media as well as new thoughts about context, form, repetition and structure to name a few architectural issues.'

While resisting the idea of an overarching 'style', Lynn does accept that there is an inherent signature that marks his work: 'Now that I'm 15 or 20 years out of school, I can for the first time start to imagine having a signature. That doesn't mean that I'm not working on the same things I was doing back then; however, I think that expression comes out of a deep engagement with a discipline.' And when pressed about self-expression he declares: 'Anything I do is self-expressive, but I do always try to begin with the extension of some previous architectural arc or trajectory. I like to look at the history of our discipline and try to locate the contemporary and future issues that are most

RIGHT SLAVIN HOUSE, VENICE, CALIFORNIA, USA, 2004

The Slavin House applies two of Lynn's design techniques: 'bleb' and 'blob'. In this case the 'bleb' was applied to achieve the unique form of the house's facade with inward opening courtyards, and for a new type of column developed in collaboration with Klaus Bollinger and composing of two continuous, extruded and radially bent steel tubes, braided and looped through one another to function simultaneously as horizontal and vertical members.

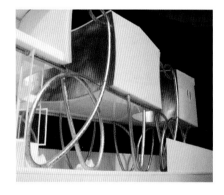

ABOVE SLAVIN HOUSE, VENICE, CALIFORNIA, USA, 2004

Lynn explains his design for the Slavin House: 'Continuous filets and radial tangents enable the curvilinear basket structure to both support and create hollow courts. The flowing continuity of upper and lower levels, of roof and ground and of voided, hollow structural baskets engenders a new kind of porous, domestic space that folds together indoor and outdoor spaces, structural frame, void light wells, solid figures, translucent bounding envelope and an undulating ground plane.'

poignant. I am interested in my expression as a designer, but I am more interested in how this connects and extends the discipline of architecture.'

His collection of high-profile projects such as the Embryological House, the Alessi Tea and Coffee Piazza (2000), the Ark of the World Museum and Visitor's Centre, San José, Costa Rica (2002), and the Sociopolis Apartments project (2009) and are all imbued with Lynn's commitment to design process regardless of their scale or context. 'When it comes to doing a church, or a single-family house for an art collector, or a public housing project for 500 people,' he explains, 'there is another layer of stuff which is this institutional content of what the architect needs to communicate about its contents, and conversely about architecture; they're two independent issues which coincide over the top of each other and that's always really tricky to reconcile.[23]

However, it is his philosophical and mathematical underpinning that is reflected in Lynn's relationship with aesthetics: 'My geometric predilections lead me towards totally monolithic, organic, synthesised things, and so my aesthetic is not an aesthetic of collage or composition. For me, the notion of beauty is very connected to both history and rigour. Near symmetry is more beautiful than perfect symmetry, so I try to achieve near symmetry using massing and composition. Assembly of elements in rhythms of variation and undulation is beautiful, so I try to incorporate this as well rather than slick unarticulated surfaces. I do not

The Blob Wall is a collaboration between Greg Lynn and
PANELITE which evolved as a textured panel used for
dividing space in the Slavin House. It is fabricated in
lightweight plastic and colourful, modular elements
that are custom-shaped using the latest CNC
technology. The blob unit, or 'brick', is a tri-lobed
hollow shape that is mass-produced through rotational
moulding. Each wall is assembled from individually
robotically cut hollow bricks that interlock with
exacting precision.

The design of the individual elements in Lynn's set of
flatware proceeded through the use of specialised
software invented for the animated film industry. The
final set is manufactured using a computer-controlled
3-D printer that builds the pieces in micro-layers of
sintered tool steel and bronze. The finished parts are
then silver-plated directly from the printing machine.
Thus no tools or polishing are used in the manufacture
or production.

believe beauty is subjective; it is aesthetic and I have an aesthetic discourse that drives my
work. It is certainly not by happy accident as it might have been two decades ago.'

Ultimately, Lynn returns to a refinement of technique to describe his own experience of
beauty, exclaiming: 'I still love it when the mastery of the medium comes into contact with
the expression of the artist. Every day I try to view my work from that point of view, but
when I actually witness it in painting or architecture, it's just transcendent for me.'

Interviews
Gritti Palace Hotel, Venice, Italy, 10 September 2004
Started at MOCA's exhibition Skin+Bones: Parallel Practices in Fashion and Architecture,
and continued at Lynn's Office, Venice, California, USA, 15 December 2006
Email exchange, 27 July 2008

Notes

1. Lynn's aesthetic language marks a distinct shift from the forefather of the digital architecture movement, John Frazer, who
borrowed terminology and referenced ideologies from the field of genetics. Many digital architects are still using the language
Frazer introduced in the 1990s while teaching at the Architectural Association (AA) in London (although he developed this
language much earlier through his computational design processes in the late 1960s), and as described in his book: John Frazer,
An Evolutionary Architecture, Architectural Association, London, 1995.

2. The University of Illinois at Chicago (1991–2), Columbia University Graduate School of Architecture (1992–9), Ohio State
University (1995–6), UCLA (1998–present), ETH Zurich (1999–2003), Yale University (2002–present) and the University of Applied
Arts, Vienna (2003–present).

3. Lynn graduated from Miami University, Ohio, in 1986.

4. 'Differential geometry is a mathematical discipline that uses the methods of differential and integral calculus to study problems in geometry. The theory of plane and space curves and of surfaces in the three-dimensional space ... formed the basis for its initial development in the eighteenth and nineteenth century. Since the late nineteenth century, differential geometry has grown into a field concerned more generally with geometric structures. It is closely related with differential topology, and together they make up the geometric theory of differentiable manifolds.' http://en.wikipedia.org/wiki/Differential_geometry

5. Terms such as 'folding', 'intricacy', 'supple', 'pliancy' and so on.

6. 'An intricate structure ... is a collection of components that communicate with each other and all change simultaneously ... the aim is to produce an intricacy .... if I change one thing that would have been a second or third level decision it can ripple through the entire structure and change every aspect of the building including the controlling geometry.' Greg Lynn, interview with L'Architecture d'Aujourd'hui board, *L'Architecture d'Aujourd'hui*, 349, Nov/Dec 2003, p 108.

7. A spline is a drafting tool consisting of a flexible rubber or leather strip to which is attached a series of evenly spaced discs with coordinates for reproducing curves at a variety of scales with precision based on the continuous interpolation of a curve through fixed points.

8. 'The New York Five' refers to a group of five New York City architects who emerged in the late 1960s: Peter Eisenman, Michael Graves, Charles Gwathamy, John Hejduk and Richard Meier. Their work was exhibited in New York's Museum of Modern Art (MoMA) in 1967.

9. Intuition derived from a calculus-based technique.

10. The word 'rigour' is constantly peppered throughout Lynn's conversation, recalling its origin within mathematics where it describes the process of mathematical proof by means of systematic reasoning. It is where language meets logic – a great pursuit of Lynn's through his thinking process as well as through his pure computational formal design process.

11. Lynn here refers to Gilles Deleuze's discussion of Henri Bergson in the chapter 'Intuition as Method', in Gilles Deleuze, *Bergsonism*, trans Hugh Tomlinson and Barbara Habberjam, Zone Books, New York, 1991.

12. The Predator was a collaboration between Lynn and Fabian Marcaccio. The three-dimensional painting substituted a standard canvas with a clear formed plastic with paint laid down using a new technique Lynn and Marcaccio developed over three years.

13. Lynn's articulation of the term 'skin' originated with the Predator installation – a key project in upgrading the notion of surface to the modulated skin as a relief surface, as in an animal's skin where the pattern and relief are intricate with the form.

14. 'My Embryological House research or any number of recent projects ceased to be about an animation or digital design process and have instead become about putting tens of thousands of parts into communication so that when you change one part it distributes the effect across all the other parts ... the aim is produce an intricacy ... All mathematics for this is over 300 years old. It is calculus, but architects have never been able to design as calculus. They have been able to analyse it for structure or so, but never intuitively design the things [along calculus].' Greg Lynn, interview with L'Architecture d'Aujourd'hui board, *L'Architecture d'Aujourd'hui*, 349, Nov/Dec 2003, p 108.

15. Greg Lynn, *Intricacy*, University of Pennsylvania Institute of Contemporary Art, Philadelphia, PA, 2003.

16. Office dA is a Boston-based architecture firm. Its principal partners are Monica Ponce de Leon and Nader Tehrani.

17. Bernard Cache of the Objectile studio based in Paris was an influential pioneer in production methods based on software and technological tools.

18. Terms such as 'shred', 'bleb' and 'teeth', for example, are related to techniques for placing openings, volumetric pocket-making and connecting between corresponding surfaces. All three terms are related to 'skin'. Skin is an elaboration of a surface where pattern and relief are intricate in their relationship with form [like animal skin]. 'Lattice' is the major structural articulation of surface and so on. Within different projects, Lynn combines techniques to pursue his visual concepts. For example, he describes the Ark of the World as being a combination of three techniques together: skins, lattice and flowers. The Embryological House employed three techniques: 'blob', 'bleb' and 'shred'; the Sociopolis residential project (2004–): 'teeth', 'flowers', 'strand'; the Slavin House (2004): 'bleb' and 'blob' and so on.

19. The Predator, Blob Wall and the Slavin House's 'bleb' columns all evoke accessible connotations and imagery. The origins are varied: 'bleb' is a term derived originally from digital software, as is the 'blob', although 'blob' is an English metaphor for shapeless form or a soft lump.

20. 'William Bateson invented the term genetics and described it as follows: "If all you have is random mutation and external selection, if an environment is based on gradients like temperature you would expect that all individuals would be continuous gradients. So you would just go from one species to another continuously where individuals would be unique for their environment. Instead you get these groups and you get jumps from group to group," and Bateson called this "discontinuous variation".' Greg Lynn, interview with Yael Reisner, 10 September 2004.

21. It is a position that continues to confront many of his contemporaries as well as his mentor, Peter Eisenman: 'I remember showing the Embryological Houses at an earlier conference and Eisenman stood up and said, "Greg, you've lost it".' Greg Lynn, interview with Yael Reisner, 10 September 2004.

22. However, Lynn's early texts have sometimes caused him concern. He explains: 'Every day, I regret the discourse I introduced in Animate FORM and the related projects in it as it had too much the apologetic scientific tone of an amateur looking for justification of their design decisions.' Greg Lynn, email to Yael Reisner, July 2008.

23. Lynn uses the word 'tricky' to describe his belief that the unity of content and form must be kept intact, and yet any external consideration to his computational design process creates difficulty for his design system.

Sulan Kolatan & William Mac Donald

CREATIVE IMPURITIES

KOL/MAC LLC, THE NEW YORK-BASED ARCHITECTURAL STUDIO of Sulan Kolatan and William Mac Donald, engages in highly inventive, speculative work inspired by the intersection of contemporary culture and scientific discourse. Their practice embraces a complete computational process where a project's production – from early sketches, working drawings and the final product – is designed solely on computer, allowing a smooth interface for their strategy of working with key collaborators across the digital realm.

In juxtaposition to the majority of their digital peers who value consistency and 'purity'[1] through design methodologies derived from mathematically based processes, KOL/MAC LLC prefer to categorise themselves as 'lumpers' – a term they discovered in the science section of the *New York Times* and reappropriated to describe their work which 'looks for correspondences between seemingly unrelated things and phenomena.'[2] The strategy marks a significant departure from the current digital landscape by embracing the notion of 'impurity' and relying on lateral and intuitive thinking within a wholly computational framework. KOL/MAC LLC also engage directly with scientific applications through their growing interest in the relationship between network theories and computer software.[3] Most recently, they have been investigating biotechnological ecologies and conducting research projects with the ambition of moving beyond conventional sustainable technologies and towards cutting-edge ecological solutions.

OPPOSITE OK APARTMENTS, NEW YORK, USA, 1997

As 'digital architects' KOL/MAC LLC embrace a complete computational design process where the project is produced using the computer as a design tool from early sketches, developed drawings, models, working drawings and through to the final product.

Mac Donald is American-born and was educated internationally, while Kolatan originates from Turkey, qualifying as an architect in Aachen before moving to New York to pursue post-graduate studies. This cultural diversity is also reflected in their physical appearance: Mac Donald is a calm, large presence in a black suit, talking with great clarity, while the elegantly dressed Kolatan speaks more animatedly with the air of an intellectual and youthful European woman. The couple continue to balance their practice and research with teaching positions at Columbia University, New York,[4] and various invited international professorships. In addition, Mac Donald holds the position of Graduate Chair of Architecture and Urban Design at New York's Pratt Institute.

After founding their practice in 1988, Sulan Kolatan and William Mac Donald refined their 'lumping' design strategy[5] while teaching at Columbia University during the 1990s. Their research developed a unique system that enables them to utilise a richer computational language to create form that moves beyond the usual digital preference for thin, refined surface and flat ornamentation and embraces volumetric compositions – curved or angular – within individual projects.[6]

As William Mac Donald explains: 'Lumping proliferates horizontally, by blending between already "matured systems"[7] across different categories;[8] it opens this field of synthetically generated material to intuition, interpretation and evaluation as architecture. Excess, in this instance, means ambiguity. Significant lumping affords productive leaps – it has rules and consequent yields.'[9] To this end, KOL/MAC LLC reintroduce elements of 'pre-digital architecture' in their work – engaging the speculative operations of lateral thinking and the subjective nature of reliance on the architect's 'eye', while utilising a computational framework to give their design process rigour and definition.

Certainly, Mac Donald responds to the notion of intuition with great enthusiasm: 'I think it's impossible to argue that any creative process occurs without the input of intuition.' Kolatan agrees, but places it within context: 'Our work, however, is very process-based in order to make it rigorous, because if it's purely based on intuition it becomes too subjective.' This approach positions the architects within the role of 'author/editor' as well as designer. 'We prepare the "ground"[10] in which to work. Then we select the relationships between things in a manner that yields the best architectural and aesthetic outcome,' Kolatan explains. 'This process of evaluation is consistent all the way through so we're constantly valuing and editing. For us the computation and the software provide the opportunity to extend that "prepared ground" all the way into the construction phase, which is a great advantage for the way we work. So the design sensibility or design intelligence[11] carries throughout.'

Mac Donald concurs: 'For us it's very important that the process isn't about translating an idea into an architectural form, but that the idea itself is transformed; that is, the process of transformation[12] begins and ends in architecture. I think it's a radical shift in thinking![13] I'm not sure if it's a causal relationship to using software, but I do think it's a type of

BELOW OK APARTMENTS, NEW YORK, USA, 1997

The parametric model is generated by using 'the ingredients' of the 'genetic pool' of the project called 'base' (old houses) and 'targets' (forms of existing objects). A target – determined by forms or data (multi-indexing) related to a range of functionality – could be a curved form, and when blended within the computational process some parts of it will disappear and other features will remain.

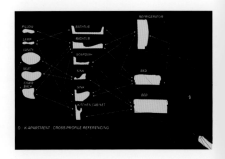

This diagram provides a glimpse into an element of
KOL/MAC LLC's design methodology and breaks down
the distinction between space and programme to
generate a compelling aesthetic where the sink
transforms into a metallic dividing wall and the floor
becomes bed then bath.

LEFT RESI-RISE, NEW YORK, USA, 2004

The architects utilise a computational framework to give their design process rigour and definition. Mac Donald says: 'We think it's impossible to argue that any creative process occurs without the input of intuition … Our work, however, is very process-based in order to make it rigorous, because if it's purely based on intuition it becomes too subjective … This strategy allows for an open and speculative system for content and form making.'

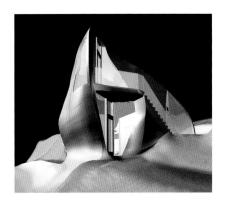

KOL/MAC LLC's research has developed a unique
system that enables them to utilise a richer
computational language to create curved or angular
forms. As Kolatan describes: 'If one were to describe
digital processes in terms of geometry, it's really about
topology, and topology doesn't actually differentiate
whether a surface is curved or angular.'

intelligence that is specific to contemporary conditions today.' Mac Donald's position is
strengthened by his reference to the belief held within scientific practice that breaking
down a consistency often creates the best platform for ingenuity. As he suggests: 'You
have certain intentions in terms of the speculation or experimentation, and then you set
up the groundwork to test further.'

While this process may facilitate a rigorous investigation, KOL/MAC LLC are also conscious
that their methodology should aspire to engage with current preoccupations. 'There's an
emergence of a type of "pop science" that affects almost every branch of our culture, and
for us engaging with the current cultural context is far more important than being
"digital". We try to be very aware of cultural discourses and analyse where we are at this
moment, where we are going as a society, and how that affects architectural practice,'
explains Mac Donald.

Kolatan acknowledges that their practice is continually influenced by cutting-edge
scientific theories that capture the imagination of a wider public audience: 'While we
don't have any particular interest in being purely scientific, we are intrigued with the
issues that engage our general community. One such issue is "network theory" because
we think that there is a direct influence between network theories and computer
software. Understanding the pragmatic and performance aspects of networks interested
us because of how it effects the way we think of our working process, as well as how

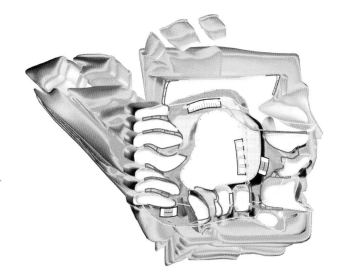

KOL/MAC LLC engage directly with scientific
applications through their growing interest in the
relationship between network theories and computer
software. This interest has led to their investigations of
biotechnological ecologies with the aim of moving
beyond conventional sustainable technologies and
towards cutting-edge ecological solutions.

LEFT RESI-RISE, NEW YORK, USA, 2004

The Resi(dential) Rise apartment tower project was initially exhibited at the Centre Pompidou's 'Non-Standard Architectures' exhibition in Paris. Kolatan explains: 'We planned to use the excessiveness of the project's skin by turning it into some kind of metabolistic element, where it would store and recycle energy and deal with water and air circulation both inside and outside.'

we think about the position of architecture within society. I think that in the future there will be the ability for clients or end users to much more actively take part in the process through these kinds of interfaces.'

Kolatan and Mac Donald are also preoccupied with new ways of using biological technologies in the structural, operational systems and physical presence of a building to investigate how architecture can become responsive within an environmental agenda. Their 'high-performance' Metabolic Wall (2005–) recalls ideas first explored in their Resi(dential) Rise (Resi-Rise) apartment tower project (1999–2004), which was initially exhibited at the Centre Pompidou's 'Non-Standard Architectures' exhibition in Paris (2003–04). Kolatan recalls: 'In the Resi-Rise project we planned to use the excessiveness of the project's skin by turning it into some kind of metabolistic element, where it would store and recycle energy and deal with water and air circulation both inside and outside. This would not only produce a beneficial effect on the interior units, but also on the exterior, and one could start to conceive that buildings could have a positive effect on the city.'

The idea was never completely resolved within the Resi-Rise project, but provided the background to Kolatan and Mac Donald's pursuit of the creation of a new kind of 'high-performance' building skin or wall that engages directly with biotechnologies. Kolatan expands on the concept: 'We think the topological surface of the "wall" could become a substrate for biological matter, such as micro-organisms, which ecologically clean; this cleaning activity produces energy which could be used within a building's surface. So, in

OPPOSITE INVERSABRANE HIGH-PERFORMANCE ECOLOGICAL BUILDING MEMBRANE, 2005–

Kolatan explains the concept behind the 'high-performance' wall: 'We think the topological surface of the "wall" could become a substrate for biological matter, such as micro-organisms, which ecologically clean; this cleaning activity produces energy that could be used within a building's surface.'

SULAN KOLATAN & WILLIAM MAC DONALD **239**

the long term, it may be possible to view a structural wall less in technological terms and more from a biological perspective.'

The concept is clearly one that resonates with Mac Donald, who animatedly describes the system's potential: 'One of the aspects of the exterior cladding material we are using is that it is antiseptic so, for example, you could actually encourage the growth of photosynthetic rather than photovoltaic materials, which would actually absorb light and then produce it directly, in terms of energy. It is also completely waterproof, so this is actually a huge vessel for containing grey water for the systems of the building. So, the concept provides the basis for a high-performance ecological system and, rather than just using "green" materials, we decided to try and see what we could do with a very proactive attitude towards the environment.'

Kolatan and Mac Donald's inclusive attitude towards the notion of impurity – including biotechnologies – marks a stark departure from the position of their digital design colleagues such as Bernard Cache, Mark Goulthorpe or Greg Lynn,[14] although they do share one major preoccupation: an outright rejection of any suggestion of deterministic formalism within their body of work. Like their peers, KOL/MAC LLC employ computational processes to find a diverse range of strategies to create their architecture rather than a deterministic process where the work directly reflects one's will.[15] As Mac Donald suggests: 'I think that working in a very methodological way creates a liberating condition and allows for a sensitive relationship to architecture as a cultural practice. Of course, architecture is still a constructional practice as well, but non-deterministic processes push it towards a kind of betterment of the environment. It's done within such complex terms these days that I think it is very difficult to continually impose one's sole will. In the end, the question must be: Is that approach really bettering the environment for those that participate in it?'

KOL/MAC LLC take a flexible and inclusive approach by rejecting the pursuit of deterministic design, and characteristically they ground themselves in a progressive tradition. As Mac Donald articulates: 'Ultimately, our most important responsibility is to speculate. So once you put yourself in that role of speculation – with a sense of responsibility to your profession – then I think you get closer to the idea of how you should operate in the world. Suddenly, this becomes the most important thing and speculation becomes a necessity rather than just a desire, and a responsibility to progress.' However, he concedes that this position is not completely detached from aesthetic values: 'The rigour is also, without question, to produce something that is interesting and worthwhile in terms of an aesthetic position, and we are very conscious of the way we make things and how they look.'

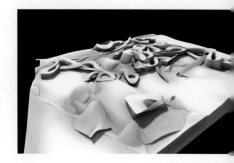

ABOVE GRAND EGYPTIAN MUSEUM, CAIRO, EGYPT, 2005

In the Grand Egyptian Museum competition scheme, KOL/MAC LLC use sand in many forms. The building walls are concrete panels cast onto the landscape, and sand-filled, synthetic blankets help stabilise the dunes.

BELOW GRAND EGYPTIAN MUSEUM, CAIRO, EGYPT, 2005

KOL/MAC LLC's work also embraces colour, as Kolatan explains: 'If digital discourse equates topology or topological architecture with the use of the computer, then we feel it's also important to establish the relationship between colour and the RGB world of the computer. ... The fact that one can expertly blend and intensify colour is very much part and parcel of the medium of the computer.'

In this conversion of a pre-existing military barracks
into a contemporary art and architecture museum, the
architects use a new generation of environmentally
responsive shotcrete containing both structural
(composite fibre) and ornamental (metal powder)
admixtures with a parametrically changing steel frame
that adapts to the Klein bottle-like geometry of the
new addition.

Kolatan extends the aesthetic discussion to include 'ambience', suggesting the term as a
useful framework for further debate: 'I think the notion of ambience is a much broader
issue than just a visual one. Creating ambience includes emotional, sensory, tactile and
haptic space that goes beyond the physical aspects of architecture. It also includes
temperature, lighting and everything that contributes to making a sensory environment.'
Specific titles for each project and the use of vibrant colour also contribute to each
design's ambience. 'We always name our work,' Kolatan says with a smile. 'There is the
Tub House, for instance, and the Malibu, Shingle and Golf Course houses. By naming them
we try to establish particular qualities, whether casual or formal. It also underwrites our
desire not to be neutral, but to make a conscious choice that includes the colour range,
and of course that has an effect on a project's ambience.'

Interestingly, KOL/MAC LLC's notion of ambience brings with it a clear signature that
opposes the preference of the digital parametric architects, such as Goulthorpe, who
advocate that the parametric design process abolishes the architect's identity. However,
as Kolatan states: 'The particularity or signature of ambience is crucial to a concept and
you can't think of that in a generalised way.' She expands: 'For example, if digital
discourse equates topology or topological architecture with the use of the computer, then
we feel it's also important to establish the relationship between colour and the RGB

LEFT FONDS RÉGIONAL D'ART CONTEMPORAIN
(FRAC), ORLÉANS, FRANCE, 2007

Like their peers, KOL/MAC LLC employ computational
processes to find a diverse range of strategies to create
their architecture rather than a deterministic process
where the work directly reflects one's will. As Mac
Donald suggests: 'Non-deterministic processes ... are
done within such complex terms these days that I think
it's very difficult to continually impose one's sole will.'

world of the computer. How can the designer materialise that kind of RGB thinking within
their work? The fact that one can expertly blend and intensify colour is very much part
and parcel of the medium of the computer.'

Certainly, KOL/MAC LLC's innovative lumping design methodology continues to provoke
the core digital fraternity who remain suspicious of any 'impurity' within the design
process. Yet Kolatan is adamant that the inclusion of intuitive elements within their
practice does not result in a dilution of the work: 'In terms of political correctness there
is always this puritan idea that you can't combine serious intellectual pursuit together
with sensory aspects within the design process – it's seen as indulgent. They are
considered mutually exclusive, and that's the problem! So, as an author, you find yourself
pegged in one camp or the other. However, we are optimistic that we are moving beyond
this deeply ingrained aversion because we realise that it's not very smart to work within
those kinds of restrictive categorisations.' Mac Donald concurs and neatly captures the
pervading uneasiness with acknowledging lateral thinking and aesthetics within
architectural discourse: 'It is a kind of erotic taboo among architects. It's too sensual and,
therefore, people feel that it should be kept behind closed doors' they don't want to
actually talk about it or confront it.'

Interviews
Bartlett School of Architecture, University College London, 19 March 2004
KOL/MAC LLC studio/apartment, New York, 17 October 2006

ABOVE ROOT CHAIR PROTOTYPE, 2008

Kolatan and Mac Donald's inclusive attitude towards
the notion of impurity is a stark departure from the
position of their digital design colleagues such as
Bernard Cache, Mark Goulthorpe or Greg Lynn. Their
unique methodology requires clear modes of
computational procedure to be invented and scripted to
embrace the notion that intuitive leaps within the
design process are valid.

Notes

1. KOL/MAC LLC's approach is provocative, particularly in the early period of digital discourse from 1995 and onwards when practitioners such as Bernard Cache were promoting a pure and logical digital process that rejected any notion of 'fluid thinking'. Later, Greg Lynn referenced ideologies such as 'Bergson's intuition' that advocated following procedural performance related to technique rather than relying on lateral thinking.

2. See *AD Contemporary Techniques in Architecture*, Vol 72, No 1, Jan/Feb 2002, p 77.

3. Marking a significant factor that moves their work beyond the quasi-scientific methodologies of their computational peers.

4. Kolatan and Mac Donald met while completing Masters qualifications at Columbia University in 1988.

5. The term 'lumpers' references a technique used in scientific practice where researchers look for correspondences between seemingly unrelated things and phenomena. This is characteristic of lateral thinking in science, art or any creative activity.

6. KOL/MAC LLC seek to clarify the enduring misperception that digital processes are intrinsically linked with the 'blob'. As Sulan Kolatan explains: 'If one were to describe it in terms of geometry, it's really about topology, and topology doesn't actually differentiate whether a surface is curved or angular ... the continuities implied are of a different sort than at the level of the curvilinear or angular.' Sulan Kolatan, interview with Yael Reisner, 19 March 2004.

7. A 'mature system' could be a 'target' or 'base' chosen by the architects. For instance, a target could be a curved form, and when blended within the computational process some parts of it will disappear within the manipulation and other features will remain.

8. The ingredients of the 'genetic pool' are called 'base' (old houses) and 'targets' (forms of existing objects) and are part of mature systems. A digital blending is a blending between already matured systems across different categories. The relationship between the system and its potentiality ... is the object of mental speculation.' KOL/MAC LLC, *AD Contemporary Techniques in Architecture*, op cit, p 77.

9. The 'targets' they blend into their process could be forms or data (multi-indexing) related to a range of programmes (functionality), allowing the architects to include their intuition within the design process. Therefore, forms and programme are blended continuously and within the architects' control, allowing a sense of ambiguity within their design. This strategy allows for an open and speculative system for content and form making.

10. Kolatan and Mac Donald prepare the ground throughout their entire design process, effectively enlarging the 'genetic pool'.

11. 'The term "design intelligence" is the design sensibility of an architect – the acquired taste that one develops in an intuitive, subjective and ultimately personal way.' William Mac Donald, interview with Yael Reisner, 19 March 2004.

12. All of the digital studios seek to 'transform' rather than 'translate' – a notion they see as belonging to the past. KOL/MAC LLC's technique of transforming ideas is their 'lumping technique'.

13. Prior to the digital era, architects often expressed a formal idea directly within their architecture. However, digital architects *transform* an idea through a rigorous computational process. A resonant example of the pre-digital approach can be seen with Oscar Niemeyer's scheme for a theatre exterior, an extension for the Ministry of Education and Health Building, Rio de Janeiro, Brazil (1948). Niemeyer's sketch of a woman's body was translated directly onto a building's silhouette. Although not built, the project was published as a photomontage. See David Underwood, *Oscar Niemeyer and the Architecture of Brazil*, Rizzoli, New York, 1994.

14. The difference between the KOL/MAC LLC's work and that of Cache, Goulthorpe and Lynn is marked by their engagement with lateral thinking and active manipulation within their digital process as well as their engagement with scientific applications such as biotechnologies.

15. Advocating a 'non-deterministic' approach is an attitude that can be traced back to the 'downfall' of German Expressionism in the 1920s and continued to be influential through the second half of the 20th century. Since 1990, John Frazer – recognised as the forefather of digital architecture – has imbued his students at London's Architecture Association (AA), through his agenda of 'Evolutionary Architecture', with the non-deterministic values that he first developed in the late 1960s. It is an attitude that continues among the digital architects of the early 21st century.

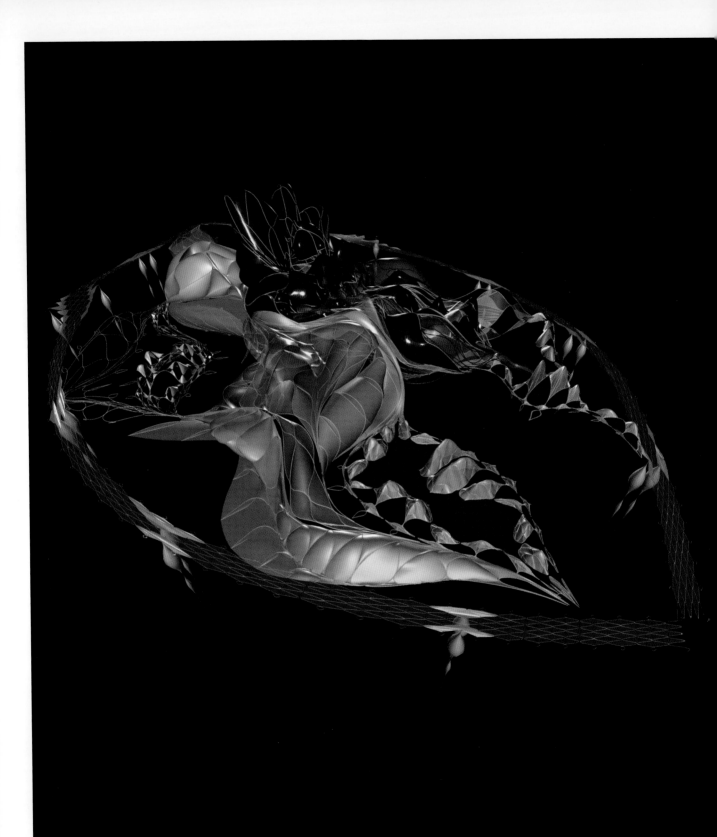

Hernan Diaz Alonso
DIGITAL VIRTUOSITY

ARGENTINEAN ARCHITECT HERNAN DIAZ ALONSO enjoys playing the role of the archetypal South American male, striking a memorable figure with a strong physique, black moustache and small beard, wearing heavy silver rings and bracelets and often photographed holding or smoking a large cigar. Despite his image, Diaz Alonso proves a direct and straightforward conversationalist revealing a routine of rising early to work in quiet solitude and a modest approach to living – drinking little and eating mainly traditional Argentinean food.

Born in Buenos Aires in 1969, Diaz Alonso graduated from the National University of Rosario with a degree in architecture, although he is quick to suggest that his architectural career happened more by lack of opportunity to pursue his boyhood passion for film-making rather than a call to an architectural vocation. Despite his early ambivalence, he went on to complete the Advanced Architecture Design Program at Columbia University in New York as a student of Greg Lynn and Jeffrey Kipnis. Proving a gifted student, he graduated from the prestigious course with honours and was awarded the Excellence of Design Prize and the SOM Travel Fellowship selection.

As a second-generation maverick among the fast-moving digital culture pioneered at Columbia[1] during the 1990s, Diaz Alonso developed his unique computational design approach with the use of computer animation software[2] combined with his passion for cinematics. His revolutionary approach of combining cutting-edge computational processes with an engagement with form, image and expressive authorship is undoubtedly due to the influence of working with two influential yet disparate mentors – as a student with Greg Lynn (1999) and in the late Enric Miralles' office (1996) – coupled with his innate belief in the importance of the architect's intuitive contribution. He also worked as a Senior Designer at Peter Eisenman's office (2000–01) before starting his own firm, Xefirotarch, in Los Angeles in 2001.[3] He is revered as a brilliant virtuoso by his staff and students who admire him for his ability to engage with the

OPPOSITE BUSAN CONCERT HALL, BUSAN METROPOLITAN CITY, SOUTH KOREA, 2004

Diaz Alonso is quick to defend the importance of play within his architectural process: 'Architecture for me is sort of a game ... I don't vindicate the notion of fun and play.' A self-described 'Romanticist', he embraces the notions of intuition, self-expression and emotion within his computational process. 'I think that architecture is extremely personal so I don't try to hide my personal qualities ... I believe in a highly individual approach and not in the detachment of the outdoor script.'

latest animation software with a fresh and innovative approach, unencumbered by non-deterministic processes or notions of morality.

Hernan Diaz Alonso's ability to fuse complex ideologies and cutting-edge computational processes with a sense of irreverence and play is perhaps best illustrated in his choice of name for his practice. He recalls a casual conversation with friends about one of Umberto Eco's novels, *Foucault's Pendulum,* and its theme of intellectual games and fun. 'I wanted something more like a name of a rock band or something that doesn't mean anything,' he explains. 'I remembered the conversation on Eco's book and the reference to the term "sefirot" within the text. I liked it because it wasn't English or Spanish and it didn't mean anything in particular.' Distorting the term to become Xefirotarch, Diaz Alonso freely admits that he neglected to make the connection of Sefirot[4] to Jewish mysticism or mathematics, explaining: 'A couple of years ago an interviewer asked me why I chose a religious meaning of mathematical numbers for the name of the practice, but actually the absolute truth was that I just liked how it sounded and that nobody would be able to pronounce it correctly!'

This sense of youthful irreverence permeates Diaz Alonso's body of work and he is quick to defend the importance of play within his architectural process: 'Architecture for me is sort of a game. I don't vindicate the notion of fun and play. I think that kind of a childish

ABOVE BUSAN CONCERT HALL, BUSAN METROPOLITAN CITY, SOUTH KOREA, 2004

It was not easy for the young architect to break away from Columbia's emphasis on pure computational processes and intellectual discourse and to find a method of working that suited his natural inclinations. As he explains: 'I always understood myself more as a designer rather than an intellectual.' It wasn't until 2002 that Diaz Alonso found the confidence to completely embrace his interest in the image.

attitude towards working is important.' A self-described 'Romanticist', Diaz Alonso embraces the notions of intuition, self-expression and emotion within his computational process: 'Intuition is also an important element within my work and it's a form of intelligence that I am interested in. How can architecture be a vehicle to express emotions for the author; how do you introduce the conditions to do that? So this idea of playing, games and a romantic sense of expression is something that I really enjoy. I think that architecture is extremely personal so I don't try to hide my personal qualities. I believe in a highly individual approach and not in the detachment of the outdoor script.'

Diaz Alonso's path to an architectural career was an indirect one, beginning with a boyhood passion for film and culminating in an awakening of his architectural vision. As he recalls: 'I never actually wanted to be an architect; I wanted to be a film director when I was 18 years old. At the time all the universities were publicly funded in Argentina and so many of the private film schools had closed. So I agreed to do a year of architecture before I applied to start film school and my interest evolved from there.' As a 19-year-old student he was shown the catalogue of the 'Deconstructivist Architecture' exhibition at New York's Museum of Modern Art (MoMA) where he saw the work of Zaha Hadid and COOP HIMMELB(L)AU for the first time. 'I remember thinking "Wow, there's something else to architecture!" Soon afterwards somebody brought me a book about Archigram's projects; at the time I didn't really understand the significance of the work but I was completely seduced by the images so I became excited about architecture and forgot about film school.'

ABOVE SUR INSTALLATION, PS1 MOMA, NEW YORK, USA, 2005

'The image is something that is produced by others at the end of the process while we will start to speculate from the very beginning so that the image itself becomes the genetic code.' This statement marks one of the most important factors in distinguishing the unique character of Diaz Alonso's work from that of other digital architects. His 'cinematic image' has character, rhetoric and an individual touch – qualities rejected by the Modernists for many years and, more recently, by most digital architects.

RIGHT SUR INSTALLATION, PS1 MOMA, NEW YORK, USA, 2005

'I'm absolutely shameless about the heavy use of rendering within our work and the fact that we use shadow, reflection and so on as a vehicle for the direction of form. We work with computer renders in a generative way from the very beginning of a project where we will start to speculate with colour, reflection and so on. This starts to dictate the manipulation of the geometry and the form according to the effect that we are trying to produce through the image.'

He attributes his individualistic approach to the influence of working with the late Enric Miralles and the pure computational logic introduced to him by Greg Lynn at Columbia University's Advanced Architecture Design Program:[5] 'I've been lucky to work and study with amazing people. Enric was my hero and the architect who I admire the most. I've always tried to incorporate many of the things I've learnt from them. Greg and Jeffrey Kipnis were my teachers and I worked for Enric[6] and Peter Eisenman after graduation so these four amazing guys influenced me early on in my career.'

It was not easy, however, for the young architect to break away from Columbia's emphasis on pure computational processes and intellectual discourse to find a method of working that suited his natural inclinations: 'The whole year at Columbia was fantastic ... the studio seminars ... and it was the pinnacle of the Deleuze and Guattari discussion and so on. I read and talked about them but I never felt quite comfortable because I always understood myself more as a designer rather than an intellectual.' It was not until he completed the U2 Tower competition (2002) that Diaz Alonso found the confidence and clarity to break away from a purity of process and completely embrace his interest in the image: 'When we did the U2 Tower competition in Dublin everyone started to talk about the picturesque and the figurative that was present in my work. So it was the first time I realised that I could liberate myself from the intellectual process with my interest in cinematic behaviour and the way that image could produce form.'

LEFT SEROUSSI PAVILION, MAISON SEROUSSI 'SEINGEMER', LA MAISON ROUGE, PARIS, FRANCE, 2007

As Diaz Alonso explains: 'It seems to me that the forms that I want to pursue are almost impossible to achieve through physical investigation. I think you can get the complexity of the form, but I don't think you can get the complexity of the image-driven logic of the form that I'm interested in.'

As his work progressed, Diaz Alonso lost interest in the CAD/CAM direct production process that many digital architects employ. Instead he aspired to develop cinematic sequences that led – among other things – to a preoccupation with the creation of affective cinematic imagery as a significant part of the design process. He thus benefited from the mechanisms that come with the familiar world of the cinema: triggering associative thinking, memory, illusions or mood.

As a result, Diaz Alonso's work has created a new approach to the architectural design process within digital culture, where the image is embraced as a primary generator for the work. As he explains: 'I'm absolutely shameless about the heavy use of rendering within our work and the fact that we use shadow, reflection and so on as a vehicle for the direction of form. We work with computer renders in a generative way from the very beginning of a project where we will start to speculate with colour, reflection and so on. This starts to dictate the manipulation of the geometry and the form according to the effect that we are trying to produce through the image.' Continuing, he suggests: 'The difference between my work and the way that other people work with these tools is that the image is something that is produced at the end of process[7] while we will start to speculate from the very beginning so that the image becomes the genetic code.[8] So we start to define[9] whether something will be a shiny material or opaque, or whether we're going to have colour or no colour, what kind of shadow is produced, how much articulation are we going to produce and so on.[10] Now the challenge is how do you translate that in the real world?'[11]

Diaz Alonso believes that we are witnessing a changing of the guard within the contemporary architectural condition his generation has identified and embraced: 'I think there are three critical shifts that have developed over the last 15 years that I'm most interested in. The first is the shift from representation to simulation. The second is the

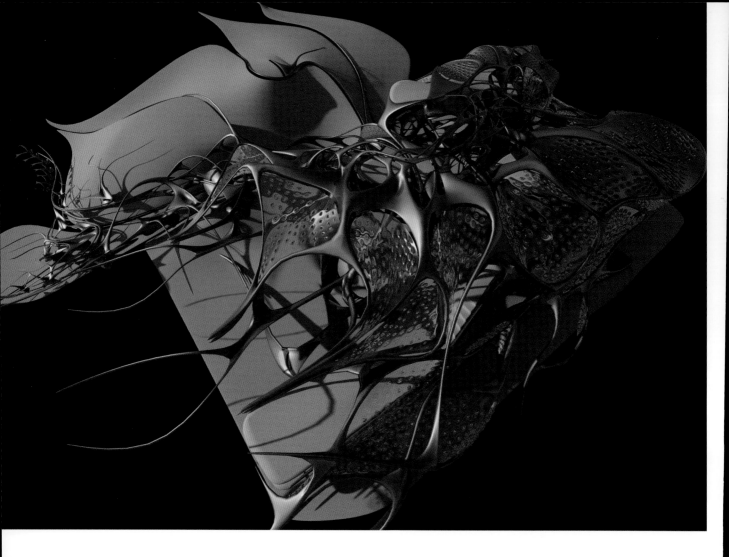

ABOVE STOCKHOLM CITY LIBRARY, STOCKHOLM, SWEDEN, 2007

As Diaz Alonso explains: 'I am not interested in reinventing the genre; I just want to work faster and more aggressively to create more complexity and beauty. It is a sense of irresponsibility as well; it can't be highly ethical or absolutely moral.'

move to a kind of generative internal logic that grows into the form. And the third is the transfer of power from the generation of architects who have viewed computers with the attitude of "OK, what can this software do for me?" to younger architects such as myself who view it as "What can I do for the software?".'[12]

Characteristically, he turns to a rock music reference to illustrate his point: 'Jimmy Hendrix, for example, didn't invent his famous guitar sound simply because it was a pedal system. Now, I have a lot of friends who have an electric guitar with a pedal, but they don't play like Jimmy Hendrix. So there is a sensibility that comes with the ability of how to use the equipment. And I think this illustrates the mental change in the way that my generation approaches work. I think that we have absorbed the technology and the technique to a degree that we can keep shifting the sensibility.'

Diaz Alonso is interested in the resultant form, and the image of that form, rather than a discourse regarding process. Consequently he is critical of the self-righteous nature of many architects in the manner in which they claim the importance of process to their work: 'The purity of the work lies in the final effect.'

Continuing the music analogy, Diaz Alonso suggests: 'In the development of digital culture, I think Greg is more like Charlie Parker or Dizzy Gillespie in the way that they broke a whole new genre of jazz – new sound, new things. I think the work of my generation is more like John Coltrane or Miles Davies in that we're not inventing a whole new genre, but taking certain factors of the genre and corrupting it to make it faster, more disturbed and to incorporate other sounds. So it's not so much an obsession for innovation, it's much more an obsession for variation or an obsession to create different roles.'

His commitment to creating a dynamic, non-static cinematic experience within his architecture is all consuming, suppressing the conventional concerns of the architect to play a very minor role within his process. He declares: 'I don't actually have any interest whatsoever in the material aspect of architecture. When we build then we deal with that aspect, but it's not something that interests me for investigation. As a result we have

'As architects, we hold this idea that the coherence of the process provides a sense of morality, and that idea is something that doesn't interest me whatsoever,' exclaims Diaz Alonso. 'The quality of work we produce has nothing to do with the process; it's not good simply because of the process. I think in my work there is an obsession about the production of the image and the final aesthetic.'

been avoiding doing any physical models in the office. I think it has to do with my ambition to keep everything in a kind of dynamic and cinematic logic. Every time you make a model you produce a frozen condition.' He recognises the contradiction suggesting: 'I know it's kind of a paradox for an architect and I want to build my projects, yet at the same time the built reality can also produce a huge amount of disappointment. It seems to me that the forms that I want to pursue are almost impossible to achieve through physical investigation. I think you can get the complexity of the form, but I don't think you can get the complexity of the image-driven logic of the form that I'm interested in.' As a result, Diaz Alonso understands that he is much more obsessed with image than the physicality of form. At the opening of his pavilion at MoMA's PS1 (2005), he recalls: 'I saw the opening, took a picture and never came back. I didn't have any interest whatsoever to see it again. I like seeing the pictures more than seeing the object in reality.'

Unlike his digital predecessors, Diaz Alonso completely rejects the inherent morality attached to the purity of computational processes where one's artistic inclination is repressed. As such he is unapologetic in using his taste and aesthetic to corrupt the logical processes: 'I am not interested in reinventing the genre; I just want to work faster and more aggressively to create more complexity and beauty. It is a sense of irresponsibility as well; it can't be highly ethical or absolutely moral. I think being socially responsible is not only about action; doesn't architecture also directly affect human behaviour? It can also be about proving that the nature of the work you produce can communicate to people in a different way. So I think there is more than one way to contribute to working with a social attitude.'

Certainly, Diaz Alonso is ultimately interested in the resultant form, and the image of that form, rather than discourse regarding process. As a consequence he is critical of the self-righteous nature of many architects in the manner in which they claim the importance of process to their work. 'The purity of the work lies in the final effect. As architects, we hold this idea that the coherence of the process provides a sense of morality, and that idea is something that doesn't interest me whatsoever. This is not to say that the work doesn't have a very precise technique process, but the quality of work we produce has nothing to do with the process; it's not good simply because of the process. I think my work holds an obsession with the production of the image and the final aesthetic that is produced.'

Intriguingly, he also draws an analogy with abstract Expressionist painting to explain his manipulation and mastery of technique.[13] 'It's not a lack of authorship,' he states, 'it's more about the ability to surprise myself and keep it playful, in the same way that Jackson Pollock, when painting, held control but also allowed a margin of unpredictability. So that interests me a lot because I've always wanted to keep that killer spirit within the work and surprise myself.' Diaz Alonso has, thus, developed access to layers of randomness within an inherent system, embracing the tremendous freedom facilitated within the computational process while benefiting from the new sensibilities that grow with new software, new technologies and refined technique.

Describing what he terms an 'excessive virtuosity', Diaz Alonso embraces the quality of 'awkwardness' within his work and introduces what he considers a sense of 'harmony'. He claims the meaning and logic of his architecture are an afterthought and certainly not predetermined. This attitude, unlike that of many of his peers, liberates his architecture from the heavy processes and the overworked reasoning that underpin the methods of others. As he explains: 'I don't need to define the rules for my working process. I am interested in total liberation. For me it's more like a wild horse; you get on and see where it takes you.' Of course, you still have your technique to ride the horse. And in the Romantic tradition, Diaz Alonso prefers not to dissect his work: 'I always try to refuse to talk about the processes behind the work because I like the notion of separating the "magic from the magician". I think that the trick is more interesting than the method.' However, he agrees to be drawn a little further on his process: 'We always work with two or three typologies at the same time, and the corruption or contamination of these typologies is a technique

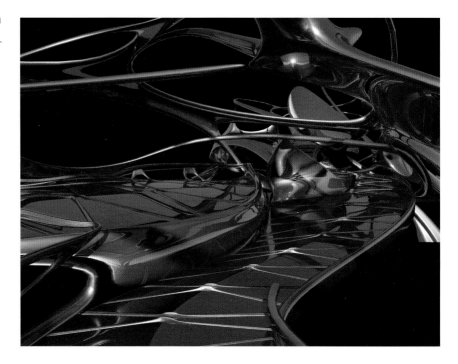

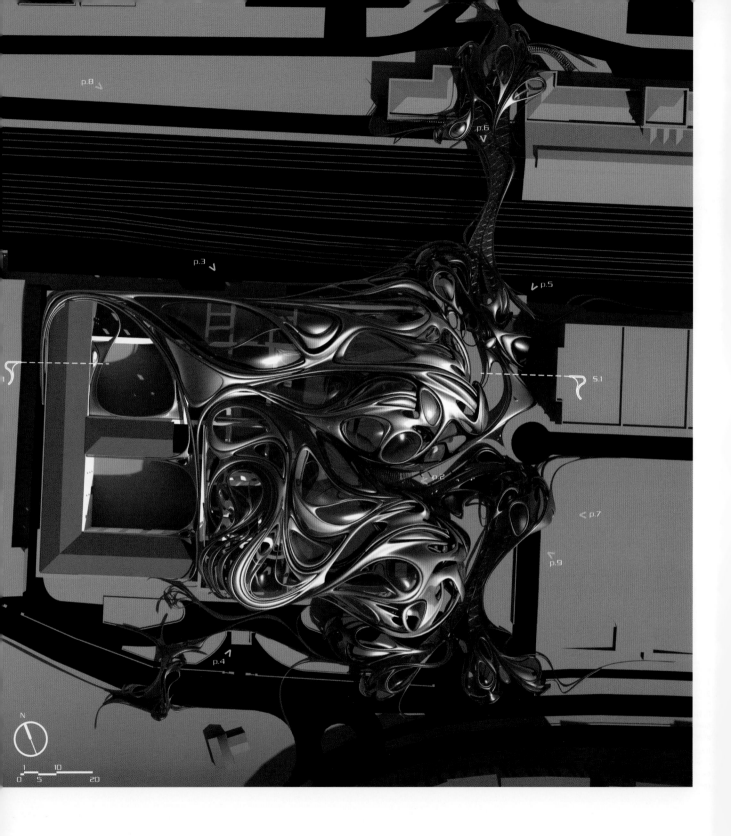

Diaz Alonso has developed access to layers of randomness within an inherent system, embracing the tremendous freedom facilitated by the computational process while benefiting from the new sensibilities that grow with new software, new technologies and refined technique. He claims the meaning and logic of his architecture is an afterthought and certainly not predetermined.

Intriguingly, Diaz Alonso draws an analogy with abstract Expressionist painting (as does Frank Gehry) to explain his manipulation and mastery of technique. 'It's not a lack of authorship,' he says, 'it's more about the ability to surprise myself and keep it playful in the same way that Jackson Pollock, when painting, held control but also allowed a margin of unpredictability.'

which we use all the time. They produce a kind of awkwardness because there are certain aspects of the work that can seem out of place and out of proportion.'

Undoubtedly Diaz Alonso has produced some of the most compelling architectural imagery of recent years, and when pressed to discuss the aesthetic qualities of what is obviously tremendously dexterous form-making he responds in a manner typical of his persona: 'I think that my work can be defined in two categories – some projects are grotesque[14] while some of them are horrific, and I think they represent different problems. My view of the grotesque doesn't have an aesthetic value per se; it's more about a place in time in the same way that the work of painter Francisco Goya was described as grotesque simply because the work didn't fall under a known aesthetic of the time.' Elaborating, he continues: 'So the grotesque is more about an emergence of a new form. For example with the U2 Tower I can clearly see the grotesque because it wasn't something I was looking for – it just happened and can't be quickly defined. It's like the opposite of cute. It's something else – it's not beautiful, it's not ugly yet there are other qualities that are difficult to describe so for me grotesque falls into that condition.'

Diaz Alonso returns to a cinematic analogy to continue his explanation: 'For me the notion of the "horrific" describes the opposite of elegant or precise – it's the idea that you can choreograph, orchestrate and organise the sensibility so it's playful in that sense. For example, when Alfred Hitchcock was putting together the shower scene in the movie *Psycho*, I think he was having fun with it; there is something horrific and scary, but at the same time a kind of adventure and playfulness comes into it. So, ultimately, there is a

BELOW HISTORY MUSEUM OF POLAND, WARSAW, POLAND, 2009

'I think being socially responsible is not only through action, doesn't the architecture also directly affect human behaviour?' asks Diaz Alonso. 'It can also be about proving that the nature of the work that you produce can communicate to people in a different way. So I think there is more than one way to contribute to working with a social attitude.'

RIGHT 'PITCH BLACK' EXHIBITION, MAK, VIENNA, AUSTRIA, 2007

In the Romantic tradition, Diaz Alonso prefers not to dissect his work: 'I always try to refuse to talk about the processes behind the work because I like the notion of separating the "magic from the magician". I think that the trick is more interesting than the method ... Design always concerns a translation between forms and formats of image. More than "textuality" or even "iconography", its very form is a secondary function of how it performs as an image.'

kind of a condition that makes us want to see horror movies or take a ride on a rollercoaster.' He concludes: 'For me this is an aesthetic problem. I don't aspire to inflicting a horrific feeling in people through my architecture, but what's really interesting for me is the possibility of something horrific and grotesque revealing a different kind of beauty, and to create a different kind of an effect and condition on the people that experience my work.'

Interviews

Xefirotarch studio, Los Angeles, 16 December 2006

The Building Centre, London, 29 January 2007

Notes

1. Particularly associated with the pioneering use of computer animation software.

2. Alias Studio and Maya.

3. Diaz Alonso currently also holds the position of Design Studio and Visual Studies Professor at the Southern California Institute of California (SCI-Arc) where he coordinates the Graduate Thesis. He is also a Design Studio Professor at the Graduate School of Architecture, Planning and Preservation (GSAPP) at Columbia University, and a Visiting Professor at the University of Applied Arts in Vienna.

4. The novel *Foucault's Pendulum* by Umberto Eco, published in 1988, is divided into 10 segments represented by the 10 Sephiroth, and is full of esoteric references to the Kabbalah, Alchemy and Conspiracy theory (see http://en.wikipedia.org/wiki/Foucalt's Pendulum). Sephiroth means 'enumeration' in Hebrew. The sephiroth in the Kabbalah of Judaism (Jewish mysticism) are the 10 attributes that God created through which he can manifest not only the physical but also the metaphysical universe. The mystical state of the 10 Sephiroth also has significance in a numerological sense. Between the 10 Sephiroth run 22 channels or paths which connect them and when combined make the number 32, which makes reference to the 32 Qabbalistic Paths of Wisdom and also the 32 Degrees of Freemasonry (see http://en.wikipedia.org/wiki/Sephirot).

5. Diaz Alonso credits Lynn as the most interesting 'digital architect', but suggests that even though he was influenced by Lynn, 'I also always made a conscious effort to create my own formula. Though Greg and Peter Eisenman advocate an extreme, hardcore methodological process within their work, it was never actually in my nature. It took me some time to make peace with those two worlds and that's where my "romantic" sensibility comes to the fore. The only thing I'm interested in and obsessed with is to make a difference; where my work is different from the others. It has nothing to do with tools because we use the same tools.'

6. 'Working with Enric Miralles helped me to understand that you could be a fairly normal guy in your personal life and still do extreme and radical work. It took me a while to make peace with that because I am a totally boring and normal guy in my personal life and I put all my energy into my work. On a personal level this was one of the most important lessons learnt from Enric.' Diaz Alonso also recalls an anecdote while working in Miralles's office: 'One Saturday morning, Enric showed up super well-dressed and smoking a great cigar. So one of the guys asks: "Hey, Enric, are you going to a party or something?" And he replied: "No ... Today I'm going to do a beautiful drawing." That simple statement for me is the essence of Enric's joy of life and a lesson about a way of thinking.' Hernan Diaz Alonso, interview with Yael Reisner, 16 December 2006.

7. Greg Lynn and Mark Goulthorpe both represent the pure computational approach to the arrival of forms. As Ali Rahim has confirmed: 'Experimental designers [among the digital architects] capitalised on this accretive learning, which develops through a project, suspending the reflection of concept/image-object/image relationships.' See Ali Rahim, 'Introduction', *AD Contemporary Processes in Architecture*, Vol 7 , No 3, May/June 2000, p 7. This prevalent suspension of the image was as thus released by Diaz Alonso through his work.

8. This is one of the aspects that differentiates Diaz Alonso's work from most of the digital architects. His cinematic imagery has a character, rhetoric and an individual touch – all qualities that the Modernists rejected for years, as have most contemporary digital architects.

9. In a brief to his students for his Vertical Studio in the fall semester (2006) at SCI-Arc, Diaz Alonso writes: 'Design always concerns a translation between forms and formats of image. More than "textuality" or even "iconography", its very form is a secondary function of how it performs as an image.'

10. Diaz Alonso suggests that he lost interest in the CAD/CAM direct production process that most digital architects employ. Instead he aspired to develop cinematic sequences, which led to the creation of affective cinematic imagery – among other preoccupations – as a significant part of the design process. He thus benefited from the mechanisms that come with the familiar world of the cinema: triggering associative thinking, memory, illusions or mood.

11. Diaz Alonso recalls: 'When we worked on the PS1 project for MoMA we were obsessed that the project would capture certain conditions and the image would produce it, so how can we achieve those levels or conditions? I was absolutely obsessed that the final object would look as close as possible to the renders and, as a matter of fact, when I started to send images of the project to friends, everybody said "Wow! Nice photomontage!"' Hernan Diaz Alonso, interview with Yael Reisner, 16 December 2006.

12. As Diaz Alonso explains: 'There is a transfer of power in terms of permanence, so a lot of how the work progresses is revolutionary in technique and in relation to what technology allows you. There is a kind of interaction, and of course there is a sensibility that comes with it.' Interview with Yael Reisner, 16 December 2006.

13. Frank Gehry also references abstract painting within his work.

14. Mark Goulthorpe wrote about the grotesque in his essay 'Misericord to a Grotesque Reification', in *AD Architecture + Animation*, Vol 71, No 2 , March/April 2001, p 57. He reintroduces the notion of the 'grotesque' as an animation phenomena and its popularity among digital architects who used software designed for animation. In doing so he quotes Ernst Gombrich who suggests that animation produces an effect in us, as a psychological rather than simply a physical manifestation. As Gombrich explains: 'Animation ... in design ... imbues the shape with life and therefore with movement and expression ... animation not only uses monsters, it generates them ... the principle of animation rules in the world of the grotesque.' Ernest Gombrich, *The Sense of Order: A Study in the Psychology of Decorative Art*, 2nd edition, Phaidon, New York,1984, pp 261–2.

Suggested Reading

For further exploration of the difficult relationship between architecture and beauty, the authors suggest:

1. Reyner Banham, *Theory and Design in the First Machine Age*, Architectural Press, Butterworth-Heinemann, Oxford, (1960 first edn) 1997.
2. Bill Beckley with David Shapiro, *Uncontrollable Beauty: Toward a New Aesthetics,* Allworth Press, NY, 1988.
3. Isaiah Berlin, *The Roots of Romanticism*, Princeton University Press, Princeton, New Jersey, 1999.
4. Beatriz Colomina, *Privacy and Publicity: Modern Architecture as Mass Media*, The MIT Press, Cambridge, Mass, 1996.
5. Peter Cook, *Primer,* Academy Editions, London, 1996.
6. Adrian Forty, *Words and Buildings*, Thames & Hudson, London, 2000.
7. Martin Jay, *Downcast Eyes: The Denigration of Vision in Twentieth-Century French Thought*, University of California Press, Berkeley and Los Angeles, 1994.
8. Arthur I Miller, *Insights of Genius: Imagery and Creativity in Science and Art*, The MIT Press (pbk edn), Cambridge, Mass, 1996.
9. Walter J Ong, SJ *The Presence of the Word*, Yale University Press, New Haven and London, 1967.
10. Peter Osborne, *From an Aesthetic Point of View: Philosophy, Art, and The Senses*, Serpent's Tail, London, 2000.
11. Juhani Pallasmaa, *The Eyes of the Skin: Architecture and the Senses, Polemics*, John Wiley & Sons, Ltd, Chichester, 2005.
12. Juhani Pallasmaa, *The Architecture of Image: Existential Space in Cinema,* Rakennustieto Oy, Helsinki, 2001.
13. Wolfgang Pehnt, *Expressionist Architecture,* Thames & Hudson, London, 1973.
14. Marvin Perry, *An Intellectual History of Modern Europe*, Houghton Mifflin Company, Boston, 1993.
15. Colin Rowe. *As I Was Saying, Recollections and Miscellaneous Essays*, Volume Two, Cornelliana, The MIT Press, London, 1996.
16. Colin Rowe, *The Architecture of Good Intentions: Towards a Possible Retrospect,* Academy Editions, London, 1994.
17. Alan Sokal & Jean Bricmont, *Intellectual Impostures: Postmodern Philosophers' Abuse of Science*, Profile Books, London, 1998.
18. Leon van Schaik, *Mastering Architecture: Becoming a Creative Innovator in Practice*, John Wiley & Sons, Ltd, Chichester, 2005.
19. Leon van Schaik, *Spatial Intelligence: New Futures for Architecture*, John Wiley & Sons, Ltd, Chichester, 2008.
20. Mark Wigley, *White Walls: Designer Dresses, The Fashioning of Modern Architecture*, The MIT Press, Cambridge, Mass, 1995.
21. James Wines, *De-Architecture*, Rizzoli International Publications Inc., New York, 1987.

Index

Picture credits

The author and the publisher gratefully acknowledge the people who gave their permission to reproduce material in this book. While every effort has been made to contact copyright holders for their permission to reprint material, the publishers would be grateful to hear from any copyright holder who is not acknowledged here and will undertake to rectify any errors or omissions in future editions.

l = left, r = right, t = top, b = bottom, m = middle

Cover design by Jeremy Tilston, The Oak Studio Ltd

p 5 Left-right, top-bottom:
© Susan King; © Zvi Hecker, photographer Hiepler, Brunier, Architekturfotografie; © Photographer Alexander Cook; © Juhani Pallasmaa Architects, Helsinki photographed by Adolfo Vera; © Photographed by Lebbeus Woods; © Gaetano Pesce, 2008; © COOP HIMMELB(L)AU Wolf D. Prix / W. Dreibholz & Partner ZT GmbH, photograher by Elfie Semotan; © Morphosis Architects, photograher Mark Hanauer; © Eric Owen Moss Architects; © Antonio Olmos; © Zaha Hadid Architects, photographer Steve Double; © Odile Decq; © Mark Goulthorpe, photographer Bernard Barc; Courtesy of Greg Lynn Form; © KOL/MAC LLC, Sulan Kolatan and Bill Mac Donald; Courtesy of Hernan Diaz Alonso, photographer Monica Nouvens

p 6 Left-right, top-bottom:
© Gehry Partners LLP; © Zvi Hecker Architect; © Paul Ott Photografiert; Courtesy of Juhani Pallasmaa, Photo Balthazar Korab; Courtesy of Lebbeus Woods, photographer Alexis Rochas; Courtesy of Meritalia; © Hélène Binet; © Nic Lehoux; © Eric Owen Moss Architects; © SMC Alsop; © Werner Huthmacher/Artur/View; © Odile Decq- Labtop; Courtesy of Mark Goulthorpe; © Greg Lynn FORM; © KOL/MAC LLC; © Hernan Diaz Alonso

p 12 © Maralles Tagiabue EMBT; pp 13, 14, 15, 16 © Yael Reisner; p 19 © Marjan Colletti, *The Basking – a House in Hampstead, London,* MArch, the Bartlett, UCL, 1999; p 20 © Aniko Meazaros; p 22 © CJ Lim / Studio 8 Architects Ltd; p 23 © Image by Philip Beesley; p 25 Courtesy of www.andreasgreber.ch; pp 30, 32 © Tim Street-Porter / Esto/View; p 134 © Tim Street-Porter; pp 31, 35 © Susan King; pp 33, 34, 39, 40, 41 © Gehry Partners LLP; p 36 © Thomas Dix /Esto/View; p 37 © Karin Hessmann/Artur/View; p 38 © Juergen Benkelman/Artur/View; p 44 Courtesy of Zvi Hecker © Zeev Hertz; p 45 © Zvi Hecker, photographer Hiepler, Brunier, Architekturfotografie; pp 46, 47, 49, 50, 51, 53, 55 (r) © Zvi Hecker Architect; p 48 © Rudolf Klein; p 52, 54, 55 (l), 56 © Michael Krüger, Architekturfotografie; pp 58, 60, 61, 62, 63, 64, 65, 69 (b), 70, 71, 72 © Peter Cook; p 59 © Photographer Alexander Cook; pp 66, 67, 68, 69 (t) © Paul Ott Photografiert; p 76 Courtesy of Juhani Pallasmaa, Photo Rauno Träskelin, 1938-39; p 77 © Juhani Pallasmaa Architects, Helsinki photographed by Adolfo Vera; p 78 Eino Makinen © Alvar Aalto Museum (1958); p 79 © Museum of Finnish Architecture/ Jussi Tiaine; p 80 Courtesy of Juhani Pallasmaa, Photo Rauno Träskelin, 1993; pp 81, 82, 86, 128, 179 (l), 181 (r), 182, 184 (t), 185, 187, 189 (l) © Hélène Binet; p 85 Courtesy of Juhani Pallasmaa, Photo Balthazar Korab; pp 88, 90, 91, 92, 93, 94, 95, 96, 97, 98, 100, 101, 102 (t) Courtesy of Lebbeus Woods; p 89 © Photographed by Lebbeus Woods; p 99 Courtesy of Lebbeus Woods, photographer Alexis Rochas; p 102 (b) Courtesy of Lebbeus Woods, photographer Reiner Zettl; pp 104, 106, 107, 109, 110, 113, 114, 115 © Gaetano Pesce Office; p 105 © Gaetano Pesce, 2008; p 108 Courtesy of Meritalia; p 111 (l) Courtesy of Gaetano Pesce Office, p 111 (r) Courtesy of Gaetano Pesce Office: permission Cassina S.p.A. Products and photos with thanks to Tavolo Sansone, Sedia Dalila, Archivio Storico Cassina, Ph. Mario Carrieri; p 112 Courtesy of Gaetano Pesce Office, Photo Liderno Salvador / Bracciodiferro (Cassina); pp 116, 118 © COOP HIMMELB(L)AU; p 117 © COOP HIMMELB(L)AU Wolf D. Prix / W. Dreibholz & Partner ZT GmbH, photographer by Elfie Semotan; pp 119, 120, 121, 122, 123 (l) © Gerald Zugmann/ www.zugmann.com; p 123 (r) © Armin Hess, ISOCHROM; pp 124, 125, 139, 140 (l), 184 (b) © Roland Halbe; p 126 © Martin Kroll/Artur/View; p 127 © Stefan Mueller-Naumann/Artur/View; pp 132, 135, 136 (b), 150, 151, 152, 153, 154 (l) © Tom Bonner; p 133 © Morphosis Architects, photograher Mark Hanauer; p 136 (t) Courtesy of Morphosis architects, photographer Brandon Welling; p 137 Courtesy of Morphosis architects, photographer Farshid Assassi; p 138 © Kim Zwarts; p 140 (r) © Lawrence Anderson/Esto/View; p 141 © Nic Lehoux; pp 142, 143, 144 Courtesy of Morphosis Architects; p 145 Courtesy of Morphosis Architects, photographer Michael Powers; p 146 Courtesy of Morphosis Architects, photographer Carlo Lavatori; pp 148, 149, 154 (r), 155, 156, 157, 158, 159, 160 © Eric Owen Moss Architects; pp 162, 164, 165, 166, 167, 168, 169, 170, 171, 172, 173, 174 © SMC Alsop; p 163 © Antonio Olmos; pp 176, 178, 180, 181 (l), 183, © Zaha Hadid Architects; p 177 © Zaha Hadid Architects, photographer Steve Double; p 179 (r) © Paul Warchol; pp 186, 188, 189 (r) © Werner Huthmacher/Artur/View; p 190 Courtesy of Zumtobel Lighting, Zaha Hadid Architects; p 192, 196, 197 (t) © Odbc/Georges Fessy; p 193 © Odile Decq; pp 194, 195 © Odbc/Stephane Couturier; p 197 (b), 198 (r), 199, 200, 201 © Odile Decq- Labtop; pp 198 (l), 204 © Odbc; p 202 © Odbc/Jswb; p 203 © Odbc/Polaris Gallery; pp 206, 208, 209, 210, 211, 212, 214 Courtesy of Mark Goulthorpe; p 207 © Mark Goulthorpe, photographer Bernard Barc; pp 218, 220, 221, 222, 223, 224, 225, 226, 227, 228, 229, 230 © Greg Lynn FORM; p 219 Courtesy of Greg Lynn Form; pp 232, 234, 235, 236, 237, 238, 239, 240, 241, 242 Courtesy of KOL/MAC LLC; p 233 © KOL/MAC LLC, Sulan Kolatan and Bill Mac Donald; pp 24, 244, 246, 248, 249, 250, 251, 252, 253, 254, 255, 256, 257 © Hernan Diaz Alonso; p 245 Courtesy of Hernan Diaz Alonso, photographer Monica Nouvens; p 247 Courtesy of Hernan Diaz Alonso/Xefirotarch